ITALY

AND THE

COMING WORLD

DON LUIGI STURZO

Here is a book that mirrors the thoughts of President Roosevelt when he said:

"The Italian people are capable of self-government. We do not lose sight of their virtues as a peace-loving nation. We remember the many centuries in which the Italians were leaders in the arts and sciences, enriching the lives of all mankind. Italy should go on as a great mother-nation contributing to the culture and the progress and the good-will of all mankind—developing their special talents in the arts and crafts and sciences and preserving her historical heritage for the benefit of all peoples. We want and expect the help of the future Italy toward lasting Peace."

It has been near to the author's heart to give a faithful interpretation of the "Spirit of Italy" since the Roman Empire carried civilization to the uttermost ends of the then known world up to the day when Mussolini's intuition led him

(Continued on back flap)

to declare war on France and G.
Britain, and later on the United States.
This picture of the Italian people serves
to introduce an illuminating analysis of
the causes that led to Italy's participation in the First World War on the side
of the Allies and in the present struggle
on the side of Hitler. No one who is interested in the post-war world can
afford to miss the brilliant and penetrating chapters on "Italy and the Allies," "Italy and Democracy" or the
frank exposition of the problems of
"Monarchy or Republic" and "Church
and State." Profound knowledge, ripe
wisdom, ardent patriotism and the true
"Spirit of Italy" pervade this all important treatise on the Italian character, the
Fascist adventure and the role played in
it by other Powers. Abiding faith in
Man guided by Providence makes firm
the promise that Italy will again take
her rightful place among the nations of
the world as a free, powerful and independent Republic. Something of the
spirit of '76 breathes in these pages
written by a liberal and philosophical
priest and publicist, by a great Christian-Democrat. American readers will
be the richer for this outstanding contribution to practical politics and constructive Democracy by one who fights
under the banner of Liberty and the
Rights of Man.

ITALY

AND THE

COMING WORLD

OTHER WORKS BY LUIGI STURZO

Organizzazione di Classe e Unioni Professionali. Cultura Sociale, Rome, 1901.

Sintesi Sociali. Cultura Sociale, Rome, 1906.

Dall'idea al Fatto. Francesco Ferrari, Rome, 1919.

Riforma Statale e Indirizzi Politici. Vallecchi, Florence, 1923.

Popolarismo e Fascismo. P. Gobetti, Turin, 1924.

Pensiero Antifascista. P. Gobetti, Turin, 1925.

*La Libertà in Italia. P. Gobetti, Turin, 1925.

*Italy and Fascism. Harcourt, Brace, New York, 1927.

*The International Community and the Right of War. Richard R. Smith, New York, 1930.

*Il Ciclo della Creazione. Bloud et Gay, Paris, 1932.

*Politics and Morality. Burns, Oates and Washburn, London, 1938.

*Church and State. Longmans, Green & Co., Inc., New York, 1939.

Les Guerres Modernes et la Pensée Catholique. L'Arbre, Montreal, 1942.

*The True Life—Sociology of the Supernatural. The Catholic University of America Press, Washington, D.C. (St. Anthony's Guild Press, Paterson, N. J.), 1943.

*L'Italia e L'Ordine Internazionale. Giulio Einaudi, Turin, 1944.

*Inner Laws of Society—A New Sociology. P. J. Kenedy & Sons, New York, December 1944.

Spiritual Problems of our times. Longmans, Green & Co., Inc., New York, 1945.

*Various essays and studies in reviews and symposiums.

The books marked with an asterisk have been published in London, Paris, Cologne, Madrid, Buenos Aires, Turin, and Rome.

ITALY
AND THE
COMING WORLD

By

DON LUIGI STURZO

Introduction by
SUMNER WELLES

ROY PUBLISHERS · NEW YORK

Translated by
Barbara Barclay Carter (Lic. ès L. Paris)

PRINTED IN THE UNITED STATES OF AMERICA
BY J. J. LITTLE & IVES COMPANY, NEW YORK

TO THE FRIENDS OF ITALY

EVERYWHERE

WHO LOVE THE BEAUTIES OF OUR LAND

HER HISTORY RELIGION CULTURE AND ART

BUT STILL MORE THE

INDUSTRY INTELLIGENCE GENEROSITY AND SINCERITY

OF HER PEOPLE

THESE PAGES

ARE DEDICATED

EVEN IN THE LONG AND DARK DAYS

OF TYRANNY AND TRAGEDY

THEY NEVER DESPAIRED

NEVER LOST THEIR CONFIDENCE

IN A

NEW FREE AND DEMOCRATIC

ITALY

CONTENTS

CONTENTS

INTRODUCTION

B ECAUSE of my belief that the publication of this most valuable book comes at a singularly opportune moment, I have been especially glad to accept the invitation of Don Luigi Sturzo to write these lines of introduction to "Italy and the Coming World." I am confident that its contents afford much-needed enlightenment to public opinion in the United States.

Relatively little attention has been devoted by the American public in general to the question of our policy towards Italy since the signature of the Italian armistice. In part this is due to the fact that popular attention has been largely concentrated upon the events attendant upon the collapse of Germany and upon the continuing progress of the war against Japan. But too little thought is being given to what United States policy towards Italy should be. There is too little consideration of the most effective means by which we can help the Italian people to become a democratic and stabilizing factor in that new Europe which is in the dawn of a profound change.

Of the views which have been publicly expressed regarding these issues, a large percentage express the feeling that United States policy should be primarily based on a studied system of retaliation because of the part which the Italian people played during the earlier years of the Second World War. There is a tendency to identify the policy which should be pursued towards Italy with the policy to be followed with regard to Germany. There is little apparent recognition that Italy can never become, for geographical, economic and racial reasons, the spearhead of any future threat to peace. There is relatively little realization that the policy of this Government towards Italy should logically be a policy designed to further the national interests of the United States by hastening the political and economic reconstruction of Europe.

People are apt to remember solely that the Italian people were led by their Fascist leaders into war with the United States. They dwell upon the wholly contemptible course pursued by Mussolini and his Fascist crew. They too often overlook the fact that a great majority of the Italian people were bitterly opposed to Italy's entrance into the World War, and that they were altogether opposed to the subsequent declaration of war by Italy upon the United States. They attribute little, if any, importance to the part which the Italian people themselves played in the overthrow of Mussolini, and to the material assistance rendered by Italian forces of resistance and by Italian troops in the final assault by the United States upon the German armies in the Mediterranean theatre.

It is, however, tacitly admitted that American policy in Italy from the conclusion of the armistice up to the present time has been lamentably unsuccessful. The United States has acquiesced in decisions laid down by the British Government. In the political field, as well as in the economic field, the course so far followed has been almost grotesquely inept. There is as yet no sign of remedial action.

These lines are written on the eve of the meeting of the Chiefs of Government of Great Britain, the Soviet Union, and the United States. In the Europe of today there are few more urgent requirements than that the policy so far pursued towards Italy should be radically revised, and that agreements should be reached upon definitive but just peace terms so that the Italian people may be rescued from the predicament of the political, economic, and territorial uncertainty in which they still find themselves. The liberal and democratic forces within Italy have been consistently weakened as a result of our recent attitude. The United States is afforded an opportunity to assume the leadership in establishing a United Nations policy toward Italy which will promote regeneration and democracy in Italy.

At the conclusion of the First World War, Lord Grey of

Fallodon wrote these words, which are singularly applicable to Italy at this time. He said:

"The history of the French Revolution, the experience in our own time of the Turkish and Russian Revolutions, show that, bad as despotism is, doomed as it is to work its own ruin, the first-fruits of its overthrow are not love and liberty."

"The Italian people are inevitably destined to pass through turbulent days as a result of almost a quarter of a century of Fascist despotism. They will not overnight be able to install a democratic government and a social and economic system which will bring with them the liberty and the security which they have so long desired. It is now more than ever that wise help and friendly understanding on the part of the people of the United States will be of real and lasting value. If it is forthcoming, it will be long remembered by the Italian people. The ties of friendship between the peoples of Italy and of the United States endured through many decades. They are increased in strength because of the many millions of Italians who have come to the shores of the United States and who have become worthy and patriotic citizens of this country. To no nation in the world of today are the Italian people in their present distress more disposed to look for leadership in the establishment of a just but constructive policy towards Italy, than to the United States."

Don Luigi Sturzo is singularly qualified to present the viewpoint of the new Italy to the people of this country.

He is a Catholic. He was ordained a priest more than fifty years ago. To many who have been misinformed, or who are not familiar with the story of modern Italy, it will probably come as a surprise to learn from this book that Don Sturzo believes that the highest interest of the Italian people will best be served by the abolition of the monarchy, and by the establishment of an Italian republic under a most liberal form of constitutional government. It will come as an equal surprise to read the exceedingly progressive views which he advances for the solution of many of the social and economic problems with which the Italian people have so long been

beset. Too few are familiar with the long years of honorable
service rendered by Don Sturzo to the cause of the working
man and woman in Italy, and with the leading part which he
played in the creation of the Christian Democrat Party, a
party established to further the achievement of the social objectives for which he has so persistently and valiantly fought
throughout his life.

There are views expressed and conclusions reached by Don
Sturzo in this book with which I individually disagree. There
are others with which I find myself in profound agreement.
But whatever the individual response may be to the arguments which Don Sturzo sets forth, there can be no question
that the views contained in this book are the expression of
the sincere belief of a liberal and experienced Italian who
seeks only the highest welfare of the Italian people. They are
however not only the beliefs of an Italian patriot. They represent the convictions of an enlightened European, in the
broadest sense of the term.

This book will help to destroy the dangerous illusion which
still persists in so many American minds that the regeneration of the Italian people requires the imposition upon them
of our own particular brand of democracy. As *Italy and the
Coming World* makes clear, the Italian people, long before
the unification of Italy, have understood the meaning of the
term "democracy". If their own ability to evolve the kind of
democracy which is truly an Italian democracy is stimulated,
in the right manner and at the right time, a new and democratic Italy will be created. In such an Italy human freedom
will be secure. Such an Italy can play no inconsiderable part
in the successful establishment of that free and peaceful world
which the United Nations have pledged themselves to set up.

The policy of the United States should be so shaped as to
further the attainment of those objectives which Don Sturzo
has so well expressed in these words:

"Postwar Italy must strive to avoid bloody uprisings and
outbursts of partisan fury and class hatreds. But if she is to
resume a normal life, apart from all the economic and politi-

cal measures that are urgently needed, she must have the sense of her own personality, to be remade, reconstituted, regained. The people, united in purpose and determination amid the diversity of trends and opinions, must rise again. Its banner must be democracy, its aim the second Italian Risorgimento within the European and international order. To give back faith to the people, the country itself, the regime to be established, the forces to be used, must be given back into their hands, making to live anew the ideals that correspond to the traditional conception of the spirit of Italy.

"Within this setting the monarchy would be nothing more than an expedient and a mechanism that might be useful or harmful. Neither Victor Emmanuel III, nor Humbert II, can aspire to become the heroes and the saviors of Italy in the eyes of a people engaged in reconstruction. They would represent that past which must perish. And if the monarchy falls with them and the republic is proclaimed, perhaps with all the inconveniences that a change of regime brings, it will serve to mark in history the opening of the new epoch in which the spirit of Italy will be born again."

SUMNER WELLES

ITALY
AND THE
COMING WORLD

1

The Spirit of Italy

ITALY, IN THE VERY HEART of the Mediterranean, with her far-flung coasts on the Tyrrhenian, Ionian and Adriatic seas, her variety of crops, her uneven soil, her contrasts of climate, her mixed population, received from nature and matured through the ages, characteristics and functions all her own, a mission that can best be described as the spirit of Italy.

For the peoples of the Levant, of Europe and of North Africa, the Mediterranean was the center of commercial and cultural communications, of progress and of the development of civilization, until the Europeans themselves were in time able to reach India and China on the one hand and, on the other, crossing the Atlantic, to discover the American continent, range uncharted seas, occupy other lands and circumnavigate the world. Even after the discovery of new continents, the Mediterranean—albeit of less commercial and political importance—remained the center of activity for a large part of Europe, North Africa and the Near East. Little by little the barrier opposed by the Crescent to the spread of European civilization in the world was broken down by war, by penetration, by revolution in the subjugated countries, by occupation of a large part of Africa by the Western powers. The cutting of the Suez Canal completed the task, gave the Mediterranean an outlet to the Red Sea and linked it to the Indian and Pacific oceans.

Seas and rivers have always been the highways of civilization, and the lands washed by them its centers. On its European side the Mediterranean has three peninsulas as well as adjacent islands great and small. The Greco-Balkan, the Italian, the Iberian peninsulas, all three face Africa. It is impossible to imagine a natural setting more favorable to the development of young peoples and nascent civilizations. Every island in the Aegean has its myths, its heroes, its poetry, its history, as have the Greek, Ionian, Sicilian and Italian peoples. Etruscan civilization, as far as one can gather from the mystery that surrounds it, reveals not only a lofty culture and mastery of art, common to all Mediterranean peoples, but a spirit of speculative inquiry anteceding that of the Greeks.

This same spirit pervaded the civilization of the peoples of Sicily and southern Italy, later known as greater Greece, where Greek philosophy and poetry assumed a more intimate and speculative character. In those days northern Italy was inhabited by Gallo-Celts, and shared the cultural and mystical outlook of northwestern Europe.

Rome became the center of the then known world. She carried Mediterranean civilization northward to Gaul and Britain and to the confines of Germany, eastward to the Hellespont, Asia Minor and Persia. The civil and political part Italy played in Roman times was important only to the extent in which she participated in the intense life of Rome; thus was brought about a moral unification of the Italian peninsula which later had other imperial centers such as Ravenna and Milan.

Meanwhile there had been infused into Greco-Roman civilization the ferment of the Jewish people, scattered throughout the shores of the Mediterranean. From this came the seed of the Christian religion which, after two and a half centuries of persecution renewed and intensified in all the provinces of the empire, finally won the right of public worship and free preaching by the Decree of Toleration in A.D. 313. Not long thereafter Rome was abandoned by the emperors. The senate still continued to sit there, an appanage of the city that was still mistress of the world. But the senate was no more than a memory of the past, whereas the Papacy gave to Rome the consciousness of being the See of Christianity.

Italy, as a province of the empire, could not be maintained as a unit politically as she was geographically. Part passed under the sway of Byzantium, part remained under the emperors of the west, later to be occupied and divided by barbarian kings who sought to achieve military unification. The history of those times is grievous indeed. The ideal Italy endured, despite political division, barbarian occupation, religious schism. Thus was born a new Italy, molded by Greco-Roman tradition, by Christianity, by the influx of Nordic invaders who while contributing fresh energies ended by being assimilated. The whole of Europe was shaken by this mixing of peoples who passed into Europe from Asia, sweeping from north to south, from east to west. Italy remained an ideal point of convergence in the conflicts of migrant peoples and a laboratory of ethnical and cultural forces. Apart from Augustine, who was to some extent Roman and Italian, Ambrose, Jerome, Leo the Great, Boethius, Benedict and Gregory the Great were in those days, as they have been for posterity, the spiritual beacons of the world.

In the seventh century the Arabs, won to the faith of Mohammed, advanced into the Mediterranean and sought to conquer the peninsulas, the bulwarks of Europe. The Balkans were defended by the Byzantine empire. As strongholds Italy still held Monte Cassino, Benevento and Rome, but Sicily was overrun and a breach made in greater Greece. Spain succumbed almost entirely and opened the door to the invasion of France, checked by the armies of Charles Martel and Charlemagne.

And then emerged the Italian cities of the sea, mistresses of the Mediterranean for long centuries: Venice and Genoa, Pisa and Amalfi. In the renaissance of the eleventh century appeared the communes of the mainland pregnant with democracy, the vindication of communal liberties in the face of feudal lords and later of Popes and emperors; the universities, harbingers of cultural revival, especially in law and philosophy; the arts reborn to express the spiritual youth of the people of Italy arising from the racial blending of Latin, Slav, German and Arab. And over all breathed the spirit of Christianity that in the travail of centuries had fought and overcome the pagan traditions of Greece and Rome, and those of the barbarians.

Whereas pre-Roman Italy was universal through the art and culture of Etruscans and Greeks, and Roman Italy pre-eminent in politics, administration and law, post-Roman Italy won universality through the Papacy. Leo the Great, Gelasius I, Gregory the Great and Leo III upheld the Latin tradition as something that unified the whole of the West and created a new civilization, while Benedict founded and spread monasticism that was the decisive element in the various revivals throughout medieval Europe. From this same spirit of universality sprang the idea of empire, first with Leo III when in A.D. 800 he crowned Charlemagne, creating the Franco-Roman empire that was doomed to failure; then with John XII, who in a time of crisis and certainly with no high ideal or hope, crowned Otto I and brought into being the Holy Roman Empire. It is true the tradition of imperial Rome lived in the consciousness of the Italian people; but the Byzantine emperors were too far off, too remote in culture and interests and the Papacy felt it could not hold its own in the broils of a fragmented Europe, in a constant making and unmaking of frontiers, in internal and external strife, under the ever-present threat of the Mohammedanized Arabs and the still pagan peoples of the north. The idea of Christendom as a religious and cultural entity found a counterpart in that of a political federation or jurisdictional-military rule. The two lights, the sun and the moon, or the two swords, the spiritual and the temporal, were taken as symbols of this two-fold unification under Pope and Emperor. Italy "seat of the Papacy" and "garden of the Empire" became the center of attraction of both, and alas for many centuries their battle-field.

The Italian communal renaissance, unique of its kind, was

the birthcry of liberty, the first experiment in democracy in
a Christian setting, the first broad and living achievement of
popular art. The Italian communes were grafted on the universal conception of empire and Papacy, retaining their own
personality and taking sides now for one, now for the other,
assuredly in accordance with their own interests but giving
to these a new life and a universal scope. The struggles
against the Swabian Emperors, Frederick Barbarossa and
Frederick II, in the twelfth and thirteenth centuries
were epical and shaped the history of northern and central
Italy where every commune was a kingdom and every city
had a great history. Meanwhile in the south the Normans,
having driven out the Arabs and overcome the Greeks,
ceased to be a dominant minority and became acclimatized
and assimilated. They contributed to the renaissance of activity and art, an architectural flowering that has remained
unique under the name of Arab-Norman.

The universalism of Italy's golden age bears the imprint
of Christian revival, of Francis of Assisi, Thomas Aquinas,
Bonaventura of Bagnorea, Dante Alighieri and Giotto: almost four centuries of philosophy, philology, poetry and art,
upon which Petrarch, Boccaccio, Lorenzo the Magnificent,
Ariosto, Tasso, Fra Angelico, Perugino, Leonardo da Vinci,
Raphael, Francesca di San-Sepolcro, Michelangelo, Tinto-
retto, Titian, Palestrina, Monteverde, Columbus, Marsilio
Ficino, Galileo and a thousand others left the indelible stamp
of Italian universality.

Even the Italy of the counter-reformation was universal.
Whereas the renaissance was universal through its spirit of
freedom, of culture, of art, and the diffusion of its language
throughout the educated world, the counter-reformation
opposing the nationalist withdrawal upon themselves of the
countries of the Protestant reformation and their rejection
of all foreign influence had its period of universality not only
with its saints (suffice to mention Philip Neri and Charles
Borromeo), but with its music from Palestrina to Carissimi,
Scarlatti and Caccini; its baroque architecture of deep inner

spiritual significance whose chief exponent was such a genius as Bernini; its painting from Caravaggio to Tiepolo; its Platonic and prerationalist philosophy with Ficino, Telesio, Bruno and Campanella.

Thus it was that even in the seventeenth century, which already showed a decline, Italy in the midst of her internal misfortunes, of foreign domination and political tyranny, was still able to assert her universal function in science, culture and art. For a time Italy continued to transmit the ideals of art and learning of the renaissance, the ideals of art and Catholicism of the counter-reformation to Europe and even to America.

* * *

All this had its counterpart. The sense of universality, like historical or political sense, is not a quality of the masses but of the elite. The call of a mission not only geographical and economic, but spiritual and cultural, is felt not by the many but by the few, even though achieved by the whole. These elites constantly interchange their ideas, activities and functions, in co-operation or in conflict. These conflicts take on the colors and passions of the time, place, party or faction, and as such are particularist, although their import becomes or will become historically universal. Thus Italy, which from the fall of the Roman Empire to the nineteenth century, played so large a part in the development of western civilization and in the religious, cultural and artistic activities of Christendom and mankind, never existed except as an ideal unit, never existed as a political entity.

Prior to the fifteenth century we cannot speak of nationality in its political sense for any European country, although in many their language and literature were fully developed. Roman municipalities, feudal communes, free cities and petty lordships had been the political forms of the age. The difference between Italy and the other countries, France, for instance, was that the latter crystallized around the strongest reigning house which, over-riding the Carlovingian and feudal sub-divisions, centralized political power, crushed the various factions, annexed or subdued the many dukedoms into which ancient Gaul had been divided, and extended the monarchy over the greater part of the territory that became known as France. This notwithstanding the first sign of true national life in France came with Joan of Arc, who may well be looked upon as its foundress. The same thing happened in England with the Tudors, in Spain with Ferdinand and Isabella, and later with Charles V.

Italy was too long and narrow, too diversified. Italian was the language of culture, whereas the dialects remained the common speech and even found their way into literature. Italy had many autonomous centers of power with their own history, their own economic and political life so intense that certain cities of the Middle Ages and early Renaissance were as important in Europe as the kingdoms of the north and west. Venice, Florence, Genoa, Milan, Turin, Rome, Siena, Naples, Benevento, Palermo were each of them worth a kingdom. How could political unification even be thought of? Local particularism was far better suited to that Western universalism whereby Italy lived. Moreover, with the spirit of its various parts, a unified Italy was inconceivable either as a federation (as each center had its own policy and interests) or even less as a single monarchy which would have dominated all the separate principalities and historic republics, and deprived the Pope of his territory. Historically such a thing would have been absurd. Even Machiavelli's ideal was unsuited to the Italy of his day.

For a federation or unification, a national policy would have been essential. Conflicts between Popes and Emperors which divided Italy into Guelfs and Ghibellines had scarcely subsided when foreign domination began. If this intrusion was not without its uses to a divided and disturbed Italy, as it created units larger than the medieval communes, from the point of view of economic exploitation and political subjection, it was the worst thing that could happen to a people. A policy of liberation could not be the work of foreigners, or brought about by foreign aid. But no Italian prince or republic was strong enough to contend with France or Spain or later with Austria. So now one, then another of these foreign states ended not only by occupying Italian provinces, but by imposing foreign princes of European royal houses or bound to them by family ties, new or old. Thus Italian policy fell into line with that of Madrid or Vienna or Paris.

The colonization of the New World gave greatness to Spain, to Portugal, to France, to the Netherlands, to England—rivals also in the highly profitable slave trade—while Italy was becoming more and more shut up within herself. Only Venice survived with her memories of the past and the remnant of her trade with the Levant.

If Italy, already enslaved, was still producing men of the first rank—churchmen, statesmen, poets, painters, musicians, architects, sculptors, scientists, even warriors—this was due to the natural rhythm of a past that was not dead. It influenced the succeeding period, from the second half of the seventeenth century onwards.

This was the time when civil and ecclesiastical authorities, often in conflict with one another in matters of jurisdiction, were united in their distrust of any innovation, intellectual or political. This tended to subdue the cultural vitality of Europe; but a new current of thought arose in France where the break between Jansenists and Jesuits led to a wide cleavage between the intellectual classes and the mentality of the reformation and counter-reformation, and in the eighteenth century a critical spirit spread from France throughout Europe and all civilized countries.

However, while France led by Descartes was veering toward formal rationalism, in Italy there arose an intellectual giant, Gian Battista Vico. He forecast the coming age, gave a new meaning to history and sought its laws, set philological criticism on the way to discover its inner significance, aesthetics on the way to realize their universal character. He revived the theory of natural law, setting it in that of the development of civilization by means of law. His philosophical concept based on historical reality viewed as an inner process, involute yet rational, and on the work of Providence, would have been enough to give the right orientation to modern thought. Instead modern thought turned aside from the constructive path to follow Descartes' formal rationalism, Kant's critical epistemology, Hegel's idealism and Comte's positivism. Vico was opposed to Descartes who left living reality out of consideration, and might have been the corrective of Kant in so far as Kant withdraws from pure reason in favor of practical reason. Above all he anticipated Hegel without falling into pantheistic idealism, and while platonizing and combating the formal abstractions of the scholasticism of his day, he never parted company with sane Aristotelian-Thomist realism. He was the type of Italian free from exaggeration, working in the furrow of classical Christian thought and renewing it by modern historical orientation.

Vico did not have the success he deserved. His thought was misunderstood and distorted in Italy and abroad. The Catholics were afraid of his audacities and of some of his views that were not in line with tradition; the anti-Catholics made use of his theories, forgetting the principal: the action of Providence. Finally in recent times both Catholics and idealists have claimed him for their own glory. The Vico period was that of the most acute crises. The outpourings of Italian thought and art, although they still circulated through Europe, no longer resounded as in former centuries.

Even the Papacy, entangled in jurisdictional disputes with the absolute monarchies, attacked by the encyclopedists and by political and social reformers, remained on the defensive, giving way for the sake of appeasement and at the same time maintaining the institutions of the past that bound the clergy to the social and economic structure of the aristocracy. Among the Popes of the time only Benedict XIV stands out for breadth of vision and loftiness of mind. Beccaria, the famous penologist, was the last universal Italian whose name crossed the Alps, as the precursor of the new revolutionary era that was approaching. Genovesi, philosopher and economist, became known only through French circles: the center of international culture had passed from Italy to France. From France came the revolution that was not only French but European. From France, for a time, Napoleon was to decide the fate of the world.

The last Italian of universal spirit although of poor philosophy was Alfieri, the dramatic and satirical poet. But he never attained the artistic level of Racine or Corneille, and his schematic classicism was no longer in tune with the preromanticism that was at the gates. His voice remained for Italy a proud protest against tyranny and a summons to liberty. He was not alone. Parini in Milan, Goldoni in Venice and the reformers, theoretical and practical, such as Romagnosi, Filangeri, Gioia and countless other forerunners of the new Italy sought to supersede the servile, adulatory, academic style that by long moral and political subjection had weakened Italian fibers, degraded the ideals of the educated classes and reduced to nought the political importance of the nation.

*   *   *

Two hundred years too late and after the bitter experience of French occupation under the First Republic and Napoleon, Italy felt the time was ripe to solve the problem of her constitution as a nation, all the more so as in 1815 the Congress of Vienna had riveted and reaffirmed Austria's hold on northern Italy (even including what had been the territory of the great Republic of Venice) and restored all the petty sovereigns connected with the Hapsburgs.

The principle of the independence of peoples and their national unification would have remained barren without the vindication of political liberty. Italy was forced by events and by her very past to fight on three fronts: the political, against Austria and her satellites; the national, against the division of the country into various autonomous states, the heads of which neither wished to lose their sovereignty nor to break away from Austria; the constitutional, to insure the

participation of the people in public life. To these three
fronts was added a fourth, the Papacy which apart from any
other problem was bound up with the *status quo* established
by the Restoration. In the movements for national unity and
liberation from foreign rule, the most influential leaders of
Vatican policy at that time saw nothing but conspiracies of
secret societies, revolutionary agitations and anti-Christian
ideologies. In those days the memory of the French revolution was something worse than the idea of bolshevist danger
after the First World War.

On the contrary, taken as a whole, Italian aspirations were
legitimate and accepted by men of the highest repute, even
Catholics like Caesare Balbo, Alessandro Manzoni, Abbé
Rosmini, Father Ventura and many others known as the
neo-Guelfs (including Gioberti, for all his vacillations). They
wished to reconcile the rights of the Papacy to independence
and liberty with the like rights of the Italian nation, and
bring about a federation of all the states of the peninsula and
at the same time the liberation of the provinces occupied by
foreigners.

Naturally the currents were various, the motives diverse,
the methods conflicting. But whereas the idea of political
unification and national life was particularist, and could not
be otherwise for the very fact that every historical achievement, perforce limited by time and space, is particular, the
motives and ideals that dominated the Italian Risorgimento
were universal because human. Independence and liberty
were ideals for which the North American and South American colonies had fought long before Italy. These same ideals
had inspired the Greeks to rise against Turkey and fight
unequal and heroic wars, to which flocked from Italy and
many other parts of the world the most chivalrous volunteers.

The story of the Risorgimento is a page worthy of the
Italian tradition, both in its moral and political aspects and
in the philosophical, poetical and artistic revival that accompanied it and in which the names of Manzoni and Verdi won
universal fame, as did the principal actors in the achievement

of political unity, Cavour, Mazzini, and Garibaldi. But if the civilized world remembers the greatest names and often exalts them as symbols and myths, even harmonizing their antagonisms and conflicting ideas, it is the duty of Italians to remember the immense number of men worthy of respect and even of fame who from every part of the peninsula and with widely divergent political ideals contributed to the Italian Risorgimento and to the constitution of the nation as a unified and morally conscious state. If mistakes were made—and what historical epic is free from mistakes—they entered into the reality of events and became motives for renewed activity.

Once national unity had been achieved, political and economic problems overshadowed idealism. The new Italy seemed smaller than the old, the new men of lesser stature than the Fathers of the Risorgimento. There were no more heroic battles or martyrs on the scaffold, only speeches in parliament, bureaucracy in the ministries, profiteers in public works. North and South did not get on well together; conscription brought uprisings in Sicily; Bourbon political brigands were the remains of legitimist opposition in the southern provinces. The seizure of Rome in 1870 increased the tension between Church and State; the financial situation became serious; Italy was isolated from the international world where at first she seemed an intruder. There were even those who thought the new kingdom would be short-lived.

Looking back today on the difficult period from 1870 to 1900 during which the men of the Risorgimento disappeared one by one leaving successors who were no longer of their stature, one must admit that the second and even the third political generation kept faith with the fortunes of the new Italy, served the country with sincerity and integrity whatever mistakes they made, and knew how to combine the ideals of liberty with those of national dignity, the universal humanitarian and peaceful ideals with those of national interests.

By this we do not mean to deny the errors that led the new Italy into the dark days of martial law and mistaken colonial adventure nor the anti-clerical complex brought about by the clash between the new Italy and the Papacy. This latter question will be fully dealt with in other chapters. Here we would merely place on record the fact that the crises through which the new Italy passed as soon as she had become a national state did not in any way vitiate the ideals in which she grew up; nor did they prevent Italian culture from playing its full part in the development of that European and universal spirit which in the nineteenth century was being created side by side with the national spirit of the various countries.

Measures that had to be taken immediately for the new system of public schools and the reorganization of secondary schools and universities were in general well inspired, with a program that was a happy medium between historical classicism and modern technology. Had it not been for positivist exaggerations and a blind faith in "progress" and "scientism" —a state of affairs by no means peculiar to Italy but rather a general disease of western culture during the latter half of the last century—the new Italy would have better overcome the intellectual crisis of the time. Unfortunately the narrow concept of a state school, the mistrust (only partly justified) of free initiative, the tendency to identify the official policy of the ministry of education with positivist school of thought, did an ill service to the country and obliged it to react in what was at times a partisan spirit.

The cultural and artistic level of this period was mediocre and the few who rose to European fame in science, law, poetry and art were survivors of the preceding generation. Manzoni was silent. Verdi on the contrary was producing masterpieces. Carducci taught and wrote poetry; with his pagan classicism he passed for the interpreter of the new Italy, he was only partly so and certainly not in his evocation of the Rome of Livy. It is usual today to underline the few religious phrases and the broad universal aspirations in his works, while it is debated of him (as of Bergson) whether in his last years he was reconciled to God at least in the secret of his heart. In music new stars were rising: Puccini and

Mascagni toured the world, Perosi brought the oratorio back to life and gave a new voice to sacred music, Toscanini expressed the universal genius of Italy in his magical interpretations.

The inheritance of the nineteenth century, as bequeathed to all civilized countries, was one of faith in man, in the progress of science, in the ethics of pure freedom, in the dialectics of history, whether idealistic as with Hegel or materialistic as with Marx. Immamentism affected even the religious world, in Protestant countries with liberal Christianity (a final effort to humanize faith) and in Catholic countries with modernism, which emphasized the naturalist concept in the history of the dogmas and in the life of the Church.

Many non-Catholics and free-thinkers followed the trend of liberal rationalism and arrived at two opposing viewpoints: positivism, which had famous exponents in philosophy with Ardigó, in criminology with Lombroso, in sociology with Pareto, in history with Ferrero; idealism with Antonio Labriola as an original interpreter of Marxism, Benedetto Croce who gave new life to Hegelism and his antagonist Giovanni Gentile, the champion of actualism. Among Catholics modernism had a certain following among the younger clergy, its best known and most persistent exponent being Buonaiuti; while in the orthodox camp there was the neo-Thomist revival which resuscitated and improved the Aristotelian scholasticism of the period prior to Leo XIII, and received a new impetus from the Catholic University of Milan. Giuseppe Toniolo was the exponent of social economy, of Christian democracy, of organic sociology, and had many followers. In the sphere of legal and ethical studies Contardo Ferrini stood out as a man of great promise. In natural law Taparelli found neither followers nor imitators. In history and philology the outstanding figures were Mgr. Ceriana, Cardinal Capecelatro, Nicola Festa and Gaetano de Sanctis. In literature the followers of Manzoni and Carducci were mediocre. Abbot Tosti was a poet rather than a historian. Fogazzaro overshadowed all his contemporaries by his original and glittering personality but today save by a few he is forgotten by both Catholics and liberals, although once the target of their admiration and attack.

Now from a distance of half a century we see that in this initial period Italy was seeking to find herself. As in all periods of transformation, personal or collective, something in the nature of involution is natural, a kind of obscure sense of diminished stature and a quest for new forces to refashion a new life.

The most visible part of this new life was its political aspect; a collective life intense and yet uncertain, conflicting and without clear aims. This life was narrowly national, one could almost say provincial, in view of the jealous care taken to safeguard the recently won unity against perils from within and without, real or hypothetical. So the universalist trend of Italian thought and consciousness may be said to have been obscured by nationalism (the word was not yet in use). This notwithstanding, whether by her prevailing classical formation, or her innate good sense, or Catholic influence (dominated for twenty-five years by the great international figure of Leo XIII), Italy, even when she had become a political nation, never repudiated her bimillenary mission of universality.

2

Italy and the First World War

AFTER 1870, two policies were open to the new Italy: a "stay-at-home" policy or that of a great power. The former was the more popular and in the early days of the kingdom the most expedient, in view of the uncertainties and difficulties of readjustment. If, on the contrary, Italy had then embarked upon a policy of adventure, occupying Tunisia, as some wished, pressing for the liberation of the Trentino and Trieste, taking part on either side in Balkan affairs, it might have led, as many feared, to a combined intervention of Austria and France, in agreement with clerical elements on both sides of the Alps, might have restored Rome to the Pope and at the same time arrested or compromised the development of the new state. Whether such fears were exaggerated or not, Italy had yet to rebuild her economic and political structure, restore her finances and reorganize an army and navy in keeping with her Mediterranean position. To do this required not only time but the strength to break through the isolation in which she found herself after 1870, and to stabilize normal relations with all the European powers.

The alliance with Germany and Austria in 1882 seemed a necessity, as Italy had no other alternative in view of the diffident attitude of France. The Triple Alliance was not popular. Intellectually and morally the country inclined more toward France, despite strong resentment over the occupation of Tunisia; and felt a traditional hostility to Austria which

16

still held the Trentino and Trieste.* It was natural that France should resent the step taken by Italy. France, who had done nothing for an alliance with Italy, feared that the alliance with Germany might contain clauses hostile to herself. As a matter of fact nothing was farther from the truth. Italy would never have embarked upon so absurd a policy, contrary to the wishes of the people. The treaty was purely defensive. Italy took a difficult step in drawing closer to Austria, but it was prudent to leave to future events the problem of the Trentino and Trieste and concentrate on consolidating what had been so laboriously achieved in thirty-three years by the territorial, political and moral unification of the new state.

The intent of Berlin and Vienna was to neutralize Italy in case of European conflict, and if possible to have her as an active ally on a basis of compensations. So at the first renewal of the treaty in 1887, Italy found no difficulty in obtaining the insertion of Article 7, by which the three powers affirmed their desire to co-operate for the maintenance of the *status quo* in the Levant, but if in the course of events this *status quo* "in the territory of the Balkans, of the Ottoman coasts and islands, of the Adriatic and of the Aegean became impossible" and Austria or Italy found it necessary to proceed

---

* Serious apprehensions were aroused in Italy by a Germany victorious over France. Even the Catholics, by no means well disposed toward France with her anti-clericalism for home consumption and her clericalism for export, were far more concerned over Bismarck's *Kulturkampf* and the predominance of Lutheran Prussia. Ruggiero Bonghi, one of the most clear-sighted men of the historic Right and a friend of Manzoni, wrote after 1870: "And there are still men who dare to assert that all confidence can be placed in the peaceful character of the Germans when the clearest lesson of their history past and present is that no people is more easily intoxicated, none more tenacious in its intoxication, more obsessed with its own importance, more incapable of distinguishing right from wrong in its own cravings. It was necessary for the sun of German science and German virtue to rise over Europe and illumine the world, for the naked principle of conquest to be restored to honor, a principle professed with infinite impudence by the most cynical and fortunate statesman in Europe [Bismarck] and a countless host of professors, and for us to hear that it was useless for the common people to protest as a whole generation would be held under an iron yoke till the advent of another, more patient or tamer or more subdued." Verdi who was no politician but who voiced popular opinion, has in his letters even stronger passages against the Germans, with a broad understanding of the French spirit, even in times when French public opinion was not kind to the new Italy.

to temporary or permanent occupations, they undertook to reach "prior agreement along lines of mutual compensation." This article was always maintained in subsequent renewals of the treaty and was in force when the Austro-Serbian war broke out in 1914.

Italy, although treated as a weak but not negligible partner, took care to comply faithfully with the treaty, without thereby serving the aims of the Central Empires. So she made it her business to maintain good relations and enter into agreements with other powers. A period of tension between Italy and France, marked by misunderstanding and friction under the Crispi government, was succeeded by one of good relations due to Visconti Venosta, one of the most enlightened statesmen of Italy. He aimed at an international policy of conciliation, as was evident at Algeciras where he sought to mediate between Germany and France. He was followed by Prinetti who, in the face of the continued uneasiness of France, declared explicitly that were she the victim of aggression or better still of direct provocation, Italy would observe strict neutrality. He repeated officially that the treaty of the Triple Alliance contained no protocols or additional articles directed against France.

The first serious test of the treaty in the relations between Italy and Austria came in 1908 when the government of Vienna, without informing Rome and without seeking the prior agreement stipulated in Article 7, proclaimed the annexation of Bosnia and Herzegovina. The reaction of Italian public opinion was most vigorous. Tittoni, then Minister of Foreign Affairs, did his best to appease it and sought compensation in agreements with Russia, which were put in writing at Racconigi the following year.

From 1900 onward, Italian policy aimed at achieving the conquest of Libya which, under agreements reached and renewed with the various European powers, had fallen to her lot in Africa from the crumbling Ottoman Empire, and was the counterpart of what France, England and Germany had already taken with or without title. Italian colonization of the coast of North Africa went back to the beginning of the Risorgimento, when political exiles and refugees found a haven not only in Malta but in Egypt, in Tripoli, in Tunisia, and in Algiers. Considerable emigration of artisans, peasants and traders followed and was the more readily welcomed as the political aims of the Italian government were so undefined. The latter in 1882 declined England's offer to collaborate with her in maintaining order in Egypt against Arabi Pasha, just as it had previously declined Bismarck's suggestion that it occupy Tunisia, fearing a conflict with France already long established in Algeria.

The Libyan expedition in 1911–12, caused by the Turkish government sending arms to the Mohammedan population of Tripoli to attack the Italian colony that flourished there, was the logical outcome of ten years of Mediterranean policy on the part of Italy. Here again it was clearly seen how despite understandings, agreements and treaties, a time comes when the jealousies and particular interests of each and every power gain the upper hand. Germany did not want the complete defeat of her protégé Turkey; Austria was opposed to carrying war into the Adriatic where Turkey had strong naval bases in Albania; France openly showed her resentment; England sold arms to the enemy.

The Libyan expedition furnished a propitious opportunity to the league of Balkan countries against Turkey. The first and then the second Balkan wars followed, in the course of which Serbia, Greece, Rumania and Montenegro enlarged their possessions, whereas Bulgaria at first victorious was later beaten; Turkey succeeded in retaining the zone between Constantinople and Adrianopolis, and Albania won autonomy and was made a principality. During the second Balkan war in 1913, the Austrian government wished to intervene against Serbia and in accordance with Article 7 of the treaty consulted the Italian government. Giolitti who was then Prime Minister replied that the Triple Alliance was defensive and not offensive, that Italy would not intervene in the war.

What did not happen in 1913, unfortunately came to pass in 1914.

It was natural after what had occurred in 1913 that the Austrian government should not only seek no agreement with Italy, but should maintain the strictest secrecy in the preparation of the aggression against Serbia; and that in the period between the assassination of the heir to the throne at Sarajevo and the declaration of war upon Serbia, she should reject all intervention by foreign powers and all peaceful advice. Vienna was determined to occupy Serbia, whose strength seemed a real danger to the Southern-Slavs then under the rule of the Hapsburgs.

After Austria had declared war on Serbia and then on Russia, the Italian government on August 2 declared its neutrality, and the semi-official press explained that this was because the Austrian note to Serbia was communicated to Serbia before informing Italy, in spite of the obligation laid down in Article 7 of the Triple Alliance treaty which forbade Austrian operations in the Balkans without prior agreement with Italy. This was the officially inspired interpretation, accepted by the majority of Italians. Only a small and noisy nationalist minority dissented, maintaining that Italy should join the Central Empires not because she was obliged to but to safeguard her own interests. This was resented by Austria and Germany. Austria at first denied that she was under any obligation to consult Italy; later she admitted that the occupation of the Balkan provinces made it necessary for her to compensate Italy and negotiations to that effect were begun.

On the other hand, France, England and Russia rejoiced at Italian neutrality, which indeed was in accordance with previous understandings and as far as France was concerned to explicit undertakings. As a result Italy refrained from sending troops to the French frontiers, either in Italy or in Libya. This was of enormous advantage to France, freed from the necessity of detaching any part of her armies to guard Italian frontiers.* The fate of France was hanging in the balance, just when the Germans were reaching Compiègne (September 5) and the victorious battle of the Marne (September 6–14) was beginning to take shape. Shortly thereafter the foreign minister who had upheld the thesis of neutrality, Marquis San Giuliano, died and was succeeded by Sidney Sonnino.

*   *   *

Italy waited till April, 1916, to decide whether she would continue neutral or enter the war. Only on May 23 did she formally denounce the treaty of the Triple Alliance and declare war on Austria, and later on August 26, 1916, on Germany as well. The period of neutrality was necessary for political, financial and military preparation. Italy had but recently emerged from the Libyan war. More than anything it was necessary to prepare public opinion. The neutralist current was strong, headed by Giolitti and followed by the majority of socialists and fairly reinforced by Catholics of the Right.

In such circumstances Italy naturally sought to settle the old problem of the *"terre irredenti,"* the Trentino and Istria. This claim was just as legitimate as that of France for the return of Alsace-Lorraine. No one could deny the Italian character of the cities of Trento and Trieste and most of those provinces, any more than the fact that Austrian policy had deliberately slavonized these lands of Italian speech and history. Besides it was only right that in a Europe armed

* It is amazing that between the two wars British, French and American historians, journalists and public men, even British members of parliament, kept on repeating that in 1914 Italy failed in her treaty obligations to the Central Empires and that Italian policy was tainted with Machiavellism. Gratitude is not a political virtue but the search for truth is a duty alike of historians and of public men who are concerned with historical facts. The basis of Italian policy in the Balkans during the entire period of the Triple Alliance was to maintain the defensive character of the treaty. Italian neutrality in the First World War was more than justified. And what can be said of the allied journalists who in connection with the Badoglio government's declaration of war on Germany in October 1943 (after the governments of London, Washington and Moscow had recognized the co-belligerency of Italy) unjustly criticized Italy saying she was "accustomed to betray" and recalling the First World War.

to the teeth, in which Austro-German influence could not be minimized even in the event of defeat, Italy should make herself secure within frontiers that Dante had recorded in the *Divine Comedy* and nature traced with impassable mountains.

What many (including the author) could not tolerate was the narrowly national outlook of the Salandra government, in times pregnant with the fate of nations, in matters that touched the very principles of civilized life. When Salandra took over the ministry of foreign affairs *ad interim* after the death of San Giuliano, he said that he would follow the same line of policy and added that to do so "demanded boldness not in words but in deeds, a mind free of all preconceptions, of all prejudice, of all feeling other than an exclusive and unlimited devotion to our country, a sacred egoism for Italy." Those were ill-considered words that isolated the problem of Italy from that of the world. This *sacred egoism* (there can be no such thing as sacred egoism) has been thrown back at us on many occasions; morally it weakened Italy's rightful claims.

No less clumsy than the phrase was the way the negotiations were conducted. In order not to incite further the opposition of those who favored neutrality and also to fall in with the wishes of certain nationalist groups, it was necessary to treat with Austria on the basis of concessions, promising in return Italian neutrality for the entire duration of the war. Those who favored intervention were opposed to such negotiations which they considered shameful; it would have been more honest and more dignified to wrest from Austria the unredeemed territories by force of arms, than receive them as the price of a neutrality that would prevent assistance to France, the victim of aggression, and support of Belgium and Serbia actually overrun. Italian volunteers were already in France!

This was the view that prevailed. But the insistence of Sonnino that the treaty of London should define all the advantages to accrue to Italy at the end of the war—as if anyone could predict how and when the war would end—the secrecy with which the treaty was surrounded even after Italy had entered the war and maintained even in regard to the United States *(until the bolshevists published the text of the treaty); the pretense of claiming the Dalmatian coast to which Italy had absolutely no right, were so many mistakes that weighed heavily on Italian policy. We all know that the game of diplomacy is nearly always played on the outskirts of ordinary morality and often far beyond, but when the future of Europe and of Italy herself as a free and democratic country was at stake, the country was thrown into a war to the death for a few areas to which its claim was dubious and that were of little worth, owing to Sonnino's shortsightedness and Salandra's incapacity to rise above national realism to a wider vision of events.

Fortunately there were men who soon rose above selfish and nationalist considerations, who saw what was at stake in the war. In opposition to Sonnino's views, a current of opinion was thus formed that clearly foresaw the collapse of the Hapsburg empire, the rise of new nationalities, the triumph of democracy, the need of a federation or League of Nations. Even before American intervention and the formulation of Wilson's fourteen points, the yeast was working in Italy as in France. Benedict XV in his message to the belligerents on August 1, 1917, referred explicitly to disarmament, arbitration, sanctions, the freedom of the seas, economic understanding, a supreme court and other matters. In Rome an agreement was reached with the national minorities of the Austrian empire on terms stipulated in the pact of Rome, and the government authorized the formation of a Czechoslovak legion on Italian soil.

Although the fraternal help given by Italy to the Serbs, Montenegrins, Macedonians and Albanians was considerable, and the pact of Rome raised the hopes of the Croats, Slovenes,

---

* Wilson said he had no knowledge of the treaty of London. This was true as far as official diplomatic cognizance was concerned, but not as to actual "lay" knowledge.

Slovaks and Czechs, the government's policy in regard to Dalmatia, Vallona and Fiume aroused doubt, mistrust and controversy. A closed Adriatic was a historical anachronism, just as if the English in the twentieth century had thought to regain Calais they had lost in the sixteenth century. Commercially, neither Trieste nor Fiume could live if their hinterland were blocked by states hostile to Italy. Sonnino imagined that after the war Austria would remain powerful and be Italy's enemy. So he hastened to claim Dalmatia, Vallona and the island of Saseno so as to fortify the entrance to the Adriatic. To maintain this view of Italian defense when the Austro-Hungarian empire was falling to pieces and even after its collapse harmed rather than helped the affairs of Italy.

All this was clear to the democrats and liberals and to the group of Christian-democrats, but not to the conservatives and nationalists and the many who were ignorant of foreign problems. Unfortunately the attitude of the socialists, save men of worth like Bissolati and Salvemini, was always hostile to the war; and after the Russian revolution took on a bolshevist tinge. For many socialists each particular political problem was then merely a matter of bourgeois interest and capitalist intrigue. Their pacifist propaganda even penetrated to the front-line trenches.

* * *

Nationalist and pacifist crises abounded in all countries during the First World War. Wartime difficulties, defeats, mutinies in armies and navies, heroic stands and glorious offensives were on every front. Many were Italy's valorous and gallant deeds among volunteers in France, on the Austrian fronts of the Trentino and Istria, at sea and wherever Italian forces were engaged with the enemy. Italy's entry into the war came at a time when the Allies were in difficulty, when the Russian armies were being driven out of Galicia, the German armies strongly entrenched on the Aisne and Lys, and England painfully involved in the Gallipoli campaign. Italian operations on the Julian and Tridentine Alps were most arduous and costly, with no apparent results. But they served to wear down the enemy.

The Russian revolution of 1917 undermined the position the Allies had gained on all fronts. The enemy's peace offensive found listeners in all countries; the working classes were in ferment. This was not the most propitious moment for the initiative taken by Benedict XV, although Vatican diplomacy had sought to prepare the ground. Events were changing the situation more rapidly than could the diplomats. The Pope's message of August 1, which contained the true bases of peace and proposed opportune practical solutions, fell to the ground not merely because of opposition in Italy, France and England, and even in America, but because public opinion was no longer disposed to listen to voices of peace. The Central Empires on their part delayed replying; they would have had to make concessions on many points and waited for the hostile reaction of the Allies to justify their position. By then American intervention had raised the hopes of the Allies, not only materially but by the emphasis given to the moral values of the Allied war aims, by the idea that the war to end wars was being fought, provided German militarism were definitely crushed.

The assumption of power in Russia by the Marxist bolshevists a few months later made a deep impression on the working classes, all the more so as pacificist propaganda had not ceased. An Italian socialist leader had launched the slogan "Out of the trenches by November!" and at the end of October by an unhappy coincidence the Italians gave way before the Austrian offensive without fighting and abandoned the Caporetto area. The name has remained in the minds of non-Italians as a disgrace to our soldiers and a symbol of the whole war fought in Italy. It is sad to record this, but ignorance, antipathy, jealousy and the presumed superiority of others count for something in the forging of myths. The cause of the retreat at Caporetto was exclusively military. Caporetto was neither a betrayal by the commanders, nor a mutiny of the troops, nor an act of cowardice of the Italian soldier. It was the effect of surprise, of enemy initiative, of inadequate counteraction by the other side. No belligerent on either side but had its Caporettos, just as France had her Sedans in 1870 and 1940. Caporetto is not an Italian disgrace any more than Sedan was a French disgrace. With this difference, that in 1917 the Italian lines were immediately re-formed on the Tagliamento, the Isonzo and the Piave. Caporetto was avenged at Grappa and Vittorio Veneto. The victory over Austria was an Italian victory; much as it was appreciated the help of the Allies was strictly limited. Public morale revived at once, not only because of Italian resistance that lasted a year from November 4, 1917, to November 4, 1918; but because of two transcendent moral factors: Wilson's fourteen points of January, 1918, and the visible collapse of the Austro-Hungarian empire with the triumph of the oppressed peoples.*

The Peace Conference did not altogether reflect public opinion in the victorious countries. Never in human affairs can reality attain to the ideal; unfortunately on this occasion the distance between reality and the ideal was deliberately increased. Clemenceau, Lloyd George, Orlando, preoccupied almost exclusively with the position of their respective countries, were not equal to the occasion, and Wilson found himself ill-prepared by lack of real knowledge of the problems and men of Europe; moreover his position was weakened by isolationist opposition in America. Today from all sides criticism is heaped upon Versailles; not without reason although

* It may well be recalled here that in the Abyssinian campaign of 1895–96 the Italian soldier, although inexperienced in colonial warfare, showed great courage, faced hardships and death without wavering in his duty and gave proof of indomitable heroism. Amba Alagi is famous even among the Ethiopians as the glorious grave of Major Toselli and his two thousand odd soldiers. The name of Major Galliano is attached to the defense of Makalle. At Adowa came defeat: twenty thousand against a hundred thousand; political mistakes; tactical errors; generals who refused to withdraw in time; soldiers who met the death of heroes. Adowa and Caporetto were and still are spoken of in the same breath, because the Italian press was hypercritical of government and generals, because public opinion ill-prepared clamored in the first case for immediate withdrawal and peace at any price, and in the second (Caporetto) while fighting on demanded a parliamentary investigation (which would have been a good thing). But Cadorna was oversusceptible and his telegram had already distorted the truth in the eyes of the world.

the mistakes then made were less than those the Allied and
associated powers committed later, especially between 1931
and 1939.

All the mistakes were contained in one: the exclusion of
representatives of the vanquished countries from the Peace
Conference. Even though they wished to make the peace
terms harsh and their victory felt, the Allies should have
brought them into relation with the material and moral
possibilities of their adversaries. Psychologically free discussion between victors and vanquished would have been of
immense advantage; it would have paved the way for a reconciliation of peoples. What did not take place at the conference
inevitably happened later under less favorable psychological
and material conditions. The treaty of Locarno followed in
1925, the withdrawal of the armies of occupation from the
Rhineland in 1930, the agreements of Lausanne and Geneva
in 1932; but it was too late and meanwhile there had been
the occupation of the Ruhr, the collapse of the mark, the
refusal after 1930 to co-operate with the republican government in Germany on urgent financial matters and for the
relief of unemployment.

Another mistake was the arousing of the wildest hopes in
connection with the creation of the League of Nations, and
then undermining it from the very start by the abstention of
the United States and the initial violations of the spirit of the
League in the case of Poland and Lithuania, the deportation
of the Greek populations of Asia Minor and Bulgaria, and the
Italian bombardment of Corfu.

A third mistake was the dissolution of the war alliance that
should have become a peace alliance. America not only refused to ratify the collective peace treaty, but negotiated and
signed separate treaties with each of the vanquished States.
England refused to guarantee the frontiers of France, as
though it would have been possible for her to stand aloof
in a new war between Germany and France. Italy, wounded
in her national pride by the Adriatic question, treated
directly with Yugoslavia and reached an agreement at Rapallo

in 1920. Moreover, she was disillusioned because no colonial mandate was assigned to her, and she could not reach agreements on the frontiers of Libya, Eritrea and Somaliland provided for in the treaty of London.

With the exception of France, the victorious countries appeared almost ashamed of their actions, decreasing their psychological importance in the face of the world. Moreover revolutionary Russia and the socialist and communist parties in every country held up Versailles as the fruit of unbridled imperialism, a bourgeois and reactionary conception, violating the most elementary rights of the people who only by revolution could bring social and international peace to the world.

The specter of revolution hovered over Europe and even America, influencing the course of events. Italy was the first to feel its tragic consequences. With her weak economic structure, politically perturbed by extremist currents of revolutionary socialists and exasperated nationalists, the country went through one upheaval after another. The question of Fiume, that should have been of minor importance, was magnified into a national question. The occupation of Fiume by d'Annunzio that should have remained a literary adventure profoundly stirred public opinion. D'Annunzio was imitating Zeligowski's raid on Vilna; the difference between the two countries was that the Italian government at Christmas, 1920, sent its navy to drive its citizens and soldiers out of Fiume, whereas the Polish government did not withdraw from Vilna and obtained the benevolent toleration of the League of Nations.

There was an aftermath to Fiume. Mussolini had conceived fascism as a party at once socialist and nationalist. His first idea anteceded the national socialism of Hitler, who afterward started his movement for revenge in Germany. Indeed the two had this in common, that both relied on the social revolution of the masses and used youth as a lever of nationalist aspirations, Mussolini in a betrayed Italy, Hitler in an oppressed Germany.

The history of Italian fascism and German nazism has been written and rewritten and will yet be written a hundred times. The ancestry of the former has been sought in the *compagnie di ventura* of the fifteenth century or in falsifying the story of the Roman Empire; of the latter in the Teutonic knights or in the Germans of Tacitus. The best is to confine oneself to the peace treaties and the Russian revolution as the immediate causes of fascism, and to trace nazism to the immediate past of Bismarck and William I, that is to the formation of the German empire. We shall thus avoid all "hereditary" theories whether of race, blood or soil, memories of imperial Rome, Marx's historical materialism, Hegel's concept of the state, and eschew even the laws of Freudian complexes, for all these could be applied at will to any period of collective crisis precipitated in the name of ancient or modern or modernized myths by any popular leader or demagogue thrown up by revolutionary movements.

While Hitler and Mussolini were finding ways of agreement, Japan too overcame the postwar crisis by a strengthening of her militarist and imperialist elements and, without speeches from the Palazzo Venezia or Nuremberg, forged ahead by trade and military adventures, prepared for the supreme test.

3

Italy and the Second World War

HISTORIANS OF THE FUTURE will make the Second World War begin either with the Japanese aggression on Manchuria in 1931, the Abyssinian war in 1935 or the Spanish civil war in 1936; others perhaps with the occupation of Austria or the Munich agreements in 1938. None certainly will describe it as falling from heaven on September 1, 1939. Many there are today who, combining the First and Second World Wars, commonly refer to the "Twenty Years' Armistice." Historically, this idea is open to question, as in 1918 there was not complete Allied victory on all land and sea fronts, peace treaties of a definite nature were not signed and despite the League of Nations a new international order was not set up.

One may classify facts as causes or effects; but they are merely elements of the historical process that, as factors conditioning man's free will, can lead to a peaceful revolution just as they have led to a new world conflagration. History is not made with hypotheses, but men often have recourse to them to invalidate the theory of *force majeure,* or fatal necessity or blind determinism. If, to take the Italian instance, the League of Nations had applied economic sanctions to the full, threatening military sanctions if necessary, without tergiversation, and had made the fascist government understand that armed intervention would follow, the Abyssinian war would never have been fought, Hitler would never have attempted the occupation of the demilitarized Rhineland, and certainly neither Mussolini nor Hitler would have gone into Spain to try out new arms and new tactics.

The cleavage of policies, toward rearmament here and disarmament there; toward psychological preparation for war here and appeasement there, began with the completion of the fascist revolution and the inception of the totalitarian state in November 1926; with the predominance of Stalin in Russia in 1927; with the nazification of German youth and Hitler's influence over the male and female electorate in Germany in various local and general elections from 1927 to 1932; with the seizure of power in Japan by the militarist element and the elimination of opponents by violence and assassination from 1929 to 1932; with the various dictatorships that arose in small and medium-sized European countries from 1923 onward, among them Primo de Rivera in Spain, Pangalos in Greece, Pilsudski in Poland, Horthy in Hungary, King Alexander in Yugoslavia, Gomez da Costa and then Carmona in Portugal.

All these events were phases of a nationalist, antisocial and totalitarian revolution that developed in Europe, after the successful pattern of Russia and Italy. The former classed as a revolution of the proletariat was called bolshevism which, losing its local and Russian meaning, remained in the West as synonymous with anticapitalist and atheist communism. The second was called fascism which, losing its local and Italian meaning, stood for capitalist and anticommunist reaction. So it was rightly said that bolshevism was a fascism of the Left, and fascism a bolshevism of the Right. But both were at heart exasperated nationalism, closed to all spiritual values beyond their own symbols (hammer and sickle or fasces) which had superseded all principles of freedom, law, religion.

The words totalitarianism and totalitarian, not to be found in any dictionary prior to 1925, were first used by Mussolini to indicate the putting away of everything foreign to the fascist state and the inclusion within it of every *raison d'être* of individual and community.

Those who see politics only as the interplay of interests and influences of material power cannot understand how a few ideas without serious foundation, either philosophical or ethical, even without inner logic, can have been so potent merely because they were skillfully converted into feeling: a feeling of fear of bolshevism, of safety in dictatorship, of nationalist exaltation, of revenge for the disillusions of the war (Italy was among the disappointed), of impotence in the discouraged democracies and above all in the economic crisis that alarmed capitalist circles where, from 1929 onward, people feared the loss of their positions through the rise of the working classes and the agitation they maintained amid growing general insecurity.

Of all this, nationalist and totalitarian tendencies took advantage even in democratic and well-knit countries like England, France and the United States. At one time it looked as though the experiments of Mussolini and Hitler had found favor not only in Wall Street and in the City, as well as in the great international press, but even in the State Department and the foreign ministries of the democratic countries, where men should have been on the alert and conscious of what was growing up in the world.

The various wars that took place between 1931 and 1939 were all directed, whether so intended or not, toward the great final struggle, the duel between democratic and totalitarian countries, two conflicting political systems, two opposing forces for world dominion. Thus although no one of these wars taken by itself led necessarily to the world conflict, their concatenation was sufficient to prepare the psychological atmosphere for the explosion of the present war.

The international structure is not something that can be improvised in a day or changed overnight. It is the outcome of prolonged processes, of continuous efforts, of repeated experiments, of occasional readjustments. Because mankind has not yet reached the stage of an international community of permanent character and adequate authority, very little is needed to upset the balance between the various powers.

If Europe was able to pass forty years without war, from 1871 to 1911, this was not due to the merit of a man or the influence of a star; it was because after all the balance of power on which the politics of the period rested was not so overweighted in favor of one group or against another as to create a war psychosis in the power that believed itself able to win a swift and certain victory. The formation of a Prussianized German Empire, uniting under a single command the greatest national bloc, and the unification of Italy, had already disturbed the relations of the powers in Europe. Germany's *rapprochement* with Austria, the weakening of Turkey and the entry of Italy into the Triple Alliance, made it necessary for France to draw closer to England and Russia. Thus the forces of the first European conflict, that became a world war, took shape. The small local wars of Libya and the Balkans were enough to upset the unstable balance and create a war psychosis in the Central Empires.

The same process preceded the Second World War. Everybody well knew the weakness of the League of Nations; a new organization of such wide scope cannot form bone in a few months, but everybody knew also that it had the support of England, France and the other countries weary of war and thirsting for peace. The defeated countries came within the orbit of the League, except Germany which entered it belatedly in 1925, torn between conflicting currents, communists, nationalists, Hitlerian or national socialist, that were undermining the Weimar Republic. The specter of Old Germany rose and grew visible behind Stresemann and Hindenburg. No one thought of Mussolini as a danger, indeed he was allowed to have his way after his interventions in Corfu and Fiume in 1923 and 1924.

The United States, while remaining outside the League, had taken the initiative of the Washington Conference at which seven treaties were signed, including the Five-Power Treaty for the Limitation of Naval Armaments, the Four-Power Treaty on Pacific Island Possessions and the Nine-Power Treaty relating to China. The Washington Conference was a success and gave promise of being the forerunner of even greater achievements. The limitation of naval armaments was the first great failure and when, at the expiration of its ten-year term, the treaty of Washington came up for revision and renewal at the London Conference in 1931, dissensions between the signatory powers made agreement impossible. And it was in the Pacific itself that the first grave breach appeared. After the failure of the London Conference, Japan, in violation of the Nine-Power Treaty, occupied Manchuria and set up a theoretically independent kingdom that was actually subordinate to Tokyo.

Whether in accordance with the Nine-Power Treaty or the Covenant of the League of Nations, the signatory powers with or without the intervention of other states not directly concerned should have prevented such an act and brought Japan to reason. Their combined fleets were more than three times as large as that of Japan. Recourse was had to verbal remedies —first inquiry, then lamentations by the League. Japan left the League of Nations, slamming the door behind her, but she retained the mandates of the Gilbert, Marshall and Caroline Islands and continued to send reports to Geneva, meanwhile fortifying the islands although this was forbidden by the terms of the mandate.

Those who believe that material causes are what count, and minimize the importance of ideas and of states of mind produced by ideas, have met with hard rebuffs in the course of this century. The weakness shown by states acting in the name of the League of Nations in sustaining the very principles on which it was based seemed unimportant but its effects were incalculable. Manchuria was the fourth blow, following Vilna, Corfu and Fiume, but it was the most serious. China, a member of the League, was deprived of a wide territory and left without defense in an unequal war. A precedent to be followed by others.

* * *

General De Bono, in his *African Memoirs,* published after the conquest of Abyssinia with a preface by Mussolini, gives 1932 as the date when he received word from the Duce to prepare for the war which broke out ("broke out" is the usual word) in October, 1935. Note the coincidence: in 1932 Japan was creating the state of Manchukuo and leaving the League of Nations, in 1932 Hitler won his first great electoral successes and von Papen and Schleicher, succeeding one another as German chancellors, paved the way for nazism. No one can say that Mussolini was losing time. This notwithstanding, historians will continue to date the Abyssinian war from the Wal-Wal incident in December, 1934, and from Laval's visit to Rome in January, 1935, when the French Minister settled with Italy the questions of the Libyan frontiers, the status of Italians in Tunisia and the Djibouti railway, all of which had been pendant since 1919. At the same time Laval gave Mussolini a free hand in Abyssinia.

As the war progressed, efforts to reach a compromise never ceased. Thus there arose the so-called Hoare-Laval plan which appears to have been prepared in unofficial understanding with Mussolini, who hastened to reject it when he saw how violently English public opinion had reacted against it. And while Mussolini continued a war to the death with Abyssinia and subjugated the country in eight months, France and England were relying on the attrition of the Italian forces instead of on the political and economic resistance of the League.

When the deed was accomplished, not only did Italy remain in the League and on the Council, where she had a permanent seat, but sanctions were speedily and unconditionally withdrawn; the Negus lost, besides his empire, his legal representation in Geneva; Italy proclaimed the Empire of East Africa and to the title of her King added the more showy one of Emperor. *De jure* recognition by members of the League was lacking, but this they gave one after the other, including England. The United States did not. It had not joined in the policy of sanctions, and so continued to trade with Italy, at the same time it placed an embargo on arms so that not even Abyssinia could obtain any.

This is not the time to carp against the Chamberlains, the

Simons, the Samuel Hoares and their predecessors, Baldwin, MacDonald, or in France against Tardieu, Laval, Daladier and even Léon Blum, who himself proposed the unconditional lifting of sanctions against Italy. They and many others were already embarked upon a policy of appeasement and saw no other means of avoiding war than by giving way again and again and again.

The League of Nations it is true emerged morally defeated from its antifascist adventure, and Mussolini was extolled in Italy and abroad as the man who had the courage to brave England, hold the League at bay and win a brilliant victory over an international coalition. Even American trumpets were sounding a paean for fascism.

What happened between 1936 and 1939 is known to all. Hitler, after having left the League of Nations and wrecked the disarmament conference, knew no restraint. The military clauses of the Treaty of Versailles no longer existed for him. The warning of the powers that met at Stresa in April, 1935, must have seemed supremely ridiculous to Hitler, to say nothing of the subsequent resolution of the League with its vague threat of measures to be adopted. When the time was ripe, he not only helped Italy to resist sanctions, but proceeded in March, 1936, to occupy by force the demilitarized zone of the Rhine. France instead of mobilizing and marching, as it was her right and interest to do, protested; England washed her hands of the matter; Belgium saw her system of international defense crumbling and changed her policy to one of vigilant and armed neutrality. The Treaty of Locarno, on which peace with Germany rested, foundered in a few days. The coup had succeeded.

Those who even today would have us believe that the army rebellion in Spain was an internal affair and a preventative defense against a Red revolution, forget the initial agreements reached between Spanish generals and the fascist government in Rome in 1934, the further agreements in the Spring of 1936 between Rome and Berlin, and Hitler's desire to test *in corpore vili* new arms and new methods of warfare, while in the face of mankind he and his compeer posed as the champions of antibolshevism, winning Catholic sympathies throughout the world.

Careful examination of facts and verification of dates show that Franco's revolt preceded the attacks on churches and the murders of priests and monks, which were no novelty in Spanish civil wars. The dispatch of Italian airplanes that made a landing in French territory in North Africa coincided as to time with the revolt, and must have been ordered and organized beforehand. This is not said to excuse the revolutionary propaganda of the Reds, or the corrosive anarchism of certain Spanish parties, which had no scruples about setting fire to churches and convents. Their attitude was due not to any reaction of the moment nor to the circulation of bolshevist leaflets, but was the effect of a century-old antisocial and antireligious cleavage that had left some of the people a prey to primitive instincts. When occasion offered, as it did with a military revolt openly supported by the clergy and backed by the new crusaders, Hitler and Mussolini, popular passions erupted. It was unfortunate that except for the cardinal of Tarragona, the bishop of Vitoria, the Basque priests and a few others, all the clergy were involved in Franco's military revolt. The victims, mostly innocent monks, priests and nuns, were murdered by the thousands; churches were burned and altars profaned. But to the list must be added the many workers and republicans killed by the military, the falangists, the Spanish partisans, or put to death in prison.

The Church was blamed, but what were England and France doing? Leaving the working classes and the parties of the Left to support the republicans, they placed an embargo on arms, declared themselves neutral, and stultified themselves by debates in a Nonintervention Committee set up in London (no longer in Geneva) in an attempt to run with the hare and hunt with the hounds. If France and England had not so willed, the Spanish republic would not have been overthrown. But France and England wanted Franco to win, because it entered into the plan already conceived by Mr. Cham-

berlain for a European understanding, giving Hitler and
Mussolini everything they wanted in order to buy peace.*
Thus Geneva was reduced to silence. When a member of
the House of Commons insisted that the League of Nations
should be revived, Mr. Chamberlain gave his famous retort:
"The League! The League! It is a parrot cry." It was the end.
Mr. Eden had resigned over the question of Italian intervention in Spain and Mr. Chamberlain had hastened to sign
with Mussolini the new Mediterranean agreement in April,
1938, a pendant to the naval agreement signed with Hitler
not long before. At the same time Austria was occupied without protest either from the powers or the League of Nations.
Indeed England herself, continuing her concessions, sent
Lord Runciman to Czechoslovakia, where he was to prepare
so well the dismemberment of that unhappy country.

Munich will remain as a word of infamy and cowardice.
Hitler obtained a cheaply won triumph. Mussolini was the
"honest broker," the man who only wanted peace. Naturally
Dr. Benês, the interested party who would have to foot the
bill, was not present. France, who had a treaty of alliance
with Czechoslovakia and another with Russia, never thought
of her obligations under them and agreed that the two countries should be kept out of the Four-Power Conference, while
matters of essential and vital interest to them were being

* Mention may be made here of the initiative taken by the British Committee
for Civil and Religious Peace in Spain, of which Mr. Wickham Steed was chairman and the author a member, in agreement with a similar committee in Paris
headed by Professor Jacques Maritain, and a third wholly Spanish but also in
Paris under Professor Alfred Mendizabal. A plan for an armistice between the
belligerents in Spain was drawn up, with conditions of an international character
to be supported by England and France. We had the impression that at that time
English pressure on the fascist government would not have been unavailing. It
was when London and Rome were negotiating the Mediterranean agreement and
Mr. Chamberlain was to meet with Mussolini. The plan was submitted in March,
1938, to Lord Halifax, then Foreign Secretary. But Mr. Chamberlain refused to
mention it to Mussolini or to discuss the pacification of Spain with him. It was
not only Mussolini who wanted the fall of the republic, but also Mr. Chamberlain, to whom this event was one of the stones of his European edifice. So that
the reader may not confuse, as is often done, Negrin's government in the hands of
the extremists with the republic, it must be made clear that the above committees
did not take part for either side during the civil war, but worked for civil and
religious peace which even today has not been achieved in Spain.

discussed. After that the people of Paris and London acclaimed their saviors, scattering flowers in the triumphal path of the heroes of Munich.

What were the consequences: Poland seized Teschen from Czechoslovakia and proposed a real German-Polish alliance; but Germany in March, 1939, demanded the return of Danzig and the Corridor, occupied Bohemia-Moravia and set up the Protectorate. In April she denounced the ten year treaty with Poland signed in 1934 (an agreement that followed the unhappy Four-Power pact proposed by Mussolini, which sent Mr. MacDonald and Lord Simon scurrying to Rome). Then in April, 1939, on Good Friday if you please, fascist Italy occupied Albania, without a protest from anyone, save the allusion in the Pope's Easter address. In May following the "iron pact" that linked the fate of Italy to that of Germany was signed in Milan. Japan was soon to follow suit. Thus the Rome-Berlin-Tokyo axis was perfected in time for the new great war.

Then another step: the neutralization of Russia. England had hastened to guarantee Poland's existence, to offer her good graces to Rumania (the oil interests were involved), to restore contact with Russia so as to bring back to life the earlier treaties and understandings that had been modified at Munich a few months before. But Poland refused to allow Russia passage through her territory in the event of a German attack, and this opposition made it impossible for England, France and Russia to reach a new agreement. On the other hand it looked as though Moscow were seeking the consent or neutrality of Paris and London in the event of an occupation of the Baltic states. It is certain however that Stalin and Molotov kept the representatives of the democracies waiting while they were negotiating with Ribbentrop, with whom they reached agreement on August 23. The Second World War began on September 3, 1939. Germany invaded Poland; England and France were obliged to take up the challenge.

Italian, German, Spanish and Irish propaganda, every anti-Jewish publication in the world and all the old clericalism

that was emerging on the fringes of the war, accused England
of having wanted war for imperialist reasons, a new duel for
the territorial and economic control of the world. It was clear
enough then and it was even clearer later on that Neville
Chamberlain and his colleagues could be accused of anything
except an imperial war. They had done everything in their
power to avert war. So true was it that Hitler alone wanted
war, that he had everything ready: plans, armies, armaments, new inventions, new tactics. England went to war with
but few soldiers, inadequate and old-fashioned armament,
and insufficient forces to protect the Empire. Such were her
preparations for a war of conquest.

* * *

A little after Munich, Mr. Chamberlain himself con-
fessed that war was inevitable and that it was necessary to
prepare for it. But the peoples of the democratic countries
were not prepared for war; for a war psychology is always
created by aggression, a war of conquest, of reconquest, of
revenge. So England and France had no such war complex.
At the same time England and France felt themselves secure
from all aggression. The governments and military leaders
believed that the Maginot Line and the naval blockade were
enough to check Hitler. They relied on the defensive. Even
if Poland fell there was the neutral wall of Russia. It is true
they feared for the fate of Hungary and Rumania and also
of the Balkans; but they counted on their forces in the East
to defend French and British possessions. Was not all naval
strength in the Mediterranean in Allied hands?

In the first surveys of the war in London and Paris, Italy
was not taken into account. The "iron pact" of Milan, weld-
ing the Rome-Berlin axis, was not considered a serious threat.
What was known to antifascists, was not understood by the
governments concerned. Following his natural bent Mussolini alternated reassuring words and hostile declarations to
London and Paris. The Chamberlains and Daladiers accepted
the reassuring words and had the press told that the hostile

declarations were for home consumption. When Mussolini declared neutrality, the Allies drew a long breath. Praise of the Duce was not lacking and certain French papers sought to compare Italian neutrality in 1914 with Italian neutrality in 1939, without realizing that the former was friendly to the Allied cause and never admitted for a moment the possibility that Italy could go to war on the side of the Central Empires; whereas the latter was unfriendly to the Allies and did not admit the possibility of Italy going to war on the side of London and Paris, but did provide by the pact of Milan for intervention in the war on the side of Hitler. Italy had then just emerged from two wars, in Abyssinia and in Spain, not to mention the Albanian adventure, her army was ill-equipped and she needed time to prepare herself. It was said Hitler had given her three years to do so. When Hitler, without warning his ally, attacked Poland, young Ciano went so far as to say that it had been done before the time agreed upon. It was believed in Rome and perhaps in Berlin that once the fate of Poland was sealed and she was partitioned anew between Germany and Russia, Paris and London would seek a compromise, another Munich to stop the war. Mussolini summarized the situation in words to the effect that the Polish question being settled, the broader question of world dominion could be postponed for a few years more.

But as the Allies did not think so, Mussolini continued to prepare for the decisive step, calling the second period of waiting "nonbelligerency," a phrase that pleased the newspapers and has passed into the dictionary and into history. Naturally nonbelligerency meant that Italy was doing Germany all possible favors, up to the limit beyond which she would have provoked the hostile intervention of the opposing side. Such intervention was never seriously considered either from the political standpoint, as it was hoped that all things being equal Italy would remain neutral, or from the military standpoint, as the inaction of the armies on the Siegfried and Maginot lines seemed insuperable, and there was no desire for a diversion that might break the stalemate and give the

initiative to the Allies. The latter did not see or did not wish
to see that offensive action in the Mediterranean, in Libya
and on the soil of Italy herself would have brought them immediate advantage, besides strengthening their position in
the Balkans and the Levant.

These are not *post factum* remarks, the usual being wise
after the event. They are problems that were foreseen and
discussed at the time. At the very outset of the war, Count
Sforza had a talk with Daladier, then head of the French government. He took the view, shared by many other Italians,
that London and Paris should at once send an ultimatum to
Mussolini to make up his mind for or against them, and come
down unequivocally on one side of the fence or the other,
and in the event of his refusal proceed to attack. Daladier replied that French public opinion would not understand such
a move, as it counted on Italian neutrality. General Georges
was said to take the same view. To think that France was still
ringing with the echoes of fascist demonstrations for Nice,
Corsica and Tunis!

This episode reveals the confusion of ideas in the minds of
those responsible for English and French policy. Naturally
fascist agents abounded in both countries at war, and espion-
age on Hitler's behalf was carried on everywhere. Fascist
propaganda took on every form: blandishments, threats, sopo-
rifics, flattery, lies! It must be recognized that many in France
and England during this period wanted to be deceived. The
state of mind that in France had prevented an open stand
against Mussolini even when fascist intrigues with the Cagoulards were discovered continued unruffled. It was the state of
mind that did not allow Mussolini's name to be mentioned
during the trial of the assassins of King Alexander of Yugoslavia and Barthou, the French foreign minister; the state of
mind that hushed his name in the proceedings against the
murderers of the Rosselli brothers who were killed in France
in 1937. For Frenchmen of the Right, French civil servants,
professional soldiers and sailors, Mussolini was still a heaven-
sent antidote to communism; a man who all things considered

could if he liked say "no" to Hitler. Had he not sent Italian divisions to the Brenner Pass to prevent the seizure of Austria?

These successive events did not count, as the French press put the blame for them on the Left, the popular front and on the hostility of the French socialist party to Mussolini over the Abyssinian war and his intervention in Spain. And while Mussolini was inciting the fascist party to claim Nice and Savoy and Corsica and Tunis, claims that could only be satisfied by a victorious war against France, the French government, army leaders and press were still at the beginning of 1940 giving credit to Mussolini for his friendly non-belligerency. They refused to accept the offer of Italian volunteers in France to form an Italian Legion as in 1914. When official Paris at last opened its eyes, it was late indeed, and many of the Italians who had registered for service to France on the field of battle, fell into the clutches of Vichy, the Ovra or the Gestapo.

President Roosevelt's saying that "Mussolini stabbed France in the back" is often heard. It is inexact. Fascism began its anti-French policy in 1927, with street demonstrations demanding Nice, Savoy, Corsica and Tunis, and supporting a certain press that sought to attract the people of Corsica to fascist ideals. It revived this propaganda on the immediate morrow of Munich, either to frighten France by words, or to prepare public opinion for war. To fascist words, Daladier replied by his triumphal tour of Tunis and Corsica, and his *"Jamais!"* But if war was to come, to wrest from France, Tunis and Corsica, Nice and Savoy, it was not to be a duel between Italy and France, but a war undertaken together and in agreement with Hitler.

None are so deaf as those who will not hear! Hitler had written in *Mein Kampf* exactly what he proposed to do; Mussolini had always spoken of cannon, bayonets and wars, of the Roman Empire and fascist fortunes, of the "have" and the "have not" countries. It was plain even without saying so that the potential enemies of fascism were France and England.

The plans were ready, the division of the spoils assured, for Mussolini as well as for Hitler. England and France would have to recognize Italy's mastery over the Mediterranean—*"Mare Nostrum"*—and Italian influence in the Balkans as far as the Levant. Mussolini's intervention in 1940 was not a stab in the back. Even Mussolini was surprised at the rapidity of Hitler's advance, and he was unwilling that Hitler alone should enjoy complete victory over the democracies. I say this not to defend Mussolini, but to place the facts in their true historical perspective, and to show on the contrary what would have been the position of a democratic Italy, allied as in 1915 with France and England. But democratic Italy, which fought fascism from 1922 to 1926, was reduced to silence by exile, imprisonment, special courts and the violence of armed gangs, was ignored by the governments of London and Paris, opposed even, for it was a constant though unheeded reminder that democracies are bound together, that none can stand by itself if spiritual solidarity and freedom for all are lacking.

* * *

A most interesting historical fact and one that will well repay study is the general incomprehension of fascism. Sometimes it has been extolled with incredible fervor: "fascism gave back her soul to Italy," "a new order of society," "the keystone of European peace." At other times it has been presented as merely an internal diversion in Italian politics, good for a people who needed the big stick, constant parades, grandiloquent speeches and flamboyant gestures. Even during the war, in Anglo-Saxon countries, we have witnessed the incredible attitude of placing all the blame on nazism or rather on Germany, and of attenuating, even avoiding, criticism of fascism. There are even those who emphasize the harmlessness of fascism, or better still the advantages of a tempered fascism à la Salazar, à la Pétain or à la Franco! Finally there was an Otto of Hapsburg to accept a kind of democratic fascism or fascist democracy, which reminds one of poor Dollfuss and the unhappy Schuschnigg.

This deliberate or unconscious ignorance of the nature of fascism has ridiculous aspects. At one time before the war there were Catholics who extolled Mussolini and put the soft pedal on fascism; during the war Mussolini's name was dropped for a time or coupled (that could pass) with Hitler's, and the emphasis was placed on "semifascism," a new word current in certain Catholic circles in America. There is a fundamental confusion today between the fascist regime which is a most modern development, and the authoritarian regimes of the past, a past that is gone forever, those of paternal sovereigns and enlightened monarchs of the eighteenth century. Today the alternative is democracy or dictatorship! Intermediate forms will turn out to be short-lived hybrids because they are sterile.

In certain circles Pétain was immensely popular when he erased the "terrible" revolutionary motto of the republic— *Liberté, Egalité, Fraternité*—and replaced them by *Labor, Family, Country;* when he dissolved the trade unions (including the Christian unions) and sought to form state corporations; when he abolished parliament and all elected bodies, to have only commissions appointed by presidential authority. Between Pétain, Salazar, Dollfuss, and Schuschnigg on the one hand and Mussolini on the other, there is this difference —a fundamental difference if one would understand the history of Italy for the past twenty years—that for Mussolini fascism was not a conviction or a faith, but only a technique, a technique of power. In this Mussolini was Machiavellian, in the accepted sense of the word. Like all techniques, fascism was not subordinated to any fixed and unchangeable theory (this Father Tacchi-Ventura, the Jesuit, who for a long time was in contact with Mussolini, saw quite clearly). Mussolini created fascism as his personal instrument for attaining power, for maintaining himself in power, and for enhancing his power from national to imperial. For this purpose the cult of war was the basis of fascism as it was of nazism. It would have been impossible for Mussolini to attain any of his aims without the cult of war, without a militarized youth. Mussolini began with civil war against the socialists and the popular party, and he continued to organize everything including the national economy for the supreme aim of war. In this connection his classic phrase "What motherhood is to woman, war is to man" acquires its full significance.

Pétain the man of armistice at all costs, Salazar the man of Portugal's reconstruction in a regime of neutrality, are or were men of conviction. They believed in their methods as ethical and political sustenance for the good of the people. They were mistaken, as were Dollfuss and Schuschnigg, but not through lack of conviction. I do not put Franco on the same level because he is a product of war, a hybrid by Hitler out of Mussolini. His case is more complex and deserves to be discussed separately.* Those I have mentioned differ from Mussolini in that they believed in Fascism. Mussolini did not. His characteristic was that he was never loyal to principles; he lacked the instinct of consistency. Foreigners, on reading over the first fascist program of 1919 with its medley of socialist, anarchist, anticlerical, republican, antistate declarations, will believe this was a different Mussolini, not the monarchic, pro-Catholic, antibolshevist, corporative Mussolini of later years. To bring into being an Italy full of fascists, he used the technique of dictatorship and totalitarian ideas. Even today it is often said that fascism was a product of the postwar economic crisis, but this is a misreading of the facts.†

It is amazing that men like Mr. Hoover and Mr. Gibson in their noted book ‡ should have written that "the French attitude toward Italy drove Italy into the arms of Germany, and thereby greatly increased the menace to French safety. It began when the Italians were denied the promised lands enumerated in the secret treaty upon which they entered the war. Then followed French affronts and pin-pricks. The repeated rebuffs of Italian advances wasted the period when

---

* See *Church and State*, by Luigi Sturzo, Longmans, Green & Co., Inc., New York, 1939, pp. 512–15.
† See Appendix V, "Fascism and Economics."
‡ *The Problems of Lasting Peace*, p. 143.

Italy would have accepted almost any reasonable solution of colonial and naval questions."

They ignore the history of twenty years and even the history of the Peace Conference; they forget that the man who opposed the provisions of the treaty of London was none other than President Wilson. But apart from the controversies between Allies at the Peace Conference, Mr. Hoover and Mr. Gibson believe in a political continuity between democratic postwar Italy which never had an anti-French policy, and Fascist Italy which was anti-French, anti-English, anti-German or anti-American as occasion arose.*

This must not be taken as the criticism of exiled and impenitent opponents of fascism, unwilling to see any good in their adversaries. If events had not borne out the words of the antifascists abroad—unheeded Cassandras—some doubt might be cast upon their objectivity, but events provide irrefutable evidence, save for those who do not wish to see.

*   *   *

The main point, and this brings us back to our appraisal of the importance of Italian intervention in the war, is the fact that Hitler alone without Italy could not have attempted a world war. What happened in the five years between 1934 and 1939 was a secret revolution, understood only by those who knew the men concerned and the reasons for their actions. Neither the military occupation of the Rhineland, nor intervention in Spain, nor the rape of Austria, nor the destruction of Czechoslovakia would have been possible had Italy opposed it. But as Germany could not have given Euro-

* To complete the historical picture omitted by Mr. Hoover and Mr. Gibson, it may be recalled that in 1922–23, Mussolini agreed with Poincaré and favored the occupation of the Ruhr; that in 1925 he agreed with Sir Austen Chamberlain in the tripartite understanding over Ethiopia and Albania (Sir Austen went to Rome and Livorno); that on February 7, 1926, Mussolini contemplated an alliance with France to "check the menace of Pan-Germanism." In 1927 he had already had the idea of demanding Nice and Corsica, but really only after Laval had signed the Franco-Italian agreement and given Mussolini a free hand in Abyssinia did the Duce come to an understanding with Hitler and establish the joint lines of a war policy. Seventeen years had passed since Versailles, quite unnoticed by Mr. Hoover and his partner.

pean territories, nor colonies, nor control of the sea, nor Suez, nor Gibraltar, nor Malta, nor Tunis, war had to be made on the "haves" in the name of the "have nots," on pseudodemocratic capitalism in the name of autarchic fascism. Mussolini was obsessed by the idea that France was rotten, England senile and the United States isolationist. Here were perfectly ideal conditions in which to launch a bold war for the conquest of the world. The Axis was born of this idea.

The only time that England displayed any strength, at the outset at least, was at the Nyon Conference in 1937 in connection with the unknown submarines operating in the Mediterranean on behalf of Franco. The words "unknown submarines" were enough to show the diplomatic fear of offending Mussolini (and his comrade Hitler), both belligerents in Spain. Even this gesture, which by a euphemism we have called strong, was short-lived and at once gave place to the Mediterranean agreement between London and Rome.

On the other hand it cannot be denied that in France there were signs of decadence, or rather of fear and disintegration on the Right and on the Left. The weakness shown by the government and courts in connection with the assassination of the king of Yugoslavia, the murder of the Rosselli brothers, the bombs of the Cagoulards, were enough to feed Mussolini's arrogance and sense of strength.* But there is no

* During the first stages of the inquiry into fascist crimes ordered by the Italian Government, important revelations were made about the murders of Carlo and Nello Rosselli. These were plotted in Rome and carried out by Cagoulards in France in June, 1937. The Rome correspondent of the *New York Times* published a dispatch about it, and the widow of Carlo Rosselli, Signora Marion Rosselli, who has lived in the United States since 1940, wrote the following letter to the editor:

"I am deeply grateful to Mr. Matthews for the solicitude with which he has given me news of the first light on the mystery of my husband's and my brother-in-law's murder in France. The news that Count Galeazzo Ciano gave orders for the crime came as a complete surprise to me, but upon reflection I find it very natural (given the Fascist regime), as Count Ciano was Minister for Foreign Affairs at the moment and he needed to send the orders abroad. My conviction that Mussolini was the instigator of the crime is confirmed. What more obvious accomplice than the husband of his daughter, or one more likely to be silent for ever upon the affair?

"A suspicion that came to me on hearing of the executions at Verona has been confirmed. Two other old-time fascists were executed along with him. General Emilio De Bono and Marinelli. Both had been deeply implicated in the Matteotti

truth in the statement that once the war had started France would have welcomed defeat if it meant the end of the republic. This idea originated with and was cultivated by men like Pétain and Weygand only when defeat was at the gates, and was seized upon as a good opportunity to refashion a France according to their ideals. They totally failed to realize that a defeat accepted without resistance, when resistance is possible and a duty, can never constitute the cathartic phase of the moral restoration of a country. What happened to France in 1940 was precisely what happened to Italy in 1922: the collapse of democracy caused by a latent crisis in the ruling class, catalyzed by a sudden and serious surprise that broke down all capacity of resistance. As a social phenomenon this was neither exceptional nor new. However it must not be thought that even at such times circumstances overrule individual activity and create historic fatalism. Nothing in history is ever inevitable. If in France there had been a Churchill in place of a Reynaud, France would have been saved. If President Lebrun had not listened to Laval and had gone at once to Casablanca, as he intended, the situation would have been saved. Three years of war would have been gained. Even if the king of the Belgians had followed the example of the king of Norway or the queen of Holland or the grand duchess of Luxemburg and had gone to the Congo to continue the struggle, or into exile as did his government, Lebrun would not have had an example of surrender and might have resisted Laval's evil counsel. De Gaulle alone (*Orazio sol contro Toscana tutta,* as Dante would say) was not enough to avert the catastrophe, but he saved the honor of his country.

History, we repeat, is not made with hypotheses, but hypotheses help to clarify history. If Lebrun had not yielded, he

murder. By having them shot, Mussolini silenced two possible absolutely damning voices that might have turned against him if it were a question of life or death for them. General De Bono, especially, was Chief of Police at the time of Matteotti's disappearance and took a hair-raising part in hiding material evidence given him by the chief of the gang of murderers, Dumini.

"Among other motives to suppress Ciano, may there not have been the illusion that, by having him shot Mussolini was suppressing the fountainhead of any news that he was himself the originator of the crime against the Rosselli brothers?"

and part of his government, all the literary outpourings on the crisis and the rottenness of the French people would have remained unwritten, and people would have sung the praises of resistance under the most extreme difficulties. Likewise if England had asked for a compromise peace (as Chamberlain is said to have suggested, and the denial is not convincing) or if Hitler had gone straight from Paris to invade England, we should have in addition to the overwhelming catastrophe a flood of political, sociological, ethnographical literature to prove that France and England were both in the last stages of decay and that their democracy had carried them to disaster.

Such was the belief that fascism sought to spread throughout the world for twenty years. People now say it was all propaganda, they awoke to that fact rather late. Mussolini's technique first and later Hitler's technique was to use propaganda to weaken an adversary, better to attack him. Propaganda all too clever from their point of view, as it served to warp the moral and political standards of the whole world and to bring about the greatest tragedy of the centuries.

With this background, on June 10, 1940, Mussolini felt strong enough to declare war on France and England, and on December 11, 1941, on the United States.

4

Italy and the Allies

ITALY'S WAR, after a few small skirmishes on the French frontier that ended with the armistice of June 1940, was necessarily fought in Africa. The occupation of British Somaliland and the advance into Egypt with the taking of Sidi-Barrani were the first contacts between the Italians and the British, while in the Mediterranean there were encounters between the two fleets. After the short-lived Italian offensive, the British counterattacked and drove the Italians back into Libya. The latter sought to make a heroic stand at Bardia but in vain and before long the whole of Cyrenaica was lost. At the same time, in January 1941, the British invaded Eritrea and carried the war into Abyssinia.

The newly set-up Italian Empire in East Africa could be maintained only by a friendly England or a powerful army in Libya able to take Egypt without delay and to occupy Suez. In the absence of both these hypothetical factors, Italy's only course was to keep up small scale operations until the enemy (England) was completely defeated by other means on other fronts.

England, against all expectations, held out all through the darkest hours of the second half of 1940, so that Mussolini by one of those intuitions which were not the exclusive privilege of Hitler decided to make war on Greece. Instead of taking Egypt in a month, he hoped to occupy Greece in less time and to renew the campaign against Egypt from two directions. Also he wanted to stake a claim in Greece to offset Hitler's pressure on the Balkans. But the Greek war went badly. Too little attention has been paid to the courage of the Metaxas

government, not so much in opposing armed resistance—
after all it was defending its own soil—as for its choice to
stand by the side of England in October, 1940, when France
had fallen and before Roosevelt had been re-elected. Compared to Greece, the France of Pétain cut a sorry figure.

The Allied press has often compared the Greek and Italian
armies, to the disparagement of the latter. In Allied newspapers, the Italian soldier is always the villain or the clown of
the piece. But the difference was mainly psychological. The
Greek was defending his homeland and knew what he was
fighting for. The Italian was carrying on an aggression without conviction and without psychological or even military
preparation. He was attacking a small country that had never
done any harm to Italy, and for which so many Italians had
fought and died in the nineteenth century. Those who cannot appreciate this state of mind can have no conception of
the true Italy now the fascist mask has fallen. Moreover,
neither the military command that was opposed to the venture, nor the fascist government ever dreamed they would
meet with such strong resistance, as witness the fact that the
first Italian contingents were not equipped for a winter campaign in mountainous regions, often deep in snow. Certain
officials of the Italian Ministry of Foreign Affairs placed reli-
ance on Greek Quislings and on spies who probably pocketed
the gold entrusted to them rather than pass it on at the
risk of being put in prison or shot in the back.

All things considered Mussolini was in a bad way in
Greece, in Libya, in Eritrea, in Ethiopia, in Somaliland.
Hitler had to rush to his aid, first in Greece then in Libya,
leaving the Empire of East Africa to its fate. Thus it happened that Greece was conquered and even Yugoslavia, which
had ranged itself with the Allies after having got rid of the
regent Paul and installed the young king Peter II. At the
same time Italians and Germans won back Cyrenaica and
reached the gates of Solum in Egypt, while the British in
Tobruk repeated the Italian heroism at Bardia in the previous campaign. The Negus Haile Selassie re-entered Addis

Ababa five years after he had been forced to flee from it, and the Italians were obliged to withdraw in the direction of Gondar and Amba Alagi. In the prolonged and hard-fought defense of Gondar various psychological and nonpolitical factors combined to exalt the valor of the Italian soldier: resentment at being reputed inferior to the British or any other nation, and the desire to make a final stand before the fall of the Empire of East Africa for which so much Italian blood had been shed in vain.

*　　*　　*

Hitler's attack on Russia in June, 1941, changed the entire war situation. He believed that he could conquer Russia in six weeks, as he had conquered France, secure himself against attack in the rear, obtain access to the products of the Ukraine and the oil of the Caucasus. A wide vista of conquest and dominion opened before him, with the prospect that the day was at hand when he would be able to strike down England or make a peace that would crown his victories. His initial operations were successful, German troops advanced as far as Kharkov, which fell before them and opened the way to besiege Leningrad and threaten Moscow.

With this tragic background the various measures taken by the United States to help England culminated in the meeting of Churchill and Roosevelt on August 14, 1941, and in the Atlantic Charter. The United States was not yet in the war. Isolationism was still strong. Axis propaganda infested the whole continent of North and South America. Japan feigning a wish for an understanding with Washington was preparing to send Kurusu as emissary. The memory of those days is like an evil dream. The Atlantic Charter came as an act of faith in liberty and humanity, to be fought for and made to triumph.

If the eastern front had collapsed, everything would have been lost. The drawing together of Russia first with England, then with the United States was a necessity of war rather than a profession of friendship. Admiration for the Russian people, fighting with such intrepid valor in conditions more difficult than those which faced the French who had surrendered a year before, aroused admiration and even enthusiasm, especially among the working classes inclined to think of Russia as a class regime. Mistrust of bolshevist Russia has decreased steadily since Russia took the courageous decision not to give way to Hitler.

On the other hand Hitler's antibolshevist campaign, re-echoed by his accomplices active and neutral, did not carry conviction even in France and Spain, much less in Italy who was obliged to send troops to the Russian front. There were hopes of involving the Vatican in the new crusade, but Pope and cardinals well realized that all this crusading zeal was for military purposes and the interests by no means spiritual of those who were torturing subjugated Europe. It was assuredly not in the name of God, whom they alleged they were bringing back by force of arms to a "dechristianized" Russia.

While even in America the Russian problem was dividing public opinion, Kurusu arrived all smiles and promises. Strange to say when Vichy consented to the Japanese occupation of Indo-China, there was only the usual exchange of views, notes, reservations and protests between London and Tokyo, Washington and Vichy.

Meanwhile England, seeing how the land lay and to avoid a repetition of Indo-China, made sure of Syria with the aid of the Free French who took over the administration of that mandated territory. Acting now with greater decision, she saw to it that the Germans and pro-Germans who had infiltrated into Iraq and Iran were driven out. In November she resumed the Libyan campaign with notable success. Russia, aided by an early winter, stabilized her lines on the various fronts and prepared for renewed action.

Finally America's turn came: Pearl Harbor. It was impossible for the United States to escape the effects of a world war. Men who for two years had preached isolation failed to see the coming storm. Lightheartedly they had sold Japan high-octane gas, oil, steel, scrap and other war materials without which the sudden and devastating attack would have been impossible. The Japanese advance in the Pacific from December to May was one of those blitz-wars that stagger the imagination and hold the record for centuries. With the power of the American fleet in the Pacific shattered in an hour, that of the Royal Navy in another, the whole system of defense in that area was wiped out. In almost no time the Japanese took a number of American islands, Hong Kong, the Philippines, Singapore, Java and the Dutch East Indies, all British possessions up to Burma, closed the Burma Road, isolating China, threatened India, threatened Australia, threatened New Zealand, and renewed the war in China occupying fresh territories. It was natural that Germany should declare war on the United States and suddenly weld the solidarity of the Axis. The same might be said of Italy, although she had no immediate reasons for breaking the long-standing friendship that had always existed between our country and the United States.

The Russian winter counteroffensive was soon neutralized by the titanic battles of the spring, when Sevastopol and Kerch fell, Stalingrad was besieged and partly taken, and the Caucasus invaded right up to the mountains. But Stalingrad was for the Second World War what Verdun was for the first.

In June, 1942, Rommel launched his grand offensive in Libya, penetrated to Egypt as far as El Alamein, seventy miles from Alexandria. Fortune willed that the British Eighth Army should stop Rommel in time and hold him all summer nailed down between the sea and the Qattara. Japan too had come to a standstill, while America was able to forestall any further enemy initiative, to carry on a war of attrition at sea and in the air, with better results than were expected.

The time was approaching when the fate of war was to change on all fronts, in spite of the loss of ships by enemy submarines, especially in the Atlantic. A strategic point had to be found on which everything would depend, a central point to be a synthesis for all fronts. There could be no other than the Mediterranean. American and British troops made a successful landing in French North Africa in November, 1942, timing it with the offensive of the British Eighth Army that drove Rommel with his Germans and Italians out of Egypt, pursued them along the whole Libyan coast and caught up with them in Tunisia. Again the Mediterranean had become the decisive zone of war. Those who have complete control of it, have the key to victory. Italy almost forgotten, or remembered only as the weak member of the Axis, became the center of the strategic plans of the two contending forces. Napoleon knew it well when through Italy he struck at Austria toward whom Greater Germany was gravitating although then there was no Siegfried Line; and when Egypt and Malta were France's counterweights to hold England at bay.

Pétain, Darlan and the other military men of Vichy, had they not been obsessed by a defeatist policy, ought to have seen before the armistice and even after it when Germany was exerting pressure on France, that they still had the French navy and French North Africa that were enough to have changed the course of this war. What they failed to take into account was clear to the minds of English and American statesmen and soldiers who at last saw Africa with other eyes than in 1940, when Wavell was not given enough military equipment, yet he drove out Marshal Graziani whose army also was not equipped in accordance with modern requirements.

In November and December, 1942, the occupation of Algeria and Morocco succeeded better than could have been believed possible, but not so in Tunisia. We shall not dwell upon the mistakes that were made. We are not in a position to say, as has been asserted, that a strong policy toward Vichy would have saved the French fleet—which was later blown up in Toulon by order of the French admiralty itself—and prevented the occupation of Tunisia by the Germans and Italians. Perhaps the two events were inevitable and must be charged to the debit of the undertaking. They cost six months of war in Tunisia, six precious months that enabled Hitler to transform Europe into a fortress and prepare for the inevitable siege. The enormous advantage to the Allies was that they had seized the initiative from Hitler and forced him to alter his war plans while he was obliged to submit to the destruction of aerial bombardment in Germany and the occupied countries.

* * *

It was evident from the beginning of 1943 that the European fortress would be attacked from the Mediterranean. The conquest of the Mediterranean was to make it possible; Italy was to be the first stage. That was the time to define clearly the aims of the Allies. The meeting of Roosevelt and Churchill at Casablanca in January, 1943, took this up as one of the points to be settled immediately. A large part of the Anglo-American press warned against repeating with Italy the mistakes made with Vichy France, demanding a different policy toward Italy both as regards the internal regime and the conditions of peace.

From Casablanca came the decision agreed upon and it was "unconditional surrender." At that time the author interpreted that term to mean the certainty of Allied victory. When still engaged in Africa, with the moment of attack on the European fortress still uncertain, the Allies declared that neither Hitler nor Mussolini could hope for a peace of compromise. They entrusted the decision to the fate of arms and insisted upon military surrender on the field of battle to avoid any repetition of German denial of defeat as in 1918. But at the same time the best informed Anglo-American statesmen, the Italian exiles and those from other countries, urged Washington and London to make an appeal to the Italian people for an honorable peace, thus discriminating not in words but in deeds between fascism and the Italian people and creating a sound basis for a reconstructive policy.

The history of Allied political moves from Casablanca to

the landing in Sicily (January to July, 1943) will be written and rewritten many times. Churchill himself has admitted that errors were made with regard to Italy. Some of them could have been avoided, and some not. Who would suggest that mistakes are not made in a war as complex and as difficult as the one now being fought? Above all, historians of the present war will be put to it to explain why neither Hitler nor the Allies took into account, between November, 1942, and July, 1943, the military and political weight of Italy.

It would appear that Hitler did not attach sufficient importance to the African and Sicilian campaigns, and thought that the Italian troops, reinforced and commanded by the Germans, would hold the Allies at bay until he had succeeded in crushing the Russian front. During the winter the Russian offensive was truly audacious and favored by fortune. Hitler took his winter reverses, which after Stalingrad must have seemed slight to him, in the hope of renewed victory in spring and summer. The African affair was an interference with his plans, just as was the air bombardment of his industrial centers. But he never imagined that his vital interest was to confine the enemy to Africa and to drive him out of Sicily, even at the cost of abandoning his offensive in Russia which moreover was delayed until June. In an article published simultaneously in London and New York in December, 1942, the author pointed this out: "Hitler will no longer be able in the new year to attempt great battles against Leningrad and Moscow; there he will be on the defensive so as not to waste arms and ammunition. Russia can no longer be put out of the war by a blitzkrieg. The winter will tell on what lines Hitler can hold, and what efforts Russia can make to regain territory. But the Russian front, except in the Caucasus, has suddenly become of secondary importance to Hitler, until the day when Russia will be able to launch her great offensive." *

But Hitler entirely miscalculated the Allied forces in Africa

* See *People and Freedom* (London) December, 1942; *The New Leader* (New York) December 17, 1942; *Nazione Unite* (New York) December 17, 1942. (In Italian with a footnote.)

or else he counted too much on Rommel's ability to hold the enemy at bay, and when in May Africa was lost he miscalculated the importance of Sicily. To have on his hands in May and June, 1943, an Italy incapable of resisting the enemy and forever demanding more troops, more airplanes, more tanks and more munitions was an unbearable burden to him just when he was about to launch an offensive against the heart of Russia. So his decision was to keep in Italy only the minimum strength needed to retard the Anglo-American advance and help his unhappy comrade-in-arms to hold out, he hoped, till autumn.

Events in Italy moved fast. Unrest throughout the country was such that the fascist government failed to allay it even with threats of resuming the gangster methods of early fascism. After the African defeat, the Italian army was without cohesion or sufficient armament, above all it had lost heart. It became necessary to take a drastic decision to contain the threatened invasion, the imminence of which was announced by constant bombardments. It would seem that Hitler's idea was to withdraw all forces (the fascist government included) to the line of the Po, with an elastic defense of the rest of Italy capable only of retarding the enemy advance. As Germany was already engaged to the very limit in Russia where the German offensive kept changing into a Russian offensive, Hitler's idea was the only possible one from a tactical point of view, but by no means feasible from the strategic and political point of view.

On the Allied side the invasion of Sicily was being prepared. The first Allied landing between Pachino and Gela coincided with the launching of the Russian offensive, the former on July 10, the latter on July 12. What happened in Sicily was symptomatic: only the Germans opposed any resistance to the enemy; the Italian troops skirmished or even fought but only if their leaders were determined to resist, otherwise they surrendered; while the civilian population welcomed the Anglo-Americans as liberators with applause, flowers, fruit, helping them how, when and where they could.

It culminated in the taking of Palermo on July 23, whereas the Germans fought over every inch of the plain of Catania and the area around Mount Etna until they withdrew from Messina.

From the political point of view the Allied governments and military leaders learned little from the Sicilian experience. They interpreted the applause as a sign of relief from the danger of bombardment, hunger and the tyranny of local fascist chiefs. Its political significance was not understood. Some correspondents hastened to say that the American soldiers did not understand the meaning of the applause and objected to Sicilian expansiveness. The fixed plan was adhered to. Italian cities and centers of population were bombarded, with or without military necessity, and insistent appeals made to the people to rebel against their leaders and surrender unconditionally. All of which must have had a strange effect on people who wanted peace and wanted to rebel and were already rebelling, but who had the right to know what would be the result of rebellion.

In the meantime fascism crumbled. Disorganized militarily, undermined morally by the behavior of the people of Sicily where it and its war were being disavowed in radical and clamorous guise, fascism no longer had political control. The lack of German aid on the Italian front shattered the last illusions. The news of the fall of Mussolini's government on July 25 and the formation of the Badoglio government, hailed by explosions of joy by the whole people from north to south, was a surprise to the Allied world. The political and military event should have been equal to the blow, but it was quickly discounted because the governments of Washington and London and the military heads of the African command failed to perceive the full importance of the fall of fascism and to make good use of it.

Three basic mistakes were made: first, that no clear distinction was ever made between fascism and the Italian people; second, that of believing unconditional surrender under bombardment was tantamount to the psychological conquest of a people who were vanquished but who wanted to count themselves free because tyranny had fallen; third, that Italy in whatever way she surrendered was of little value from the general point of view of the war and could easily be left out of account. The truth is that as regards the outcome of the war and the political future of Europe, Italy was a vital point, and that once the invasion of Sicily (essential to the naval operations in the Mediterranean) and of the Italian mainland was decided upon, provision should have been made for a simultaneous occupation of the north and center by forces strong enough not only to force surrender but to free Italy quickly of the German troops of occupation.

The fall of the Mussolini government gave Hitler a sudden idea of the importance of Italy. For many months he had refrained from sending troops, thus contributing to the disorganization of the Italian army cut to pieces and mutilated in the Balkans, in France, in Russia and in Africa; he now rushed troops to Italy, occupying the most important strategic points, holding the capital within range of his guns, reinforcing the southern zone, there to await in some security the enemy troops and at the same time to attempt to reverse the internal situation in favor of fascism, already publicly disavowed by the people and by the new government.

With the rebirth of the liberal, socialist, communist, Christian-democrat and popular parties, Italian ideals of liberty and democracy were reasserted. Badoglio's government was afraid of the popular demonstrations which might hamper the efforts he was making to arrive at an armistice; even the governments of Washington and London were afraid, as they believed the demonstrations were a prerevolutionary phase, while they really were a popular outburst for peace and liberty.

5

Italy and Democracy

AFTER THE ADVENT of fascism, many writers, thinkers, lecturers, newspapermen and rumormongers of society and the street, discussed the question whether Italy could be a democracy. *Post factum*—after dictatorship had been established—there were many in Europe and America who thought that the Italians needed discipline and more or less of the big stick, in any case a strong enlightened authority, paternal if you will but of an old-fashioned paternity that made itself feared. For a time fascism was looked upon as a purely Italian phenomenon. It was the time when Mussolini himself, not to frighten the countries and the men to whom he looked for support, declared that fascism was not "an article for export." A strictly political utterance, contradicted later when fascism was making headway among the middle classes of all countries.

Small wonder that men of open mind and liberal views, progressive people leaning to the Left, and other half-way-house and fifty-fifty folk felt the same way, and feel so even today when discussing the future of certain European countries, especially Italy.

If there is a country not only with a democratic tradition but with a democratic past, among all the countries of Europe it is Italy. Although there may be some question as to whether ancient Rome was organized as a democracy, everybody must admit that for more than three centuries her internal regime was based on the two classes of patricians and plebeians, senate and tribunes, with periodical elections, with personal responsibility, with a real interest in public affairs,

with legislation that even in the pre-Christian period reflected an objective conception of justice. The famed period
of Athenian democracy was brief compared to that of Rome,
and less firmly established.

A typically Italian characteristic, that survives even today
in the traditions of history, art and philosophy, was the organization of the seaboard cities and the communes of the mainland in many of which, albeit in the forms of the age between
the first renaissance in the twelfth century and the second in
the sixteenth century, there was intense civic and political
life, a spirit of popular initiative and liberty, even of true and
unmistakable democracy, alternating with periods of fac-
tional strife.* If the Italian communes ended by passing
under the yoke of local despots and then under foreign dynasties, no country in Europe save Switzerland escaped the despotic rule that developed at the time of the religious crises,
the Reformation and the weakening of the international
power of the Papacy.

Let us turn to modern Italy, the Italy that achieved political and national unity. The Risorgimento was the work of
the middle, intellectual and professional classes, just as were
the revolutions of all other countries that, following the spirit
and the letter of the American and French revolutions,
sought liberty, constitutional government and independence.
Those of the working classes, especially in the cities, who felt
even confusedly the same ideals, took an active part in the
revolution.

Italy founded her new life on a liberty and monarchic constitution, that of the Sardinian kingdom of 1848. But where
could one find a true democracy in the Europe of that time?
The uprisings of 1848 were inspired by the necessity of breaking the shackles that tyrants in all countries had laid upon the
peoples of Europe. Men spoke of liberty. The idea of democ-

---

* The Proclamation of Florence of 1530 said: "The truly free and democratic
state is that in which all citizens without distinction have access to all offices; it
is not by their birth or wealth that men must be judged, but by their qualities
and moral worth." (Quoted in *For Democracy*, published by the People and Freedom Group, London, 1939.)

racy had crept in but only confusedly. Many feared the word more than the word communism is feared today. In France where the revolution of 1848 immediately assumed a social aspect, the Second Republic ended in blood, shed not by the royal troops (the king was a fugitive) but by the troops of the revolutionary bourgeoisie itself. In the name of the National Assembly, General Cavaignac, the Minister of War, sent the army against the workers who were asking for bread and work. In Paris the victims numbered 15,000 and Archbishop Affre was killed on the barricades when he was acting as peacemaker with the workers.

In Italy to the names of Carlo Cattaneo, one of the most ardent democrats, and Mazzini known throughout the world, must be added that of Gioacchino Ventura, Professor of Public Law at the University of Rome and General of the Theatine Order. He was one of the most courageous Catholics of his time. His funeral oration for the dead of Vienna, the revolutionaries of 1848, delivered in the Church of St. Andrew in the Valley in Rome is famous. Amid the applause of the congregation he ended by asserting: "The Church will turn with tender love to Democracy, as once she turned to Barbarism, she will place the sign of the Cross upon that savage matron, she will make her holy and glorious and say to her 'Reign!' and she shall reign." *

This idea was taken up again by Frederic Ozanam in France. Born in Milan of French parents he had been in Italy and in Rome during the fateful years of 1847 and 1848. He was a most loyal and devoted champion of the democratic ideal, although at the first report of labor unrest, many forsook him and left him alone in the breach. Montalembert, who in 1848 had been on the side opposed to Ozanam, in 1863 made his famous declaration in Malines: "The new so-

---

* Gioacchino Ventura, *Discorso Funebre pei Morti di Vienna* etc. Vol. 1 (Milan), Carlo Turati, editore, 1860. In his "Introduction and Protest" he had written: "If the Church will not march with the people, not for this will the people stay their march. They will march without the Church, outside the Church, against the Church, and that is all. Who then could reckon the woes of the people and of the Church?"

ciety or better democracy, to call it by its name, exists today,
. . . in half of Europe it is already dominant; in the other
half it will be dominant tomorrow. . . . I look before me
and I see nothing but democracy everywhere. . . . In the
new order, Catholics will have to fight but they will have
nothing to fear." * Montalembert applied the term democracy to the liberal governments of the day based on more or
less restricted suffrage in which the working classes and
women had as yet no share. But he was right in believing
that this was already democracy, although incipient and incomplete, since in its evolution it called for the integrating
and constructive measures that little by little were to be
arrived at. From the political standpoint, the half of Europe
of which Montalembert spoke was only halfway toward democracy as we know it. To Montalembert the Italy of 1863
was a democracy; to us in 1945 it was only democracy in incu-
bation, and we may say that it was not democracy.

From the liberal point of view little Piedmont was the only
country except Belgium and Switzerland that in 1848 held
fast to a liberal constitution. By that achievement it took the
initiative in promoting the unity of Italy and her independence. The constitution of the kingdom of Sardinia and of
the sub-Alpine provinces became the constitution of the
whole of Italy, including Venice annexed in 1866 and Rome
in 1870.

Meanwhile in France the dictatorship of Napoleon III had
ended at Sedan. Who then would have thought that after the
emperors and the kings that France had sought so sedulously
after the revolution, she would descend to a marshal. At any
rate the French constitution of 1875 which lasted till the
armistice of 1940 was not shaped to promote democracy in
the Third Republic. The assembly that drafted it was in great
majority monarchic and antidemocratic, its spirit was bourgeois and conservative. By a kind of historical "occasionalism"
due to the blind quarrels of the Right, of the clericals and

* See *Church and State*, by Luigi Sturzo. Longmans, Green & Co., Inc., New
York.

the claimant who refused the throne, the new regime became democratic, radical and anticlerical without ever losing its essentially bourgeois spirit. So the famous Sixteenth of May had to come in 1876 and it was not till the election of Gambetta's friend Jules Grevy as president in 1879 that the Third Republic could consolidate its democratic character

With the fall of the "Historic Right" in 1876, Italy had passed through the same phase three years earlier. It was that party which fought for the unification of the country and gave a foundation to the new state, but it was the Left that brought a program of popular suffrage, free schools, freedom of association, and a reduction of indirect taxation. Benedetto Cairoli who came to power in 1878 had already prepared a scheme for widening the electorate as a prelude to universal suffrage.

In Belgium after national liberty had been won by the revolution of 1830, the first constitution was a liberal monarchy, the bourgeois class remaining dominant up to the First World War. The prevailing spirit was conservative as in England during the same period. The participation of the working classes in Government was opposed, and the Flemish population held in subjection by linguistic discrimination. The forces of labor concentrated on social organization which, whether socialist or Christian-democrat was most advanced. Through organizations of this kind political democracy developed in Belgium, though not without struggles.

Switzerland has always had her cantons with their democratic spirit and ancient and respected traditions, but from the federal standpoint religious conflicts created an atmosphere of civil war and persecution which impeded for some time the advent of the sound democratic constitution based, as it is today, on a truly popular conception of nationality.

In this period, the second half of the nineteenth century, democratic penetration was making headway in Europe through two channels: liberalism that appealed to the intellectual, bourgeois and urban classes and socialism (to some extent and belatedly also the Christian social movement) that appealed to the working classes. Even in England, whose parliamentary tradition was unique in the world, democracy was slow to assert itself, only liberalism was prevalent. The working classes began to become conscious and to organize economically, but not politically.* No one could have thought of an English democracy in the time of Queen Victoria, of Cecil Rhodes, of Joseph Chamberlain. Gladstone was one of Europe's greatest liberals, but his outlook cannot be called democratic. Under the Disraeli government in 1884 the suffrage was extended, almost at the same time as in Italy where however the Act of 1882 retained a tax-paying qualification. But the organization of the constituencies and the two-party tradition of the middle classes in England made it more difficult than in France and Italy for the workers to gain access to political life, until labor organized itself as a party and had its own candidates for parliament.

Even America where suffrage is governed by the laws of the various states maintained for many years—and in some states continues to do so—discrimination based on a poll-tax qualification which excludes a certain number of poor whites and negroes from political life. Labor in America has not succeeded in attaining the political importance of English labor, nor in penetrating into the capitalist machines of the two parties. Their unions (especially in the American Federation of Labor) seek to promote their professional interest by using their votes to bring pressure on the two traditional parties.

When Italy returned the first representatives of the working classes to parliament—socialists, radicals and a few Christian-democrats such as Mauri and Longinotti—Germany had her socialist party and center, and even Austria and Hungary had socialists and Christian-socialists. Toward the end of the nineteenth century, the workers' advance in political life was developing in nearly every country in Europe.

In the last decade of the nineteenth century the term "Christian democracy" appeared in the social activities of

---

* The independent Labour party was founded in 1893 and from 1900 to 1906 had only one representative in parliament: Keir Hardie.

Catholics in Europe, and sought to penetrate political life. In Italy it worked as a vigorous leaven but the barrier set up by the *non expedit* * made it necessary for Catholics to keep the social and political spheres distinct. This was not easy.

When in 1900 the Christian-democrats of Italy (of whom the author was one of the promoters) published their ten-point program, each beginning with the words *"Noi vogliamo"* (we demand) it was a revelation to the Catholic and lay worlds. We were then demanding universal suffrage for men and women, the legal recognition of labor unions, progressive income taxes, proportional representation, agrarian reform and free education. Was it possible for Catholics to be so progressive, nay radical and truly democratic? Were they not all reactionaries and obscurantists? So the liberals asked themselves. The socialists in turn suspected an attempt to deprive them of the monopoly of representing the working classes. Above all conservative Catholics were in consternation: they saw a departure from all the old legitimist, reactionary, authoritarian and clerical policy.

More or less the same thing occurred in France where conservative Catholics opposed the "democratic abbés" (who does not remember Gayraud, Naudet and Lemire?) and in Belgium where l'Abbé Pottier had to leave the country and find a haven in Rome with Leo XIII. In Germany a long and bitter controversy raged over the vertical Christian unions. In Austria, Lueger tainted the Christian social movement with anti-Semitism. But the ferment was working everywhere, as a rebirth of the political and social conscience of Catholics, a fact of particular importance in a country like Italy, where Catholics constituted the majority of the population.

Leo XIII to allay public opinion which had been aroused against Christian-democrats, especially in Italy, published in January 1901 an encyclical opening with the words *Graves de*

---

* *Non expedit* (it is not expedient) was the reply given by the Sacred Penitentiary Congregation in Rome to certain Italian bishops who had asked whether the faithful could in conscience vote in parliamentary elections or present themselves as candidates.

Comuni. The intention of Leo XIII was clear; to strip the movement known as Christian democracy of all political significance, of all revolutionary tendency. This was necessary from the point of view of the Church because not a few, either from excess of zeal or inability to make a distinction between the two spheres, were upholding the social and political reforms of Christian democracy in the name of the Church, and seeking to transform Catholic action into a political movement.

At the time all this seemed like a step backward on the part of Leo XIII who five years earlier had proclaimed: "If democracy is Christian it will do great good to the world." * In that context the word democracy on the lips of the great Pope meant what it meant for everyone: a government of the people and for the people. In that sense Professor Giuseppe Toniolo had defined it emphasizing its social side, in his celebrated course of lectures on Christian democracy in Rome and other Italian cities between 1897 and 1900. But we must take into account the political atmosphere at the time when Leo XIII issued *Graves de Comuni.* Italy was emerging from the period of uprisings in 1898 when the journalist leader of Christian democracy, the priest Don Davide Albertario, had been sentenced to twenty years' imprisonment merely for supporting a strike called by Christian-democrat workers in Lombardy. A few months before the Encyclical, Humbert I had been killed by an anarchist and other outrages had been perpetrated in various parts of Europe against members of reigning houses. France was still in the throes of the Dreyfus case and there were even attempts to transform the republican regime into a military oligarchy. Anticlericalism triumphed with the laws against religious congregations, as a prelude to the denunciation of the Concordat.

The Christian-democrat movement was then misunderstood and feared. There was a demand that the Church repudiate democracy itself and give clear and decided support

* See "The Catholic Church and Christian Democracy," by Don Luigi Sturzo, in *Social Action,* No. 5, May 15, 1944 (New York).

to reaction. It was one of those moments that recur in the history of Europe when the forces of reaction seek to defend their power by calling upon the Church. Nonetheless, the idea of a democracy founded on Christian principles (it was the prevailing idea in America) was perfectly orthodox. The Christian-democrats sought to realize it against both anti-democratic regimes, those that were democratic but anti-Christian and those that were democratic in form but not in substance.

Unfortunately in Italy the *non expedit* was still in force and in 1895 Leo XIII had made the position of Italian Catholics worse by a letter addressed to Cardinal Rampolla, his secretary of state, in which he emphasized that the *non expedit* was not merely a counsel but a real and definite prohibition. The common hope of all Christian-democrats was that the Pope would some day abolish the *non expedit*. They did not think that this could be done by Leo XIII, in view of his policy toward Italy, but they set their hopes on his successor.

Italy was then in the throes of social progress in keeping with the times. In the co-operative movement the Catholics were ahead of the socialists, whereas the latter had almost monopolized the trade-union movement. The Christian-democrats were anxious to enter the trade-union field but the conservative Catholics were afraid of the workers, and some of them who objected even to the name "trade unionism" (Sindacalismo) appealed to the Holy See for a prohibition.*

Pius X, although not averse to the social movement, wanted it to be entirely under episcopal authority, whereas the Christian-democrats pointed out that the right to strike, undoubtedly possessed by organized workers, could ill be guaranteed in a strictly ecclesiastical and diocesan organization. This being the case the worker had no alternative but to join the

---

* In 1901, the author had already published an essay on Trade Unions, dedicated to Professor Toniolo; another and much more voluminous work had been written by Professor Antonio Boggiano Pico, another Christian-democrat.
Cf. Luigi Sturzo: *Organizzazione di Classe e Unioni Professionali*, Cultura Sociale, Rome, 1901.

socialist trade unions. This was warmly commended by many who feared that trade-union interests would be impaired by the Christian-democrat movement. In the initial period, between 1893 and 1898, I shared this view, but experience of the time proved it impractical. In many of the provinces, the socialists were carrying on a campaign not only of class struggle but of hatred of religion. They were preventing baptisms, church marriages, religious burials, on the grounds that the Church was in the service of the privileged classes, that she hated liberty and stood for vertical corporations including employers and workers so as to keep the latter down. It was very difficult to work with men who held such prejudices, but on the other hand the attitude of the conservative Catholics and of the official Catholic action was often reactionary. To be specific, they held to the letter and not to the spirit of *Rerum Novarum,* they favored a return to the Guilds of the Middle Ages, in the form of corporations especially vertical. This was not exclusively an Italian movement, but more particularly Austro-Hungarian. It was headed by Vogelsang who wrote *The New Feudalism and the Corporative State* (a term not invented by Mussolini) and in France by Albert de Mun, who advocated vertical unions. In Italy this unworkable "historico-intellectualist" phase was more speedily outgrown.

If under Pius X, we had to refrain from speaking of *sindacati* (trade unions) and instead used such expressions as workers' associations, leagues or unions, the latter were exclusively composed of workers and interested in the affairs of labor. When an inspired article appeared in the *Civiltà Cattolica* * which actually used the execrated words "sindacato" and "sindacalismo" it was evident that a Christian working-class structure already existed in Italy. Soon thereafter the specifically Christian-democrat "Italian Confederation of Workers" was in existence.

That was a great achievement in those days. People today have no idea of what it cost in patience and humility, obedience and sacrifice to overcome opposition all the more serious

* The well-known Jesuit review.

and bitter in that it was often inspired by zeal, by a sense of discipline, or by fear of errors falsely attributed to "modernism."

In Italy there was the case of the priest Murri who was unfrocked in 1909, not because he was a Christian-democrat, but because he had been elected to parliament in defiance of the *non expedit* and refused to submit.* In France there was Marc Sangnier whose organization *"Le Sillon"* was dissolved in 1910 by Pope Pius. He submitted to the decree and thereafter refrained from speaking of Christian democracy in the name of the Church (the point condemned). For France and the whole Catholic world he remained the representative of modern democracy that draws its inspiration from Christian tradition.

The outcome of this controversy was that when in 1919 Italian Catholics organized a political party, to which further reference will be made, they dropped the name of Christian-democrats and adopted that of popular party.† The French also in 1924 founded the popular democratic party, inspired by the same ideals. Finally when an international secretariat of all such parties was organized in Paris in 1925, it was called the "International Secretariat of Democratic Parties of Christian Inspiration." Only in Belgium did the "Christian democratic league" survive, ultimately to become a branch of the united Catholic party.

Since the time of Benedict XV, "Christian democracy" is no longer used to denote the social action of Catholics as a branch of Catholic Action (save in certain rare exceptions), nor to denote a political party composed of Catholics (save in the case of the labor wing of the Catholic party in Belgium), but only as indicating the general spirit of a social and political movement in the name of democracy and Christianity.

The charge that Catholics brought against modern democracies then taking shape throughout the world was forgetful-

---

* During the last years of his life, Murri was reconciled to the Church.

† When it re-entered the political arena after the fall of Mussolini, the heads of the dissolved popular party revived the name *(Partito della Demacrazia Cristiana)*. The French now call it the popular republican party.

ness of or even hostility to the ethical principles of Christianity. The democracy that Father Ventura sought to bless in 1847, that Ozanam sought to bless in 1848, was the same democracy to which had contributed socially and politically the pioneers of the so-called Catholic parties, especially the German center, and the promoters of Catholic Social Action, one of whose greatest leaders was Giuseppe Toniolo.

The above is no digression from the question whether and to what extent Italy could be considered democratic in those days, it is an integration. Then Catholics helped to form the democratic spirit of the new Italy, uplifting the working classes economically and morally, educating them to the use of the franchise in municipal and provincial elections, in which it was lawful for them to take part.* The banner around which the fight raged—a banner the more cherished —was Christian democracy, which to the working masses meant on the one hand the antithesis of Marxism and communism, and on the other the teachings of the Gospel. For them Leo XIII was the working man's Pope. The monument to Christian democracy near the Church of St. John Lateran in Rome was a tribute of this collective sentiment. Although the *non expedit* still remained as an obstacle to participation in political life, Christian-democrats were convinced that the day would come when that barrier would disappear, and eagerly looked forward to so propitious an event. The author expressed this desire in an address delivered in 1905 and published the following year, calling for the constitution of a political party formed by Catholics, not in the name of the Church but of true freedom and democracy. Another fourteen years had to be spent in waiting and preparation, but as events have shown those years were lost neither for Italy nor for Christian democracy.

* * *

* The author was elected municipal councilor of Caltagirone in 1899, then mayor of the same city remaining in office 15 years. For 15 years he was a provincial councilor for Catania and for 20 years councilor and then vice-president of the Association of Italian Municipalities.

If we consider the spirit in which public life in Italy was lived at the turn of the century, between 1900 and 1920, we must recognize that democracy was a living fact. The reactionary bourgeoisie, the army and the court had to give way before public opinion that demanded the restoration of the constitutional laws that had been suspended when martial law was proclaimed during the uprisings of 1898, an amnesty for political prisoners, the introduction of universal suffrage, fiscal reform and the enforcement of social legislation. All these demands were supported by what were then known as the "popular parties" *—socialists, radicals and republicans —and by the Christian-democrats. Public opinion was with them, but the old parliamentarians while willing to accept the other proposals, refused to embark upon electoral reform. Their excuse was that there were still too many illiterates in the rural districts.

At the time of the Libyan war in 1912, the liberals headed by Giolitti decided that universal male suffrage (at that time no European country had woman suffrage) could no longer be denied the Italian people. The act of 1912 came into full force at the general elections of the following year. Everybody agreed that the results were not catastrophic and that the various political parties emerged more or less in the same positions as before. All except the Catholics some of whom abstained from voting, others supported the government coalition which leaned to the Right and sought to retard the socialist advance,† while a few others voted for candidates of their own, so that there came into being a group of some twenty deputies, known as Catholic deputies, many of whom came from the ranks of the Christian-democrats or from the trade-union labor movement.

Although the extension to everybody of the right to vote is no more than a condition of modern democracy and is not

* The name "popular" adopted by the radical Left, the republicans and the socialists was soon dropped by them to be assumed later by the Christian-democrats.

† Giolitti's coalition with the Catholics, based on an attenuation of the *non expedit*, was called the Gentiloni Pact, Count Ottorino Gentiloni being head of the Italian Catholic Electoral Union. The author opposed this pact.

democracy itself,* yet the fact of being deprived of that right morally transforms it into a privilege enjoyed by those who vote as against those who do not. But the mere right to vote is not enough to make democracy function, there must be good electoral laws and well-organized political parties. Even the smallest of modern democracies like Belgium and Norway have from three to eight million inhabitants, whereas the Athens of Pericles had but forty thousand citizens and ancient Rome no more than one hundred and twenty thousand. It is absurd to talk about direct government by the people. Democracy functions through representative government, based on general elections, with one or two constitutional chambers according to the traditions of the country. The Italian electoral system of 1912, for instance, was more or less like that of the French, founded on the principle of an absolute majority in each constituency, and on a second poll known as the "ballotage." This led to combines between local groups, and was ill suited to the' functioning of national parties of a permanent character with well-defined platforms.

It is true that the bourgeois and intellectual classes, dominant in Italy between 1860 and 1882, maintained the traditional divisions of Right and Left in the chamber, but locally they depended on groups of electors linked to the interests of powerful families, or to the posts they had obtained in the municipal and provincial administrations. In view of the limited number of electors, with their tax qualifications, the two groups remained fairly well knit and firmly established. The small republican party, which represented an idealist tradition, was an anachronism in a monarchy. The first to form a well organized national party with a well-defined program were the socialists in 1892. They used a system of protest can-

---

* More than once the author has been criticized for having paid tribute in *People and Freedom* to Swiss democracy although there as in France and Italy before the war woman suffrage does not exist. But although the denial of the right to vote to a category of the people mutilates the community, it does not mean that its life cannot be democratic. The democratic spirit can exist even where the suffrage is restricted, when nonelectors can and do influence public opinion. There can likewise be a dictatorship under universal suffrage for men and women, as in Nazi Germany and Russia.

didates to make a breach in the constituencies where a candidate was unopposed. By then what was known as the wider suffrage already existed, and in the towns many of the skilled artisans and a number of industrial workers voted for the socialists. The Catholics, although still bound by the *non expedit* had an organization of their own for municipal and provincial elections with a central electoral office * which in exceptional cases also gave directives for political elections. In 1911, the nationalist party appeared, on the lines of that of Maurras in France but without the support that the French clergy was then openly giving to *l'Action Française*. It had no following among the people, in spite of attempts to organize labor. It was antisocialist, antidemocratic, anti-Semitic and was the forerunner of fascism.

Italian political life, notwithstanding the progress made by the socialist party, was dominated by the liberal bourgeoisie, divided into two groups known as democratic liberals and liberal democrats. The former stood to the Right and tended toward conservatism; the latter leaned ever so little toward the Left. The difference was small and mostly local. It was thus possible for skillful politicians to form combines that supported now one group, now the other, maintained an unstable balance, which led to ministerial crises, dissolutions of parliament and appeals to the country. In this the Italian regime was nearer to the British than to the French, where appeals to the country were traditionally avoided, so that the governments were even more unstable and out of touch with public opinion. In Italy, both under restricted suffrage and universal suffrage (save in wartime) the appeal to the country was a safety valve and sometimes was resorted to as a means of consolidating the men in power. Actually, however, those who called the elections rarely remained in power. The ease with which cabinets were made and unmade has often been cited as evidence that the Italian people are incapable of parliamentary self-government. The same charge might be

---

* The Italian Catholic Electoral Union. The author was a member of its central council from 1905 to 1910 and from 1914 to 1918.

brought against the French, with more reason. Both countries allowed parliament to intrude on the executive, and in return the executive, that is the cabinet, took many liberties at the expense of parliament, especially by means of Decree-Laws. The cause was to be found in the fact that power was in the hands of the bourgeois or middle-class parties who resented restraint by the workers' parties and by the nationalist extreme Right (in France, the monarchist Right). At bottom there was an unsolved revolutionary problem that disturbed the parliamentary life of the two great Latin countries. In France, recurrent monarchism for which the antirepublican and antidemocratic nationalism of the *Action Française* doubled on the one hand, and on the other a socialist party that refused to collaborate with the bourgeoisie except in case of war. In Italy, Catholic influence was for the most part absent owing to the Roman Question, while the conservative Right was antidemocratic and nascent nationalism was antiparliamentary; on the other hand the socialist wing, revolutionary at least in words, always refused to collaborate with the governments of the country.

Thus moral and political secessions impeded the natural evolution of the parliamentary system toward democracy and, as a negative reaction, increased the power if not the prestige of groups, known less by their platforms than by the names of their leaders—Depretis and Zanardelli, Crispi and Rudinì, Giolitti and Sonnino, Salandra, Nitti, Orlando. These men whether of high esteem or not were never swayed by personal interest or capitalist influence, they mirrored the liberal, monarchic, bureaucratic, bourgeois tradition with its dash of anticlericalism, followed by the third and fourth generation of the Risorgimento. In personal integrity they could give points to the men in government of the various democratic countries in Europe or America, although their attachment to local interests often prevented them from discerning general interests; although to win elections they did not disdain to make use of the lowest police methods and of local gangs beyond the pale of common morality, such as the *Maffia* in Sicily and the Neapolitan *Camorra*.

* * *

The First World War interrupted the movement of political regeneration, which had begun with the adoption of universal suffrage and with the courageous enforcement of social legislation governing working conditions, co-operatives, insurance, the development of agriculture, land-reclamation, reafforestation, all much in vogue between 1900 and 1914.

The war ripened the political alignment of new parties that should have played a decisive part in the fate of Italy. The first to emerge was the Italian popular party. Its birth on January 18, 1919, was a surprise to many because of its democratic spirit and lively combativity, and also because of the number of its supporters. Its platform was that of the Christian democracy of nineteen years before, with an international emphasis in support of the League of Nations, a campaign for administrative decentralization, for regional autonomy, for responsibility of political parties.

Its first campaign was for proportional representation. This had already been introduced in some European countries and had been discussed by the center and socialist parties in Germany, when preparing for the Constituent Assembly at Weimar. In Italy the fight for proportional representation had been going on for many years and the time had come to force the issue. The leaders of the socialist and popular parties in the Chamber—Turati and Micheli—reached an agreement, the prime minister, F. S. Nitti, offered no opposition as was the parliamentary rule in the case of an electoral law, and indeed favored its adoption. Although the liberals had made notable amendments to leave a free choice for candidates to individual electors and provide for the preferential vote outside the vote by list, the spirit of proportional representation remained and the first test brought to the Chamber 151 socialists combined with the small communist group, and 99 popular party votes.

Never had two parties representing the masses occupied
so many seats in parliament, nearly half, and the bourgeoisie
took fright. The majority of socialist votes came from industrial workers, railway men, dockhands, post-office employees,
the agricultural centers of northern Italy and a certain class
of intellectual extremists. The majority of popular votes came
from skilled artisans in town and country, peasants organized
in numerous Catholic co-operatives and the Italian confederation of workers, professional and petty bourgeois middle
classes and from a large and very active group of university
students.

With these two parties Italian democracy was already asserting itself in sturdy form. Unhappily misunderstandings,
prejudices, electoral and political disputes arose and from the
outset pitted one against the other. The socialists took offense
at the Christian-democrats having their own trade unions,
workers' associations and confederations, and accused them of
disrupting "proletarian unity." Hence a jealous resentment
that in many provinces had already made them antagonists at
the polls. This was followed by a further charge, easy to make
but hard to prove, that the popular party worked or might
work in the interest of the employers. This charge could not
be sustained and was soon dropped. Opposition remained
lively to not a few points of the popular party's platform,
especially the plank calling for the development of rural
small-holdings, proportional representation in administrative
elections, woman suffrage and, above all, freedom of education.

By this time, March, 1919, the fascist party had already
been formed, but it was still small and local and in the general elections of November, 1919, did not win a single seat.
In 1920, the armed fascist gangs began their raids and attacks
upon socialists and members of the popular party. The liberal
bourgeoisie, abandoning its traditional belief in freedom,
began to encourage the black shirts, supplying them with
money and arms (even arms from the military arsenals, with
the connivance of ministers Giolitti and Bonomi), favoring

them in the courts and with the police, covering up their crimes and denying justice to their victims.

Proportional representation has been and will continue to be accused of being a system that impairs the stability of government by breaking up parliamentary representation. A comparison between the number of groups in the French and Italian chambers shows that between November, 1919, and October, 1922, there were rather more groups in France where proportional representation did not exist, than in Italy where it did. If we compare the ministerial crises in France and Italy during the same period the difference is negligible. If we take periods further back when there were more or less two groups, the Right and the Left, we find that just before or after a war cabinet crises are more frequent. Piedmont, in 1848–1850, with the property franchise and single member constituencies, and France in 1934–39, with universal suffrage and single member constituencies, suffered from the same governmental instability as Italy between 1919 and 1922, with proportional representation. This shows that it is not the electoral system that splits parliaments up into small fractions, since in every vote all of them are reduced to a majority and a minority; it is not the electoral system that produces government crises which are precipitated by parliament whatever its origin and composition. No! It is the Latin conception and tradition of parliamentary government that, subordinating the executive to the sway of majorities, makes it now weak and yielding, now firm and petulant, in demanding unnecessary votes of confidence.

The questions of proportional representation and of the relationship between governments and parliament will be reopened immediately after this war in the Constituent Assemblies of various European countries. We shall hear the same arguments for and against as in 1918–20, perhaps with a different result as the myths of the past are often smoke screens obscuring the path of progress.*

* The Consultative Assembly of Algiers has proposed that France adopt proportionate representation. In Italy it is again being discussed and supported by

When fascism came to power in Italy, proportional representation was one of its first victims.* The hatred of the liberals for proportional representation was increased by the elections of 1921 when Giolitti did everything in his power to favor the fascists and lessen the influence of the popular party and the socialists. The latter had been weakened by the breakaway of the communists in January, 1921. But despite everything the prefectures could do for the ministry of the interior, the results were not according to plan. The socialists won 121 seats, the popular party 107 and the fascists only 35. Proportional representation had to be done away with. Little wonder that the liberal leaders, Giolitti, Orlando and Salandra, summoned by Mussolini to the commission on electoral reform, supported the fascist proposals that two-thirds of the seats should go to the party which obtained the greatest number of votes (but not less than 25 per cent) leaving the other third to be divided among all the other lists. In commission

Christian-democrats and socialists. *Battaglie Sindacali* (Trade Union Fights), the organ of the General Confederation of Labor, carried these words on April 23, 1944: "Concord and Proportional Representation" is the title of an excellent article in the *Popolo* of April 16, signed by C.P. We should like to reprint the entire article. We quote its conclusion: "In seeking the responsibility of the advent of fascism, almost too many come to light, but it can certainly not be charged to proportional representation. If by democracy is meant that the people govern themselves, it is necessary above all to educate the people to public life, and proportional representation gives this education by accustoming the citizen to support ideas rather than men. Active co-operation springs from respect for the decisions of the majority." A great deal of information on this subject is contained in a book by a convinced antiproportionalist, F. H. Hermans, *Democracy or Anarchy?* (University of Notre Dame, 1941). It may yet be possible to avoid the errors of the past, and yet have proportional representation.

* As the author had a paternal interest in proportional representation, he fell a victim at the same time. As the political leader of the popular party he refused to give way and not only became the object of insults and threats, but the Vatican was said to have received information that if the electoral scheme proposed by Mussolini were defeated, it would be the signal for attacks on all the churches in Italy and the beginning of an anticlerical war. Whether true or false, the rumor had the twofold effect that some members of the popular party voted for the bill, and the author resigned his office as political secretary of the party, though remaining one of the seven who directed it and an elected member of its national council. In America he found a widespread legend that in 1923 on superior orders he had retired from political life and withdrawn to the Abbey of Monte Cassino. This was a pure invention of the fascist press. The author went to Monte Cassino in July, 1943, for a fortnight's physical and spiritual rest, after which he returned to his post where he remained till October, 1924, when he left Italy, an exile.

the 25 per cent was raised to 40 per cent to obtain the assent
of the popular party.* The proposed reform was obviously
absurd. It is superfluous to recall this sad page of Italian
political history. Reference is made to it solely for those who,
not knowing the facts, today oppose the re-establishment of
proportional representation in the name of pure parliamentarism, of the rights of the majority or even indeed of democracy. Stable governments can exist either with or without proportional representation, just as dubious majorities may be
the result of any electoral system, as shown by the political
history of France, England and Italy herself. Every electoral
system has its drawbacks and none is politically perfect; but
in the evolution of the masses toward political life, every
system has had something to contribute historically according
to the stage of development of collective consciousness. Proportional representation implies practical co-operation and reciprocal tolerance that overcome the abuses of a majority or
the extortions of a minority. The time has come for the political flowering of the working and peasant classes in collaboration with bourgeoisie.

*   *   *

The electoral system is closely bound up with the organization and vitality of political parties. There cannot be democracy without organized parties, but there can be organized
parties without democracy. To many of us this seems to have
been the position of Italy and other Latin countries. If France
is an exception, this is not due to any merit of the parties but
to the almost congenital incapacity of Frenchmen to live
under party discipline. Every Frenchman is a genial individ-

* In the election of 1924, which cost the life of Deputy Giacomo Matteotti, the
fascist party by fraud and violence succeeded in gaining more than 40 per cent of
the votes and took two-thirds of the seats, the rest were proportionately divided between the popular party with 46 seats and the socialists who came third with slightly
less. The politics of the working masses in Italy had remained unchanged. Matteotti had the courage to prove to the chamber the truth about the great electoral
fraud, and he paid for his evidence with his life. The memory of that barbarous
murder will not fade, it will always recall the many other murders in Italy and
other countries by which democracy was overthrown and the way paved for
totalitarianism.

ualist and a party to himself. Apart from exaggeration the same may be said of all Latin countries. The real difference between France and other countries is that in France the bourgeoisie, the professional and the middle classes have been superior in number, quality, tradition and combativity, to those of any other country. They have molded the culture, thought, art trends, political interests and social theories of modern life.

This is why the crisis through which these very classes passed between the two world wars had such wide repercussions, beyond the boundaries of France herself. And it shows too that even a defective and incomplete democracy like that of France, where the parties were fluid and interchangeable, where there were no great men after the disappearance of Clemenceau (great in spite of his many faults), where the electoral system lent itself to all sorts of combinations and dishonest deals, managed to survive for seventy years during which it gave so much to France, that it may be considered— after those of the United States and Switzerland—the democracy best fitted to the needs of a great nation.

England, on the other hand, has a long record of well-organized parties, which have kept control of the government of the country, alternating with the swing of the electoral pendulum. No general ideas, no passions, save in rare instances, when a Gladstone or a Disraeli held the world spellbound. For the rest, we find vested interests, a kind of political caste, formed in public schools and universities reserved to the gentry, a caste rising to the hereditary peerage in the House of Lords. English politics and even the proceedings in parliament might be compared to a game of chess, played with restrained passion, intelligent concentration and measured moves. Afterward, the loser shakes hands with the winner: tomorrow their positions may be reversed.

Democracy was not born in England until first the Irish party and then the Labour party had stirred the political waters of the Thames. Aristocratic tradition bowed to the newcomer, and for a time continued its game. It took a Lloyd

George government to shear the power of the lords, to render traditional titles innocuous, to raise to the peerage and seat in that august assembly laborites and radicals, a Sidney Webb, a Strabolgi or a Snell.

Thus after the First World War the two European democracies, in France and England, found themselves on the same plane but with this difference, that England could grant her women first the vote and then complete equality, enrolling them within the organized parties, absorbing them so to speak. This France did not dare to do. She feared that the extremists, communists and monarchists would be reinforced by the new feminine vote, to the detriment of the middle parties.*

It was this same fear among the middle parties, the traditional bourgeoisie whose liberalism was more a label than a conviction, that lost Italy in 1922 and lost France in 1940.

Professor Guglielmo Ferrero was right, when in his latest book † he emphasized the destructive power of fear when it lays hold of those in power, be they dictators, parliaments, parties or ruling classes. Then the old structure of a country falls to pieces, and it is impossible to introduce a new one that will inspire confidence. This happened in France after the fall of the First and Second Republics; it happened too in the decline of the Third Republic. Italy, on the other hand, survived the shocks of the period immediately following the Risorgimento and the more severe ones provoked by reactionary governments in the martial-law period of the Nineties, because the bourgeois governing class was alone in power and had confidence in itself. Whereas, after the armistice of 1918 the masses were already organized in strong parties, and the bourgeoisie with only its small traditional groups took fright

---

* In Italy, too, women were denied the vote (in spite of the repeated insistence of the popular party), and in Italy, as in France, those who were then least anxious to give women the vote were the socialists. Now the provisional governments of the two countries have decided to give women the vote.

† See *The Principles of Power*, by G. Ferrero, G. P. Putnam's Sons, New York, 1942.

and had recourse to street violence. The fascists of 1920 in Italy were of the same stuff as the Cagoulards of 1938 in France. Generals De Bono, Graziani and others of the march on Rome in 1922 were counterparts of the Pétains, Weygands and Darlans of the armistice of 1940. The first had a Mussolini to guide intoxicated youth; the latter, even more partisan, seized the occasion of Hitler's trampling on French soil to change the hated democratic regime.

It is said that in Anglo-Saxon countries, England, the Dominions and the United States, democracy withstands the shocks of extreme tendencies because it is organized more or less on the two-way party system. I do not propose to discuss the democracies of the British Dominions (Canada, Australia, New Zealand); their traditions of freedom do not go back very far and are in themselves deserving of separate study; nor Ireland, north and south, which has more or less been in a state of latent war since 1914. The oldest of the democracies is the United States, and by the grace of men and events, it has endured and evolved ever since 1776 with unbroken rhythm, notwithstanding wars and many crises, moral, political and economic.

Whether the credit for this should go to the organization of two parties, republican and democratic, or to the system of a central government leaving wide powers of self-government to the states, or to the ways of liberty applied to politics, is a question we must leave to Americans themselves. What impresses us, however, is that generally speaking the two American parties have so far not been able to canalize the forces of labor, which during the whole of the nineteenth century were at the mercy of an exploiting capitalism and only after the last war made any serious attempt to organize. Toward the end of the First World War they obtained the right of collective bargaining and a feeble voice in production; later through the economic crisis and the advent of President Roosevelt, they won the Wagner act, which to a certain extent gave legal status to their unions. In spite of various attempts, there does not seem to be any present possibility of a real labor party as in England.*

Far worse has been and is the situation of the thirteen million Negroes who are discriminated against not only in the exercise of the franchise but also in administrative, economic, military and even religious matters. During the twelve years of Mr. Roosevelt's presidency there were notable improvements as regards labor, social discrimination, and in other fields of public life, although war has accentuated administrative centralization and increased a cumbersome bureaucracy. American democracy has still further advances to make before it can be taken as a model and before it can dispense with new and arduous efforts to overcome the political and economic domination of capitalism.

Professor Livingston† was not alone in believing that only industrialized countries and those of a capitalist social structure can enjoy democracy. What many fail to realize is that every economic structure may have a political counterpart, shaped not by fatality but by free men working in the historic course of events to give it form and life. Thus in the last century we had highly industrialized countries such as the United States, England and Germany, each with a very different form of political organization: a democratic government, with a protective tariff in America; an aristocratic or liberal government, with free trade in England; a theocratic and militarist government with dumping in Germany. And in the present century, the America of Harding and Hoover became a democracy dominated by capitalist monopolies (in spite of the Sherman Antitrust Act), saturated with political and tariff isolationism, which by its very nature was undermining the foundations of true democracy. England, for her part, has maintained the rule of the conservatives through an old and obsolete electoral system, which led to the ruin of the liberal party, and with the exception of MacDonald's administration

---

* There exists a small labor party in the state of New York, but in 1944 it had already split in two, the anticommunist group taking the name of Liberal Party.
† The translator of Mosca and Pareto.

held the Labour party out of the government until Churchill's cabinet in 1940. England and the United States were spared the hysterical phases of France and Italy, but subjected to the untrammeled sway of capitalism of the City and of Wall Street—one of the causes of the weakening of democratic faith among Anglo-Saxons, and of the policy of appeasement that led to the present war.

Another example is that of Russia. A great industrial development has been accompanied not by a democratic regime, but by unlimited totalitarianism. Today, after the test of war, all bow to Russia for her national spirit and her military and industrial preparedness: no one can say that these were the effect of previously existing democracy, or that they will be the cause of democracy in the future. If certain American sociologists who seek to link democracy to capitalism or to industrialization would study comparative history, they would see how facts contradict their theories.

Others who cling to the mechanism of two parties do not see what lies behind it. Above all, the two parties are often (especially in America) the fruit of personal or group compromises, which cannot conceal the deep internal cleavages which in fact paralyze political life itself. The third parties, which are more than one, as human psychology is the same the world over, are stifled—as happened to the unfortunate liberal party in England—by the electoral system, which facilitates the maintenance in power for long periods of one party that may be only slightly the stronger.

The two-party system is extolled as the one most likely to insure public tranquillity and the one implying greatest democratic responsibility, inasmuch as the majority assumes the responsibilities and aspirations of the minority. Those who think thus do not realize that in actual fact there are never only two parties in any democracy in the world, since opinions, trends, interests and creeds are manifold. The difference is merely political and a matter of organization, never sociological. In fact, either such opinions, trends and interests express themselves within the parties, or else they do so in parliament or Congress, but the ultimate effects are always either those of compromise or of conflict.

In every social structure, the various concrete forces are expressed in affirmative and negative terms; that will prevail which is strongest in numbers or force or reason. Thus the final decision is the one which imposes itself. Democracy is the surest method on condition that the vote be free and the final decision acceptable.

In France and in Italy the spirit of individualism with its good and bad aspects, has always prevented the bourgeoisie from forming its own parties within the structure of capitalist society. Only labor parties like the socialists, or having the social character of a labor party like the popular party (which was not a class party) have given cohesion to the electorate and expression to political programs. But whether because the Latin socialist parties (unlike the Anglo-Saxon) were revolutionary, or because the popular parties appeared too late (and in France before the war were merely the shadow of a party), the fact remains that in times of national crisis, parties representing labor are incapable of holding their own against reaction. This was true even in Germany.

Perhaps the English Labour party, after about forty years' experience, may be ready to inherit power from the bourgeoisie, but in America labor is not yet prepared for such a task. It is perhaps more backward than was the Italian working class of 1922, and the French working class of 1939. It is beyond question that communism, as understood by members of the communist parties belonging to the former Third International, inoculated western democracies with the virus of fear and very nearly disintegrated the forces of labor itself with revolutionary ideas. But what Italy has suffered through the fascist adventure has been far more the effect of fear on the bourgeoisie than of mob revolution. It was precisely the bourgeoisie that abandoned democracy and made revolution its own.

*   *   *

Those who look upon the fascist crisis as an indication of the inability of Italians to live in democracy have no historical, psychological, or sociological understanding of the complexities of Europe. When the first French democracy (if it ever was a true democracy) went from the reign of terror into the dictatorial empire of Napoleon, many of the French believed themselves unfitted not only for democracy, but for the upper-class parliamentarism of England. The restoration was welcomed as a temperate and paternal monarchy, with a trend toward absolute power.

The democracy of 1848 soon failed in France through bourgeois incomprehension or fear of the masses who were breaking in upon it. Twenty years of dictatorship under Napoleon III (the second empire) led the world to believe France incapable of a popular regime. And not alone the men of Vichy but many others, in and out of France, believe today that democracy is ill-suited to the genius of the French people. Yet modern democracy was born in France. When American democracy was born, it derived from English common law, puritanism and the French encyclopedists. Not only was French idealism not lacking, it actually was the leaven.*

Would Americans or Englishmen in the days of the first or second Napoleon have had the right to say that France was unfit for democracy? So Americans or Englishmen, today, have no right to say that Italy (because of one Mussolini instead of two Napoleons) is unfit, I do not say for democracy, but to return to democracy, to a better democracy than ever.

When historical crises have been overcome and periods are linked up, then the dark and dubious points and the tragic fates of a people on its upward way are seen with clearer eyes. After the Civil War and the abolition of slavery, America felt morally and psychologically sounder, even though still bleeding from four years of war and bitterness, that was to remain alive for many decades. And although it may be said that the

* Some believe Rousseau was the father of French and modern democracy. This is not true, not only as regards America, England and Italy, but even France. For democracy, Rousseau is a name; as Marx is for socialism; the thing itself is different.

democracy of Jefferson and Lincoln was more conscious and sounder than that of Theodore Roosevelt or Herbert Hoover, yet in the light of history, each phase outgrown is a victory won in the name of the ideal. So it will be tomorrow with France when she is able to set up the Fourth Republic, to wipe out the shame of Compiègne in 1940, to repudiate the men of Vichy. So it will be with Italy when she is able to carry forward the second Risorgimento after the totalitarian tyranny of fascism and the empty bragging of empire.

Democracy is something more than a system of elections and party organizations, it is an ideal. This ideal, common to mankind, finds expression in every individual community and in every age of history, giving to each special characteristics and a form of its own. That is why democracy, the best form of life in a political society, has taken different ways and assumed different forms on either side of the Atlantic. This is because it has had to overcome different obstacles of tradition, institutions, religious and philosophical cultural trends, economic and political interests; also because it takes on the color of the various peoples in their civil and moral evolution.

The Englishman does not proceed by sudden changes, but slowly and surely in a spirit of adaptation that has made his nation the strongest and best able to withstand political storms. That is why he has twice been able to face the German, better equipped, better disciplined and twice as numerous. The Frenchman is too logical for adaptation, the Italian, too impulsive. That is why they have always had intangible written constitutions (disregarded perhaps in practice), rigid forms of administration, a centralized bureaucracy and excessive formalism. That is how it is on paper, but in real life individualism prevails over collective consciousness and the fetters of society. Anyone who can evade the law enjoys doing so, pleased with his own cleverness (especially if he is evading the tax collector), convinced that society, even the most liberal, is tyrannical indeed not to allow him to do as he pleases. When the chains of society hamper class interests, a restive impatience turns against regimes too rigid to readapt themselves to new conditions. Hence the crises great and small in Europe from the French revolution onwards. Latin individualism has its advantages in the development of personality, the affirmation of genius, the flame of art, even in artisans and workers, and in its constant effort to overcome the social, political and economic barriers that class and party structures impose on the community.

In any case, every country will have its own democracy, every age its own democracy. A time will come when democracy will be submerged and a time when democracy will return triumphant. Those who see no good save in the uniformity and permanence of political regimes have neither historical sense nor imagination.

The Italy of tomorrow will be democratic not only because every country with an individualist spirit tends to democracy; not only in reaction against the fascist past that it will wish to wipe out; not only by instinct of imitation as victory will rest with the democracies (and Russia and China will pass or be made to pass for democracies), but because the reconstruction of the country and a return to social and political sanity make a democracy for Italy imperative.

* * *

But what democracy? There are various kinds. There have been various kinds in the past, there will be more in the future. Countries and epochs adapt themselves to existing institutions while transforming them; countries and epochs create new institutions to meet new requirements. The post-war period will see an immense psychological transformation of victors and vanquished; social values will be reassessed consciously or unconsciously. The repudiation of a cumbered past will be an act of duty for totalitarian countries (Russia included), as well as a psychological and moral necessity for the democracies themselves.

Without a true moral catharsis, it will not be possible to

create a true new democracy in which the various social classes and the various cultural groups will have confidence, and for which they will be willing to pocket their pride, sacrifice their tranquillity and contribute their labor. Thus no one must be surprised if to many Italians, after such a deep and far-reaching crisis, the words liberty and democracy do not ring with hope and social harmony. For these the words "nation," "Spirit of Italy," will have greater appeal, as for certain others "trade-unionism," or "communism."

When the period of depression and humiliation has passed —human nature does not change easily, and immediate feelings have more effect on the imagination than the soundest arguments—Italians will begin to think and will see that in politics today the only choice is between democracy and dictatorship. The semidemocracies are in fact semidictatorships, and it will be easy for them to lose the sense of liberty and become arbitrary governments like the dictatorships themselves. Those who today speak of paternal government (as in the eighteenth century) not only do not remember that the historical government of that time was not really paternal, but they do not understand what it means for a people to abdicate its own political life into the hands of an irresponsible group. In the eighteenth century there were still the aristocracy of birth, the Church and the bourgeoisie, three distinct classes, jealous of their rights, which at least buttressed that particular social structure. Not so, today. The leaders would be military men like Horthy, Pétain, Darlan, Franco or Carmona, who represent only the interests of a limited and reactionary caste, or upstarts who would be worth no more than a Mussolini or a Laval or other political adventurers, well meaning or evil minded.

Thus by a process of elimination, even the most antidemocratic in the defeated countries will come to feel the necessity of a parliamentary regime (without a parliament democracy is impossible), of a sound and honest franchise including women (without elections a parliament is impossible), and with party organizations in keeping with the economic structure and the cultural formation of each country (without parties honest elections and parliamentary life are impossible). *

This picture, if similar in outline to Italy's past from 1848 to 1922, will not resemble it in historical, psychological, moral, political and social reality. Italy will have to refashion her entire structure. What remains after the moral and economic destruction of fascism and the material destructions of the war will have to be rebuilt with the single aim to save Italy, to set her once more on the path of destiny and to redeem her.

6

Monarchy or Republic

THE QUESTION THAT was so keenly debated by our
fathers of the Risorgimento is once more agitating the
Italian people: Is Italy to be a monarchy or a republic?
Since the French revolution it has not been easy to reconcile
democracy with monarchy in Europe, and if this has been
done in northern countries, it has never been achieved by the
Latin nations.

In England, after the death of Queen Victoria and with the
advent of the Labour party, people began to speak of democracy as a living thing, for up till then its existence had been
stoutly disputed. To "make the world safe for democracy"
was a slogan of the last war, but only quite recently has the
word become current, and it was used by Prime Minister
Baldwin himself, to differentiate England and France from
the totalitarian states. All the fascisms of the world, headed by
Italy, have contributed to bring the word into use by their
contemptuous references to the plutocratic and capitalist democracies. Before the First World War Belgium and Holland
did not dare call themselves democracies. They were liberal
regimes with a popular trend. After the death of Albert I, his
son Leopold showed clearly that he had little liking for democracy although the Belgian masses (socialists and Christian-
democrats) were ripe for wider social experiments. Only the
Scandinavian kingdoms, in the last twenty years, have shown
rapid progress along the path of social democracy, as also the
British dominions, Australia, Canada, New Zealand. The
king of England, the queen of Holland, the grand duchess of

Luxemburg and the kings of Sweden, Norway and Denmark, are something more than constitutional monarchs; they are bound up with the lot of their peoples, progressively experimenting in social reforms along democratic lines.

Latin monarchies have had a different character and history. That of France was unseated more than once between 1792 and 1848. These kings were never in favor of democracy, but almost always of reaction. French monarchist parties have been and are antidemocratic by definition. From the constitution of 1812 to the abdication of Alfonso XIII in 1931 the tradition of the Spanish monarchy, even that of Isabella's branch, has always tended toward absolute power, granting concessions to the people and then withdrawing them according to the revolutionary moment. Portugal freed herself from the Braganza dynasty in 1911 but did not achieve democracy. The passage from anticlerical to clerical dictatorship has been beneficial but not happy. Salazar's antidemocracy is not directed toward a restoration of the monarchy; one obstacle less in the way of free and democratic government in the future.

After the restoration of 1815 there were no less than seven Italian dynasties in addition to the Pope and apart from the emperor of Austria, who was a foreign sovereign. Except in Piedmont, there was no real popular tradition of monarchy. As soon as the movement for unification began, opinions were divided between a confederation of states, under the presidency of the Pope (as the neo-Guelfs proposed), and a republic "one and indivisible."

After the failure of the revolts between 1820 and 1830, and after the vain promises of constitutions made by the various sovereigns, the idea of a republic won much support under the auspices of Mazzini's *Young Italy*, whereas Gioberti's *Primacy of Italy*, published in 1843, inclined many to the idea of a confederation. The words of Pius IX: "Great God, bless Italy," came as an elaborate shock to all Italians, who believed imminent such a confederation or some other form of unification. Whether the monarchs were to stay or go was not the problem of the moment: the Italian people felt that they were the nation, and this feeling was crystallized in favor of independence from Austria and constitutional government.

In 1848 Charles Albert of Savoy-Carignano gave the kingdom of Sardinia a constitution and declared war on Austria. He thus became the leader of the new Italy. Beaten at Novara, forced to ask for an armistice, he abdicated and went into voluntary exile. However insincere and vacillating he may have been toward the revolutionaries, however imprudent his attempt at improvised war, he attracted to himself and his dynasty the support of all the liberals in the country. When Pius IX took fright and fled to Gaeta, King Ferdinand of Naples withdrew the constitution he had granted, Sicily entered upon an unequal struggle with this Bourbon who had usurped her rights, and all the other petty princes returned to the harshest reaction, under the direction and with the help of Austria. Victor Emmanuel alone remained faithful to the constitution. He thus became the natural claimant to the crown of Italy; even Sicily gave up her traditions of independence. Fortune and Cavour did the rest: Victor Emmanuel became the first king of Italy and the father of his country. Many republicans rallied to the monarchy at the slogan: "The republic divides us, the monarchy unites us." Even Garibaldi gave way; even Mazzini did not oppose it. The Mazzini tradition remained as an historical memory or perhaps a warning. It had active centers and courageous exponents. It dropped the first part of the motto, "God and the people," and clung fast to the second, more or less following socialist tendencies.

One of the things most typical of the spirit of Italy—that never suffered from French "monarchitis" or Spanish "legitimitis"—was the rapid disappearance of all memory of the dispossessed dynasties and the inefficiency of the parties favoring restoration. Naples had its little group of pro-Bourbons, a few disconsolate aristocrats who made loyalty to the dynasty a point of honor; a few ecclesiastics who feared the liberty or rather the license of the new regime; a few faithful officials who rather than swear allegiance to the new king—to them a usurper—preferred to live in misery. These good folk had not the makings of a party. In the Neapolitan provinces the so-called "Bourbonian brigandage" found support for a time, helped by money from Francis II, but it was drastically repressed. Sicily had only memories of constant hostility to the Bourbons of Naples, and the final blow, the suppression of the constitution of 1812 (guaranteed by England) had stirred up various revolts, preceded and followed by petitions to London and British interventions—finally by the war of 1848. The few "Bourbonians" were looked upon as traitors to Sicily albeit she had little liking for the "Piedmontese" and even attempted a fresh revolt. In fact, there was no monarchism; the idea of Sicilian autonomy alone predominated.*

The only resistance to the new state of things came from Catholics, not in the name of legitimism, which was soon outgrown, but in regard to the Roman question and its ecclesiastical implications. Of this we shall speak in the next chapter.

As the dynasties of the past made no appeal to Italian tradition, save in Piedmont, so the dynasty of the new kingdom of Italy had no other title to the country as a whole than that of its fidelity to the idea of unity and liberty and the way it had led the enterprise of 1848–70 to a happy conclusion, in the space of twenty-two years—an achievement that seemed almost miraculous. It is useless to speculate whether the same result could have been achieved without the House of Savoy. The fact remained that it was bound up with the great days of the Risorgimento and had become popular even among the Catholic populations (apart from those that declared the king usurper and excommunicate). Most of the Catholics deplored the conflict with the Church and wished to see Pius IX and Victor Emmanuel II reconciled. "Conciliation" became the word of the moment and Italy was torn between "conciliationists" and "anticonciliationists." Not long after, in 1878, Victor Emmanuel II and Pius IX died within a few days of each other.

---

* After 1848 there was no further idea of a separate kingdom in Sicily, but many resented the central government and aspired to regional autonomy. Only at the moment of Allied occupation was there open talk of separatism.

Humbert I acceded to the throne of Italy. The old Garibaldi advised his fellow militant, Benedetto Cairoli, who had become Prime Minister, to persuade the new king "that the future does not belong to the monarchy, and that how long his dynasty lasted would depend on the advantages it brought to Italy." Giovanni Passanante's attempt on Humbert's life in November, 1878, played into the hands of reaction by impeding the democratic plans of Cairoli (who on that occasion was wounded in the leg).

What share in the politics from 1878 to 1900 is to be attributed to the king and the court, what share to economic crises, colonial enterprise and the temperament of political leaders such as Depretis, Crispi, Giolitti and Rudini, we leave the professional historians to decide. The risings in Sicily and Lunigiana in 1894, and those which spread from Milan to other parts of Italy in 1898, were not accidental occurrences nor were they due exclusively to subversive propaganda. In every revolt there is always the spark that sets off and the demagogue who profits by it; but the social and economic conditions of Italy were deplorable, and awakening of the masses was passing from the narrowly economic and local stage to the political and national one.

King Humbert was accused of wanting a reactionary domestic policy; the middle classes who feared the democratic movement clung to the monarchy and the army as to a sure shield. The proclamation of martial law was in no wise conclusive; popular unrest reached even a part of the lower middle classes, the urban artisans and the white-collar workers. Election returns (even without universal suffrage) showed the demand for a complete return to normalcy and a far-reaching program of social legislation and political reform. In this heated atmosphere the assassination of Humbert came as a shock to the whole country and as a warning to the new king.

Victor Emmanuel III enjoyed an initial period of popularity; he was believed to be democratic. The parties then described as "popular" (radicals, socialists and republicans) were able to form a coalition and were strongly represented in the chamber of deputies; they also had their own representatives in the senate and gained considerable influence in certain government departments, such as public works, agriculture, industry and commerce. They brought about the creation of a ministry of labor, and a high council of labor, a bank for co-operative societies, and introduced various legislative and ministerial measures in favor of the working classes. Finally even universal suffrage was obtained. In the previous chapter we have seen how in Italy democracy was developing and how the working classes, despite phases of restlessness and uncertainty, were emerging into public life, becoming conscious of their rights and their potentiality, organizing into political parties.

It has often been said that even in this period, which seemed so promising, the action of the reactionary bourgeoisie, of the army and the court, if not of the king personally, was such that they managed to retain the levers of command and to curb the impatience of the extreme parties, alternating concessions with reaction to prevent the coming of democracy. If we do not wish to consider Italy as an exception, all this and more was happening all over Europe. To blame Victor Emmanuel III would be excessive; it would be to look at the events of thirty and forty years ago through the spectacles of 1945. In any case, how can the bourgeoisie of those days be blamed, when the strongest labor party, the socialists, while making use of the constitutional regime and taking part in parliamentary life, proclaimed themselves revolutionaries and acted as such? Was it not the socialist party (headed by Mussolini, then the editor of *Avanti!*) which incited the crowds to prevent the departure of soldiers for the Libyan war, tearing up the railroad track or encouraging women to lie down in front of trains? And later, did they not organize the so-called "Red Week" at Ancona, which was a genuine revolt? And, on the other hand, the socialists themselves declared they did not wish to take part in the government, but were waiting the hour for revolution.

Thus it is easy to see why the bourgeoisie, the army, and

the court stood together: why they implored the Vatican to allow Catholics to take part in the political elections to ensure "social conservation," and why they showed so much hostility to the Catholic workers' associations. More than once industrialists said and wrote: "Better the socialists than the Christian-democrats."

So it was natural that the king should avail himself of Giolitti as his trusted adviser. Giolitti knew the ropes in the chamber of deputies and had great influence in the country. Besides he was Piedmontese, a loyal bureaucrat and a clever politician who could be conservative and progressive at the same time. He knew how to face opposition when he was sure of success; he knew the right moment to resign so as to return the man of the moment; he knew how to becloud the crown, making it appear that the true sovereign was the electorate, which he was trying to manipulate, and the chamber, which he had sought to form to suit his policy. The author opposed Giolitti politically all his life, and was repaid by a like aversion, but we must be objective and not attribute to Giolitti or to Victor Emmanuel more than their share of responsibility.

It is true that men like Giolitti dominated the country too long and not always to its advantage, and that the support of the monarchy, discreet but steady, played no small part in making him the necessary and at times the fatal man of the hour. We are, however, opposed to the use of the word dictatorship, too readily applied by some to Giolitti, to Depretis and even to Cavour. Giolitti was not a dictator in the modern sense, nor was any other man in Italy, not excepting Crispi, who had the instinct for it. The opposition parties could attack all Italian prime ministers, Giolitti included, with the utmost vehemence. Giolitti evaded the blows. He tried to wear down his opponents and to favor his friends to the very limit, which at election time was easily overstepped as he knew he could so with impunity.

Giolitti, like Depretis, knew how to outmaneuver liberty, without ever abolishing it (as Crispi did by martial law). But where national interest was involved, they were capable of adopting decisive attitudes and taking great responsibilities. For better or for worse, according to the point of view, Giolitti decided upon the Libyan war after Italy for twenty years had been assured of the support of the great powers in respect to this territory which was Italy's share in the spoils of the Ottoman Empire. Giolitti introduced universal suffrage. It was Giolitti, and not Nitti the democrat, who had the courage to refuse the protectorate over Albania, offered by France, England and the United States at the Paris Peace Conference, and to drive d'Annunzio and his irregulars out of Fiume by shot and shell, as under the treaty of Rapallo, Fiume was recognized as a free city.

Italian democracy, which was steadily ripening from 1900 to 1914, did not find personal obstacles in either Victor Emmanuel or Giolitti, nor in the alleged monarchic-bourgeois dictatorship which did not exist. It was handicapped by the attitude of the industrial bourgeoisie which was alarmed by the labor movement; by Catholic absenteeism, on account of the *non expedit;* and by the revolutionary ideals, although mainly verbal, of the left-wing socialists.

*   *   *

If after the First World War affairs in Italy had remained at this point, the problem of the monarchy would never have been reopened. The socialists would have allowed what they called the "republican preconception" to drop completely; the popular party would never have raised the problem of the republic, although the author, then political secretary and leader of that party, and others with him, always had ideally leaned toward a republic.

The man who after the war again raised the question of the monarchy was Mussolini. One of the points of the fascist program of March, 1919, was the proclamation of an Italian republic. But the republic did not appeal to the fascists; for them it served merely as a revolutionary threat to the monarchy. Liberals and conservatives understood this at once, but so long as Mussolini was not sure whether Victor Emmanuel would object to making him prime minister, he, discarding the republic, sought to exploit the ambitions of the Duke of Aosta. So his plan was to confront the king with a claimant from his own House of Savoy. In a solemn address at Udine, Mussolini declared he had dropped republicanism and rallied to the monarchy. That speech was the exact counterpart of another he made in the chamber of deputies, in favor of Catholicism and the Vatican as an important factor in the future of Italy.

When the fascist revolt broke out at the end of October, 1922, Victor Emmanuel found himself with Luigi Facta as prime minister. This man, amid waverings and regrets, obliged to choose between the claims of the fascists and respect for liberal tradition, chose the more honest part and together with the other ministers who had already resigned declared martial law. He was right in his belief that in a few hours and with a small force of carabineers, police and garrison troops, the fascists would have surrendered. Mussolini in Milan was keeping a car in readiness for an escape to Switzerland. The king, however, gave more credence to certain pro-fascists generals than to his own cabinet. He was afraid that his cousin Aosta, who was lurking in nearby Spoleto, would be proclaimed king; he lacked confidence in the popularity of his person and of his heir-apparent; he feared lest his defenders, in the event of resistance to fascism, be socialists and members of the popular party. He gave in. At first he deluded himself, as did many others, that once Mussolini and the fascists had been appeased, they would become a docile tool in the hands of experienced men like Salandra, Giolitti and Orlando. It was this first act of "appeasement," in the English manner, and not a *combinazione*, in the Italian manner, that inaugurated an entirely new method in national and international politics.

The king and his councilors were grossly deceived. The psychology of those who have won a cheap victory is far more complex than that of the victors of long and hard-fought battles. The fascists and their leader had to foster the belief (and what is more to hypnotize themselves into believing) that their battles had been hard fought and bitter, that their armed demonstrations through the countryside and villages, threatening working men and destroying co-operatives, forcing castor oil down the throats of unfortunate victims in the presence of mocking youths who called for second and third doses, had been heroic deeds for the salvation of the country. The entry into Rome of thirty thousand men in blackshirts, with banners and pennants, bearing the skull and crossbones, bombs and daggers as device, was staged as the triumphal outcome of battles that had never been fought, a make-believe parade that here was Caesar returning triumphant over the hostile factions.

And so it was. The king took upon himself full responsibility. He, a constitutional monarch, refused to sign the decree proclaiming martial law and, instead of proceeding constitutionally to the formation of a parliamentary cabinet, appointed Mussolini prime minister when the latter was still in Milan; and allowed him, moreover, the march on Rome, as a sign that revolt had triumphed, thus transferring to armed gangs of swaggering rebels all the constitutional powers of king, parliament and government.

We do not mean to lay the sole blame on Victor Emmanuel, nor do we wish to attentuate the faults of Prime Minister Facta. We cannot forget that among the minister were antifascists like that peerless Giovanni Amendola (who paid for his opposition with his life), Bertini of the popular party and yet others. What seems strange is that Victor Emmanuel, who in the twenty-one years of his reign had always shown himself a constitutional monarch, loyally observing the traditional rules of the Albertine statute, should himself have suddenly cast off a meticulous and formalist etiquette, to shoulder responsibility for a revolution. He must have been sorely goaded by army men, men of the court and politicians to abandon his traditional reserve—unless the idea of a claimant to the throne excited him to the pitch of overcoming all hesitation. It was said he gave way to avert civil war. To the author it seems impossible that Victor Emmanuel could have thought Italy was on the eve of civil war. However much people may have exaggerated, there was not the shadow of such a danger.

From that ill-omened day of October 28, 1922, Victor Emmanuel followed the road he has chosen: nonresistance to fascism. He resumed his role of constitutional monarch without the constitution, or with a shred of constitution. There was a moment, after the murder of the socialist deputy, Giacomo Matteotti, when it was believed that the king was inclined to withdraw his confidence from the Mussolini cabinet (there was still the political fiction of believing in the existence of a cabinet appointed by the crown) and to call upon others to form a new government. It would have been a courageous act which might have been more far-reaching than any one could have imagined. But when the king called upon them for advice the ex-leaders of the liberal cabinets—Giolitti, Salandra and Orlando—gave it as their opinion that it would be inexpedient to venture upon a change, which would be the prelude to a government dominated by socialists and popular party. The crisis was averted. The king resumed his passive position, even in the face of growing public opposition and the resistance of the rump parliament, called the Aventines. This went on until Mussolini himself in the Chamber, in the session of January 3, 1925, taking upon himself the responsibility for the murder of Matteotti and for all crimes committed "for national ends," abrogated what liberty remained and effectively established his dictatorship.

It is probable that Victor Emmanuel thus thought to save the monarchy in Italy, while fascism was exhausting itself by the effort to keep in power. If this was so, Mussolini was more cunning than the king. He created a new organ of power, the fascist grand council, which possessing neither legal authority nor executive power, soon became an instrument of control and blackmail surpassing any other power that might tend to assume a capacity and responsibility of its own. The grand council was empowered to give its view in the event of succession to the throne. This tenuous provision, which looked like a veto, was enough to keep the king and his heir subject to the fascist party. Victor Emmanuel naturally set his signature to the decree creating the grand council, and Mussolini in this devious way succeeded in making permanent the dictatorship of the prime minister under a monarch.

Future historians and professors of political science will be hard put to it to characterize this hybrid regime. In analogous cases, Alfonso XIII remained king even with the dictatorship of Primo de Rivera, and Alexander I, of the Serb-Slovene kingdom (afterward known as Yugoslavia), himself became dictator. Going back to the Dark Ages, we find Pepin the Short, who, from being major-domo of Neustria, packed the last Merovingian king off to a monastery, had himself elected king by the assembly of the Franks, and then crowned by Pope Stephen II. Mussolini had no monastery at his disposal to which he could send Victor Emmanuel III, nor an assembly prepared to proclaim him king, nor a Pope ready to crown him. The army, the bourgeoisie, the court, and part of the clergy wanted a strong government, not a change of dynasty. Thus Mussolini left the king in his place as a constitutional monarch without a constitution, and without the power to appoint his own ministers or to change the head of the government, prime minister, party leader and dictator; without the power to dissolve the chamber of deputies and appeal to the people; without a free electorate—without any of the things that could give meaning to the existence of a real monarchy. Even his right to be commander in chief of the army and of all the armed forces of the nation was denied him, as Mussolini had invested himself with this lofty function.

But it was a more grievous trial for the Italian people than for the king, because the people wanted to retain their faith in the House of Savoy at all costs, that faith that for weal or woe had led them to turn to the dynasty of the Sardo-Piedmontese kingdom during the Risorgimento, as the fulcrum of the constitutional regime and the symbol of the nation. And every time that hope failed, as over the case of Matteotti, it sprang up again, waiting for some new event or incident that would finally bring the king into collision with his prime minister. And if, in spite of everything, in any one of those twenty years the king had made some small gesture of resistance, the crowd would have acclaimed him, as it did on the evening of July 25, 1943, when Mussolini fell.

For the masses, for the good folk of every country, a king is by definition honest, benevolent, the lover of his people, just, above all parties, worthy of respect, of trust, of love. The dictator is feared, admired or despised, but the king is loved; he is the father. This is a very ancient belief, one which a thousand kings—tyrants or traitors or exploiters of their country or merely stupid—have been unable to tear from the hearts of the people, not only because there were other kings who were fathers, or heroes or saints, but because above and beyond any personal quality the king is a symbol. Will this prove to be the sole force remaining to the king of Italy now that all personal merit has vanished?

There are those who think so, and if this were merely a personal case, it would have been easy to content public opinion with the abdication of Victor Emmanuel, who would never be able to justify his solidarity with fascism, and with the renunciation of the succession by Prince Humbert, who was in the same position as his father, a field marshal by appointment of Mussolini, and one who did not blush to wear the uniform of the fascist party. The idea of a regency during the minority of the son of Humbert and Maria José, to satisfy the monarchists and not to offend others who are anxious to eradicate from Italy the name and memory of fascism, seemed to make headway between August and December, 1943. The nomination of Humbert as a lieutenant of the king has been a temporary compromise. The problem remains unsolved whether Italy is to be a monarchy or a republic.

*   *   *

We may pass over the arguments of those who, laying the blame for fascism on all, ruling classes, politicians, mass parties, industrial groups, object to seeing the

king made a scapegoat. While agreeing that all were to blame
though by no means equally, we deny that if the king lost his
throne, he would be a scapegoat: he is a culprit, and from a
political and historical point of view he is the chief culprit.

Germany in 1918, after her defeat, overthrew not only William II, the man really to blame for the war, but all the kings
and petty princes around him, his accomplices as second-
grade monarchs and generals of the army. Austria-Hungary
overthrew the Emperor Charles, whose only offense was that
he succeeded Francis Joseph, who had declared war against
Serbia. It was not the Allies who obliged these monarchs to
abdicate, but the peoples themselves, weary of four years of
war and brought to the edge of the abyss.

When Charles Albert was defeated at Novara by the Austrian armies, he abdicated, but no one then thought of setting
up a republic, and Victor Emmanuel II succeeded him. Today on the contrary the republic is being discussed because
the public opinion is different. Then the people were with
the monarchy to drive the *tedesco** out of Italy; but under
fascism the monarchy was not with the people because it allowed the *tedesco* to return to Italy.

How far this state of mind will lead to a decisive break between the people and the monarchy cannot today be foreseen.

What we know is that nearly all anti-fascist groups abroad
are for the republic; and that the same is true of many in the
underground movement in Italy as well as of part of the
young intellectuals, socialists and members of the action party
are for the republic. In the other parties (communist, Christian-democrat and liberal) the idea of a republic is freely expressed and is supported by many as a program for the Constituent Assembly.†

The current view in the United States and England among
the ruling classes—apart from progressive circles and the
masses—is that Italy must be chained to monarchy. We do

---

* Italians use the word *"tedesco"* both when speaking of Austrians and for
Germans.

† On the Constituent Assembly, see pp. 250–256.

not know for what mysterious reasons all the countries of the
American continent, Guatemala and Santo Domingo included, can be republics or "republicettes," why no one thinks
of restoring a king to Poland or an emperor to Germany, and
yet that the Italians must have a king forced upon them even
if they prefer not to have one.

All Latin countries, except Italy, do without kings. This
matter of the Latin countries has been the particular concern
of certain Anglo-Saxon and Irish Catholics who seem to have
appointed themselves the special guardians of such countries.
Some of them have imagined a kind of Latino-Catholic confederation, with kings in France and Spain. I do not remember reading whether they are looking for a king for Portugal
or whether (like geopoliticians who specialize in remaking
the map of Europe) they would lump Portugal and Spain together. Naturally, the Pope would have some sort of political
temporal function in this Latin federation, for the thoughts
of these would-be rebuilders of the Latin world are turned
more to the past than to the future. But history marches on
and, whether they like it or not, history is a development of
the past and present that conditions the free activity of men.
In the last analysis the latter are the masters of their acts, but
they cannot manufacture history out of materials existing only
in the imagination of the gifted few. France will never again
be a monarchy so long as she remains the France of liberty
and events today are driving her even farther from monarchy
and its worst substitute, "marshalism." * She is returned to
the true origins of the republic founded on "Liberty, Equality, Fraternity," even though the French continue to quarrel
among themselves for another half century.

We shall make no forecasts about the dictatorships (why are
they called semidictatorships?) of Franco and Salazar in the
Iberian peninsula. There is no danger, so long as England
exists, that Portugal will be annexed by Spain; nor indeed
that Portugal will seek out some offspring of the Braganzas

---

* Weimar Germany was undermined by the choice of Marshal Hindenburg as
president, France tottered with MacMahon and fell with Pétain.

and give him back the crown. As regards a federation, suffice to say that neither their Latin bond nor the fact that these countries are in majority Catholic will be enough to unite them, in the absence of dominant political and economic interests, as a unit distinct from the British commonwealth and even from Germany. Let us leave this task to the geopoliticians or to Mr. Ely Culbertson. And let us set aside the idea that, like a king in chess, the Pope would think of castling into a Latin zone where he would have semipolitical power, in order to rivet the idea held in Protestant spheres that the Pope and the Church of Rome are not universal for the whole world, but Latin, particularist and in geographic sense "Roman Catholic"!

*　　*　　*

The Italians have a reputation for *combinazioni,* in the sense that while affirming and reaffirming principles, they find a way to apply them without going to the extremes of conflict. In this they differ from the Spaniards, who rejecting all compromise readily come to bloody struggles and civil wars; they differ too from the French, who while avoiding civil wars perpetuate their quarrels for centuries in the name of logic. But I doubt that this time, in the case of monarchy, any *combinazione* could serve the cause of Italy or the interest of Europe.

In Italy the monarchy has no history other than from the Risorgimento onward, and that is the history of a liberal parliamentary regime moving toward democracy. In Italy there is no aristocracy and no House of Lords as in England, there is no long monarchic tradition as in Holland and the Scandinavian countries. Like Belgium, Italy was born of a liberal revolution that thought to buttress its own existence with a king. In 1830 Belgium took a pro-English German king; in 1848 Italy found a Savoyard king who was anti-Austrian and pro-French. The same thing happened in the new kingdoms of the Balkan peninsula, which went to Germany for their new sovereigns.

Lacking historic basis, the attribute of tradition, all ties with the land itself and the landed aristocracy—all the things that have made Britain the only stable monarchy in the world, the last surviving great monarchy—there is only one thing that can count: the confidence of the people. If that fails, like a sap rising from the deep earth, the institution of monarchy withers away.

There is the further fact that the northern monarchies which endure have another mainstay, less effectual today than of old but still very real—the support of the Reformed churches which look upon the king as their ecclesiastical head. Not so in the Catholic countries whose religious head is the Pope. Thus where the ancient "orders" and "estates," in which the clergy had its political, economic and social place, have disappeared (and they did so sooner in Catholic countries than elsewhere), all that remains to the king is the religious function of his consecration. The kings of Italy, however, have never had this consecration, for up to 1929 (the date of the Lateran Treaty), they were held to be usurpers and implicitly excommunicate.

The Italian clergy were well disposed toward the House of Savoy only after 1929. Sixteen years are not enough to build up a tradition, all the more so as ten of those sixteen years were years of continuous warfare in Abyssinia, Spain, Albania, from 1935 to 1939, and the present war since 1940.

If despite the periods of martial law in 1893 and 1898, despite fascism from 1922 to 1943, despite the wars since 1935, the monarchy is rooted in the hearts of the Italian people (its only title to existence), it is for that people to say when it is again free, has reflected upon its future and is in a position to make a decision. A monarchy upheld by foreign troops and coalition powers against the will of a people would be a fiction and an imposition.

What might be the intrinsic value of a monarchy in Italy in the postwar future, the Americans themselves should be able to say. In founding their democracy they took care to avoid a monarchy, a landed aristocracy and titles of nobility.

It is true that later the aristocracy of the dollar supervened, but in this world it is not always possible to avoid abuses.

If the future Italy is to be a great military power, with large armies on land, at sea and in the air, then a warrior king, who can boast the tradition among his ancestors, of great generals like Emmanuel Filibert and Prince Eugene,* might help to give character to the country, especially if surrounded by barons, counts, marquises and dukes renowned for their feats of war aims and conquest. If on the contrary, the king is to confine himself to being merely the symbol of the country, a constitutional king "who reigns but does not rule" † he can without serious inconvenience be replaced by a president who has less pretensions and can be changed every five or seven years, without much trouble or ado.

It is said that an hereditary king is a guarantee of national continuity; but the experience of Switzerland (the longest on record) and of the United States after a century and a half, go to show that national continuity resides rather in the spirit of the people and in national consciousness than in a reigning family. If the United States can indulge in the luxury of a popular presidential election every four years (and their president is not like a constitutional king who reigns but does not rule; he is the head of the administration and of the nation), there seems to be no reason why Italy, if her people so wish, should not elect a president at fixed intervals.

The attitude of Churchill toward the House of Savoy is inconceivable. Surely no Englishman in his senses can have the remotest idea that the fall of the House of Savoy could weaken the stability of the House of Windsor. In other days and much closer at hand in Paris the Bourbons fell and then the House of Orleans (we do not count the two Napoleons, who had no ancestors, not even a baron or a count). And

---

* Respectively the general of Charles V, who won the battle of St. Quentin against the French (August 10, 1557), and Prince Eugene of Savoy, the famous general of the seventeenth and eighteenth centuries, who invaded France together with the Duke of Marlborough.

† According to the French constitutional theory and that of Italy in the nineteenth century.

nothing happened across the channel. Nothing will happen if there should be a president of the republic of Rome.

Whether Italy is to be a monarchy or a republic is essentially an Italian problem. Others should be concerned only with the spirit in which the Italian people choose the new regime. That is what counts, even if the form they choose were still to be the monarchy. What Italy needs is to overcome the fascist complex and avoid falling into the discouragement of humiliation. They must take their defeat for what it is: a defeat inflicted by friendly peoples from whom Italy had turned away. The faults of these friendly peoples cannot be hidden or minimized, even if many still fail to recognize them. But the faults of the ruling classes of Italy, who adhered to fascism, upheld it, and then themselves became its victims, must be visited with moral and historical sanctions (apart from the criminals and their accomplices).

The soul of a people, exposed for twenty years to subtle and continuous poison, cannot be refashioned without a profound transformation. A cathartic action is necessary. There will be new books, new teachers, new trends, but the people must renounce all megalomania; they must overcome the inferiority complex that has led them to see themselves as downtrodden and oppressed by everyone; they must pass from a sense of national isolation and fascist-fomented egocentricism to a *rapprochement* with the other peoples, to resume their place in the world, without being dominators or dominated.

Collective ideas are not produced by moral preachings alone; common sentiments are not born by pure will power; they must be transformed into collective life, an active life truly lived, hence a life with a common purpose that becomes an ideal. If tomorrow the Italian people were to be placed in subjection to a semi-absolute monarchy, or to a capitalistic or military bourgeois clique that took over public life and prevented all democratic activity (as Franco, Pétain and Salazar have done), if the monarchy were to serve as a screen and the Church as an aid in keeping down the people, then the necessary spiritual transformation could never come to pass.

The people would take two opposite roads: that of mistrustful resignation and that of secret societies for a democratic revolution. And a third element, bolshevist psychology, would make itself felt. Even if Stalin plays the honest bourgeois with Truman and Churchill or Attlee and acts as best man to the monarchy, Moscow will remain a magnetic attraction, a myth in the fantasies of distrustful and exasperated masses, a slogan of revolt.

Postwar Italy must strive to avoid bloody uprisings and outbursts of partisan fury and class hatreds. But if she is to resume a normal life, apart from all the economic and political measures that are urgently needed, she must have the sense of her own personality, to be remade, reconstituted, regained. The people, united in purpose and determination amid the diversity of trends and opinions, must rise again. Its banner must be democracy, its aim the second Italian Risorgimento within the European and international order. To give back faith to the people, the country itself, the regime to be established, the forces to be used, must be given back into their hands, making to live anew the ideals that correspond to the traditional conception of the spirit of Italy.

Within this setting the monarchy would be nothing more than an expedient and a mechanism that might be useful or harmful. Neither Victor Emmanuel III, nor Humbert II, can aspire to become the heroes and the saviors of Italy in the eyes of a people engaged in reconstruction. They would represent that past which must perish. And if the monarchy falls with them and the republic is proclaimed, perhaps with all the inconveniences that a change of regime brings, it will serve to mark in history the opening of the new epoch in which the spirit of Italy will be born again.

7

Church and State

FOLLOWING UPON the Risorgimento, relations between Church and State in Italy were complicated by the Roman question and the presence of the Pope in Rome. Although quite distinct and in theory separate, these questions could not be disjoined in matters of state and in the feelings of the people.

Cavour's slogan, "A free Church in a free State," owed its origin to Montalembert and his campaign in *l'Avenir*, before the encyclical *Miraris Vos* of Pope Gregory XVI in 1832,* when Lacordaire and Montalembert were helping Lammenais to run the paper. These French Catholics saw all the harm that was being done in the "Restoration" period by what was then called the "alliance of throne and altar." It was all to the advantage of the throne and to the spiritual disadvantage of the altar, and ended by political and moral harm to the throne, and helping its enemies and those of the Church. The mistake of many in those days was to consider an attitude of practical expediency as good for all times and places, almost as a theoretical and universal truth. The separation of Church and State may be beneficial to both in democratic countries, but never under feudal or despotic rule. France and Italy were then emerging from absolutism; they had not achieved democracy.

There was however something more serious in the liberal trend of the time—the passing of absolute power from the royal sovereign to the sovereign people. As the sovereign

* In this encyclical various propositions supported by the editors of *l'Avenir* were condemned, although the writers themselves were not named.

people was reduced to exercising its sovereignty only for a few hours every four or five years, and even then through the intermediary of a privileged class formed of an electorate based on a property qualification, a class which claimed to interpret the wishes of the whole people, the power of the sovereign people was in fact exercised by the government and by the ruling class. Lammenais failed to see this and all his life it was on these grounds that he supported the principle and sought the realization of the "political absolute." First he extolled the all-powerful monarch, then the Pope as ruler of the world,* and finally the people, the sovereign people. To these factors of social life he attributed absolute and definite potentiality. In democracy, it was natural that monarchy and the Papacy should give way to the people, but it was not true that the people were really sovereign, or possessed of illimited powers.† By way of the people one arrived at the supremacy of the state, which in those days tended to be oligarchic even when it assumed a liberal guise. Liberty was for the bourgeoisie, not for the people or the Church. In France, the alliance of throne and altar led to a revival of Gallicanism, just as it strengthened the movement against ultramontanism in the whole of Europe during the first half of the nineteenth century when relations with the Church were regulated by traditional jurisdictional agreements.‡

It would be of no interest to retrace the history of ecclesiastical conflict in Italy from 1848 to 1870, over issues that arose one after the other, such as ecclesiastical courts or the vows of religious orders or the administration of Church charities and endowments. It was natural that each and every question should assume a political aspect and color in the

---

* We speak here of the political Papacy. This was not the invention of Lammenais. Joseph de Maistre had a school of followers in France and elsewhere, and has followers even today. We do not deny the actual influence of the Papacy in social life, but this is a moral and spiritual influence, never in *politics* in the sense of the word as used by Aristotle.

† In our view the people are the principal factor of democracy. See *For Democracy*, People and Freedom Group, Burns, Oats and Washburn, London.

‡ See *Church and State*, by Luigi Sturzo, Longmans, Green & Co., Inc., New York, 1939.

struggle against the system of absolute monarchy in alliance with the Church, an alliance it was sought to destroy in order to substitute a constitutional regime based on liberty. And as among the absolute monarchs was the Pope who ruled over part of central Italy and the city of Rome, the revolutionary political movement of the Risorgimento saw ecclesiastical questions and the papal question in the same light, all from the point of view of freedom and independence for the people in a constitutional regime. Thus "a free Church in a free State" and "Rome, capital of Italy" became two facets of the same religious problem facing the new Italy re-created as a nation in a single kingdom.

The party known as the neo-Guelfs * sought to achieve the unification of Italy by a federation of all the states that went to make up the nation and driving out the foreigners (Austria) who held Lombardy and Venetia, the Trentino and Trieste. In such a federation the Pope was to be honorary president. Abbé Rosmini † went to Rome in 1848 as a special envoy of the Turin government to discuss the possibility of such a scheme. Not long after his mandate was revoked by a change of government policy. When Pius IX gave signs of favoring the Italian cause and in 1848 granted a constitution to the Roman state, the liberals of Italy and the whole world adopted him as a symbol of liberty. The neo-Guelfs then had high hopes of achieving their aims, as all the other kings as well as the dukes and grand dukes had likewise granted and sworn to constitutions for their "beloved subjects." But when Pius IX—after a taste of revolution in which his prime minister, Pellegrino Rossi, was killed—and fearing for his personal safety took refuge at Gaeta, city of the kingdom of Naples, the neo-Guelf movement collapsed and the Austrian reaction triumphed. Soon after when the Roman republic

---

* In Italy during the Middle Ages the Guelfs were for the Pope; the Ghibellines, for the Emperor. These names came back into political and literary use in the nineteenth century to denote clericals and anticlericals in Italy, not on the religious but on the political plane.

† Antonio Rosmini Serbati, philosopher and founder of the Rosminian congregation, with branches in Britain and America, that concerns itself with education and other cultural and spiritual activities.

(proclaimed on the flight of Pius IX) and the Venetian republic were both overthrown by foreign armies, the idea of an
Italian federation was abandoned and with it any idea of a
Pope as president, even in an honorary capacity. All wanted
to see the new kingdom as one state and under one king.

Lombardy was taken from Austria by Piedmont and the
France of Napoleon III (treaty of Zurich, November 1859);
Emilia, Romagna and Tuscany were annexed in 1860; the
papal provinces of the Marches and Umbria in September of
the same year; the kingdoms of Naples and Sicily (known as
the kingdom of the Two Sicilies) as a result of the insurrec-
tion of Palermo on April 4, 1860, and the subsequent expedition of Garibaldi on May 6, 1860. Finally came the
proclamation of the kingdom of Italy on March 17, 1861,
with Rome as capital.

So Rome was to be taken from the Pope and annexed to
the kingdom of Italy. The ideal of union, the national policy
and revolutionary ferment of the Risorgimento, all converged
on Rome. The Catholics, although forming the great majority, had no party of their own. Except for zealous groups
that supported the temporal power of the Pope, they favored
territorial unity and looked to the Pope for voluntary cession.
Pius IX answered with a *non possumus* that has remained
famous.

Unfortunately, to be respected the *non possumus* of Pius
IX had to be upheld by foreign troops. The French kept
an armed garrison in the remnants of the papal states, insur-
rections were suppressed, liberals put in prison or sent to the
scaffold, military expeditions such as that of Garibaldi in
1867 were met by foreign troops. Although Pius IX sought
to defend his temporal rights and guard the tradition of a
free Papacy, he actually adopted a reactionary policy and
relied on armed force. But when Napoleon III, attacked by
Prussia, withdrew his troops from Rome, the Pope remained
disarmed. The Italian armies had no difficulty in occupying
the papal states and taking Rome on September 20, 1870.

Pius IX wished to show that his opponents were using

force and that he was resisting to assert his rights, but he avoided a useless and bloody sacrifice. He gave way under protest and shut himself up in the Vatican. The Italian troops then occupied the whole city save for what was called the Leonine area * between the Tiber and the Vatican. But in consequence of disorders and lack of security in this area, the ecclesiastical authorities allowed the occupation of the whole quarter up to the confines of the Vatican itself.

Thus ended the temporal power of the Popes, which through countless vicissitudes had served for eleven centuries as the outward and visible sign of the independence of the Roman pontificate, even when adverse circumstances had obliged the Popes to migrate to Avignon or to ask the help of kings and emperors or to submit to political pressure from the dominant states of continental Europe.

The seizure of Rome made a tremendous impression, not only in Italy but throughout the world, and was commented upon favorably or adversely according to religious or political viewpoints. The bitter controversies of the time between liberals and absolutists (reactionaries), anticlericals and clericals (known in France as ultramontanes), revolutionists and conciliationists, Freemasons and *sanfedisti*,† could not dissociate the loss of temporal power from its historical, cultural, religious and sentimental implications. There were even some who seriously thought that Pius IX would be the last Pope.

*   *   *

From September 1870 to his death in February, 1878, Pius IX remained inflexible. Believing that it was impossible for the Pope to be free in his ministry as universal pastor without being sovereign in Rome, the seat of Catholicism, and that it was his duty to preserve the traditional possession of

---

* So called because Leo IV had walled it round. It included the castle of Sant'Angelo.

† Defenders of the Holy Faith (*la santa fede*), the name given in Naples to the armed bands and followers of Cardinal Ruffo against the republicans and French of the revolution.

the Holy See, of which he was merely the trustee and faithful steward, he never ceased to protest. Moreover he believed that the seizure of Rome was a machination by Freemasonry and other secret societies to overthrow the Papacy, that the new kingdom of Italy was its result, many Catholics having been led astray by national and political ideals. The Pope was inclined to think that the new kingdom lacked strength, that it was like those produced by the French revolution and the armies of Napoleon, that a new Congress of Vienna would end by restoring the old sovereigns. There were some who looked for a French or Austrian intervention to settle accounts with the usurper. In this state of mind negotiations for a conciliation between Pius IX and Victor Emmanuel were out of the question.

The Italian parliament transferred to Rome, unilaterally decided the position of the Papacy in the new kingdom by the Law of Guarantees which remained in force from 1871 to 1929, a full fifty-eight years. The Pope refused to recognize the law, sent back the first indemnity payment the Vatican received from the Italian treasury and, having no means of meeting expenses, appealed to the charity of Catholics throughout the world, who at once began to collect Peter's pence. Pope Pius IX declared himself a voluntary prisoner and refused to set foot outside the Vatican or appear on the balcony of St. Peter's to bless the people.

Thereafter a shrewd and subtle policy was pursued on both sides of the Tiber.* Although officially all relations were severed, secret channels came into being between the ministry of justice of the Italian government and the papal secretariat of state. Ecclesiastical problems could not be left without solution, the interests of local churches, of episcopal sees without bishops or with bishops in prison or in exile, had to be dealt with. With the abolition of mortmain and particular ecclesiastic ownerships, a body was created for the adminis-

---

* *Church and State in Fascist Italy,* by D. A. Binchy, Oxford University Press, 1941, is useful also for the period preceding Fascism, although treated in broad outline (chapters 1 and 2).

tration of former Church property to be used for the benefit of parishes. Other similar measures were taken.

The main concern of the two parties, Church and State, was to do nothing that would prejudice, politically or legally, the positions they had adopted. As a consequence of the plebiscite the state considered itself fully entitled to consider Rome and the former papal states as intangible national territory, and in exercising over them all rights of sovereignty. The Holy See, anxious to safeguard its rights, would not prejudice them by any administrative action that might be interpreted as an indirect or *de facto* recognition of this claim. The thesis was that accomplished facts could not create a right, in opposition to the inalienable right of the Holy See. Between these two extreme points of view adopted officially by the two sides, there was room for possible understandings, for tacit agreements, for subtle combinations by means of able intermediaries who worked with all their might to reach practical solutions while clericals and anticlericals, in books, papers and pamphlets continued to thunder against the Vatican or against Freemasonry.*

Open conflict and friendly understanding alternated according to the opportunities afforded by domestic or foreign events. Actually the Italian government whether of the Right or of the Left pursued not only a policy of separation between Church and State (retaining however rights of jurisdiction derived from the concordats between the former states of Italy and the Holy See), but in certain spheres such as education a policy of complete secularization.

The conclave for the election of a Pope on the death of Pius IX was the most important test of the Italian government's willingness to leave the Church free in the exercise of her supreme ministry. The "Historical Left," anticlerical

---

*In those days people in Italy believed that Freemasonry wielded immense occult power. As a matter of fact, it was more in the nature of an appendage of various ministries, especially those of justice, education and the navy, for the advancement of masons, than a political instrument. But it served on occasion to encourage extreme positions in the antireligious policy of the state and to promote unrest in the country.

in spirit, was then in power. What happened surprised many. The election of Leo XIII took place in one of the freest and most serene conclaves the Church had ever known. Leo had a long and glorious pontificate. After the stormy days of Pius IX and the quasi-isolation in which he had left the Holy See, Leo XIII received homage from all peoples and all governments. He adjusted the conflict created by Bismarck's *Kulturkampf* (it was said that the Iron Chancellor went to Canossa, but not with a rope round his neck like Henry IV); he arbitrated the dispute between Spain and Germany over the Caroline Islands (which today have so much importance); he interested himself—the first Pope to do so—in justice for labor and was known as the Pope of Christian democracy; he fostered, developed and lent authority to the Thomist movement in philosophy and by his encyclicals inaugurated a new era in papal action that met the modern world with persuasion and activity, rather than with condemnation.

Toward Italy the policy of Leo XIII was not so broad as had at first been hoped. A publication by Abbot Tosti, the Pope's friend, led to the belief that conciliation was near, but Tosti was repudiated and later the *Letter of Conciliation* by Bishop Bonomelli of Cremona was placed on the Index (where it was in company with Abbé Rosmini's *Five Wounds of the Church* [1849]). Also as we have seen Leo XIII confirmed the *non-expedit*. This prohibition by keeping militant Catholics away from the polls and all public life (some Catholics joined local parties and voted in municipal elections) impede a true understanding between the Holy See and the Italian people. The governments were by definition anticlerical, even when their members were indifferent or came of devout family respectful of the Church. It often happened that the most inveterate "liberals" sent their children to convents and Catholic schools, and that their families were regular churchgoers and patronized religious institutions.

The results hoped for by the clericals, especially by those who even before the seizure of Rome had launched in Piedmont the slogan "neither electors nor elected," did not mate-

rialize except among a few small groups of reactionaries.*
They sought to boycott parliamentary institutions and to
discredit the movement for "liberty and union" in the name
of the Church. Constitutional institutions triumphed throughout Italy.

Leo XIII insisted on the policy of Catholic abstention, perhaps as a possible means of solving the Roman question, or
as a permanent protest in vindication of the rights of the
Holy See. In either case the political effect fell short of his
expectation, while the moral effect grew fainter and fainter
as time wore on and the kingdom of Italy consolidated itself
at home and abroad. The *de jure* recognition of Italy by the
governments of Madrid, Paris, Vienna, Berlin and London
put an end to all thought that foreign powers might intervene to restore Rome to the Pope. After the formation of the
Triple Alliance, when the armament race between the Great
Powers began, the Roman question had already passed from
the phase of conflict of forces and opinions toward inevitable
composition.

The elevation to the Papacy of Giuseppe Sarto, patriarch
of Venice, brought the traditional policy of Pius IX and Leo
XIII to an end. Pius X wanted to be the Pope of conciliation. If he did not succeed it was because he lacked the opportunity and perhaps the ability to break with the tradition
of the Curia or because he was absorbed by the struggle
against modernism. Above all he found no Italian statesman
who understood him or was prepared to face the hostility of
the anticlericals.

*   *   *

The new Pope Benedict XV and Cardinal Gasparri, his
secretary of state, both it is true of the school of Leo XIII
and Cardinal Rampolla,† were men with a long training
in ecclesiastical and diplomatic affairs, whose experience
of modern times enabled them to deal with the most acute

---

* Binchy writes "The Piedmontese clericals were singularly unfortunate in the
choice of their leaders." *Op. cit.*, p. 21.

† Cardinal Rampolla del Tindaro, a Sicilian, was one of the most outstanding
diplomats of the Holy See.

and difficult situations. It was barely a month after Italy's entry into the last war, and after Sonnino had insisted on the insertion of the ill-considered Article V of the treaty of London,* that Cardinal Gasparri in an interview given to the *Corriere d'Italia* in Rome on June 27, 1915, said that "As befits its neutrality the Holy See has no intention whatever of embarrassing the Italian government; it puts its trust in God and awaits a proper and equitable adjustment of the Roman question, not by foreign arms but by the triumph of those sentiments of justice which it hopes are steadily gaining ground among the Italian people." Gasparri's statement came at a most opportune moment, when efforts were being made in Germany to raise the Roman question, not in the interests of Catholicism but to widen the breach between Italy and the Holy See.

The step taken by Benedict XV on August 1, 1917, to bring about a negotiated peace, although ill-received by the belligerent governments, was appreciated when dispassionately judged for its timeliness and the wisdom of its proposals. Wilson's fourteen points the following January were along the same lines. The whole world was interested in real peace that would quench war hatreds, and none more than Italy, who should have shown her traditional balance. The Pope's help would have been useful indeed had it not been for the idea that he must be excluded from the Peace Conference, put forward by Sonnino, who lived in the past and did not realize the new state of mind of the Roman Curia and of the broad-minded men who were directing it.

In spite of everything at the end of the war it was felt that even the Roman question was ripe for solution. No one any longer thought about Rome or a cession of territory to the Vatican. The idea then current was to internationalize the precincts of the Vatican with other areas to render it materially independent. In June, 1919, during the Peace Con-

---

* By this article the other "high contracting parties undertook to support Italy in preventing representatives of the Holy See from taking any steps whatever in regard to the conclusion of the peace or the settlement of questions connected with the present war."

ference in Paris the papal nuncio, Bonaventura Cerretti, had a long talk with the Italian Prime Minister Orlando on possible bases for a solution of the Roman question.* The discussions were continued in Rome between Cardinal Gasparri and Nitti, who had succeeded Orlando as Prime Minister. Under Giolitti they were suspended and were about to be resumed under Bonomi when in January, 1922, Benedict XV died unexpectedly. As Pope he had spontaneously taken steps for an understanding with Italy. In November, 1919, he had abolished the *non-expedit* so that it was possible for Catholics to take part freely in the general elections of that month.† Soon after in 1920 he abolished the etiquette of the Curia under which no head of a Catholic state who visited the king of Italy in Rome could be received by the Pope. Thus for the first time a king of Spain, Alfonso XIII, was received by the head of the Church and by the head of the state.‡ A clear symptom that before the advent of fascism conciliation was on the way. Indeed the new Pope, Pius XI (Achille Ratti), had hardly been elected when he appeared on the balcony of St. Peter's to bless the wildly excited and cheering crowd that filled the plaza—something that had not happened since September 20, 1870. It was a sign of the new Pope's policy. But Pius XI reached the pontificate at the most agitated period of Italian political life, when the fascists

* See on pp. 235–36 of Binchy's book the curious episode of the American prelate Mgr. Kelley (now Bishop) and Colonel House that preceded the talk between Cerretti and Orlando.

† In January, 1919, the Italian popular party was founded and at once began to organize in preparation for the electoral campaign. The author had received the promise of Cardinal Gasparri, secretary of state, that the *non-expedit* would be withdrawn. Without this Catholics who observed the papal directives could neither have voted or been candidates. The withdrawal, delayed to the last moment, came in time. But it had already become effective morally from the day that Catholics could be assured that such was the will of Benedict XV. The Christian-democrats of the Italian popular party won 99 seats out of 508 in the elections of November, 1919.

‡ We may recall in this connection the incident that arose from the visit of M. Loubet, the president of the French Republic, who visited Rome in 1903. Pius X sent a diplomatic note of protest which was published through an indiscretion and led to friction between the Vatican and France. Readers should bear in mind that every court has its rules, the Court of St. James's in London as well as the Vatican.

were preparing their coup and the government was in the weak uncertain hands of Luigi Facta. October came with the march on Rome, Mussolini as prime minister, and the Italian political atmosphere entirely changed. Pius XI had to wait.

Many in Italy and elsewhere believed that the formation of the popular party had been prompted by the Vatican to bring influence on Italian public opinion in favor of a settlement of the Roman question, and that the author (as rumored at the time and repeated abroad by men with no knowledge of the facts) was the long arm of the Holy See. But at the first congress of the popular party held at Bologna in June, 1919, it was made clear that this impression was false. Three members of the congress (it was learned later that they were inspired by a member of a religious society) presented a resolution to the effect that the popular party should pledge itself to raise the Roman question and propose a solution. The author, in the name of the party, refused to accept this resolution, declaring that the Roman question concerned the whole nation and not only one party, that the solution would have to be desired by and negotiated with the Holy See and not at meetings of the party, which refused to place the resolution on its agenda. Thus the party avoided a misunderstanding that might have complicated its action and embarrassed the policy of the Vatican.

Two years later however we find Mussolini, then newly elected deputy, in a most tendentious speech extolling the importance of the Papacy in the world from the Italian point of view and proclaiming it to be the duty of the government to settle the dispute in order to make use of this moral force for the benefit of Italy. Thus, whereas it was believed that Catholics, freed by the withdrawal of the *non-expedit* would have pursued a Guelf policy, the contrary occurred. The fascists, whose program up to then had been anticlerical and revolutionary, now took up the Roman question with the very obvious intent of attracting to their ranks those Catholics who, dissatisfied with the popular party as too democratic and insufficiently concerned over the Pope's position, began to place their hopes in that bold and unscrupulous leader. In fact no one imagined that Mussolini championed the Pope's rights out of devotion to St. Peter; he thought only of winning friends and adherents. And he succeeded.

One of the first to fall into the net of Mussolini's "Vaticanism" or "Catholicism" was Deputy Cavazzoni (later senator) of the popular party, who for a time was secretary of its parliamentary group. He was informed of Mussolini's desire for conciliation and became a minister in the first fascist cabinet, but he was dropped when the congress of the party meeting at Turin in April, 1923, declared its will to "continue to fight for freedom and against the pantheistic state and the deified nation." *

The first four years from 1922 to 1926 were spent by the fascist government and party in making war upon the anti-fascists and in consolidating their power. It was part of Mussolini's plan on the one hand to win over the clergy by doing them favors; on the other to discredit and destroy the popular party, which to his mind represented the main obstacle to obtaining the support of the Church. Thus in 1925 he made Alfredo Rocco minister of justice, set up a commission of experts, laymen and priests to revise laws governing ecclesiastical matters and appointed as chairman Mattei-Gentili, a former member of the popular party who had been won over to fascism. This commission worked in silence and presented its report in 1926, a report that was praised on all sides for its broad vision and objectivity. The Pope, who had already said that this commission was unilateral, rejected its conclusions on the grounds that the rights of the Holy See should first be restored and then the reform of other laws could be undertaken by agreement between the two authorities. At first the Pope's declaration came as a cold shower to damp the en-

---

* See *Italy and Fascism,* by Luigi Sturzo, Harcourt, Brace, New York, 1927, p. 130. The Turin congress of the popular party was attacked by the fascists and by the Catholics of the Right, known then as "clerico-fascists," who urged the Vatican secretariat of state to prevent it. But Cardinal Gasparri replied that it was not his business to interfere in the activities of a party that was not dependent upon the Vatican. Nonetheless he added that it was his impression that it would be better to avoid a breach. This breach however was necessary for a democratic party.

thusiasm of Catholics and clerico-fascists. Later it was realized that something was in the wind.*

It was then that Mussolini decided to outlaw the popular
party and this was done by a decree of November 6, 1926.
It may have been merely a coincidence but since Mussolini
was always † what the Italians call *tempista,* that is had a gift
for doing things at the right moment, it seemed that any
resentment of Catholics over such an arbitrary act would pass
unnoticed. The popular party however did not perish alone,
the same fate overtook the socialists and all other political
parties. Mussolini proclaimed the totalitarian state "everything and everyone for the state." Pius XI reacted in spite of
the negotiations that were about to begin and in his Christmas allocution spoke against considering man as existing for
the state and reaffirming the Catholic doctrine that the state
exists for man.‡

Pius XI now saw clearly that the time had come to end
the dispute, and that Mussolini was the man able to overcome
all obstacles.§ On the other hand Mussolini, who did not
lack intelligence save when he was ruled by fear, understood
the full advantage that he and fascism could derive from the
solution of the Roman question. So it was that at a single
stroke he won the sympathies of nearly all foreign Catholics.

The treaty, the financial protocol and the concordat were
signed in the Lateran Palace on February 11, 1929, and were
ratified on June 7 of the same year. By the first the Pope renounced the traditional rights of the Holy See over Rome
and the provinces that had formed the papal states, recognized the Italian nation as a united state and the House of
Savoy as the legitimate reigning dynasty, and accepted the
solution of the Vatican city-state, in which he would be free,

---

* See *Italy and Fascism,* p. 132.

† Always, except of course the last time when he resigned.

‡ See *Politics and Morality,* by Luigi Sturzo, Burns, Oats and Washburn, London, 1938, p. 34. Theoretical affirmations meant little to Mussolini.

§ It is in this sense, I think, that Pius XI called him "the man sent to us by
Providence" (often misquoted as "the man of Providence"), an expression that has
been sharply criticized. Subsequently he said that he "was ready to treat with the
Devil for the good of souls."

independent and sovereign with diplomatic representation as in the past and in addition diplomatic relations with Italy. The basilicas and Vatican palaces in Italian territory were declared extraterritorial and appurtenances of the Vatican city-state. The treaty discarded any idea of internationalization and by Article 24 the Holy See declared its wish to "remain outside all temporal competitions between other states and outside international congresses held for such objects, save when the contending parties unite in appealing to its mission of peace." * The financial protocol was attached to the treaty and, in view of the heavy expenses incurred from 1870 onward and those entailed by the creation of the new Vatican city-state, it does not appear that the sum offered by the Italian government was excessive, as has been alleged. What was criticized and open to criticism was the acceptance by Pius XI of a revenue from the Italian state.

The concordat was and still is most open to discussion. It was necessary to regularize the ecclesiastical position in Italy before fascism, a hodge-podge of old concordats and customs and new unilateral laws passed by the Italian parliament but never accepted by the Holy See. The idea of Pius XI in asking for a concordat was to establish once and for all the limits of state interference in ecclesiastical affairs and to leave no issues pending and unsolved. The new provisions of the concordat, reflecting the Pope's own views, concerned religious teaching in the schools, Catholic action and religious marriages. Pius XI wished to insure permanent co-operation of the Italian state with the Church. Some interpreting the Pope's intentions rather broadly began to speak of Italy as a *Catholic state.* To certain fascists such confusion, especially in Catholic opinion abroad, was not displeasing. Others objected, saying that the state was purely and *essentially fascist.*

This was the substance of Mussolini's speech in the chamber of deputies on May 13, 1929, defending the Lateran treaty and its annexes. He flatly declared that "within the state the Church is not sovereign nor even free . . ."; indeed

* Binchy, *op. cit.*, p. 295.

he maintained that had the Christian Church remained in the East and not come to Rome it would probably have perished like many other "obscure eastern sects" and that it "became Catholic in Rome." Pius XI replied immediately, when he received students of Mondragone College, and in opposition to fascist theories concerning the supremacy of the state asserted "the state does not exist to absorb, swallow up or annihilate the individual and the family—that would be contrary to reason and nature alike." Finally before ratification of the treaty the Pope wrote and made public a letter addressed to Cardinal Gasparri in which he confuted Mussolini's assertions, reaffirmed the traditional doctrine of the Church and clearly laid it down that the Church cannot tolerate encroachment by the state.

Two years later the position of the Holy See toward fascism was made clearer (although with concessions dictated by expediency) when, in violation of the concordat, Mussolini began a campaign of persecution against Catholic action, especially among the young. Pius XI then published his encyclical, *Non Abbiamo Bisogno,* of June 29, 1931, which put a full stop to the dangerous dream of a *Fascist and Italian Catholic State.**

In conclusion, the Lateran treaty with its annexes was an historical peace settlement between Italy and the Vatican, but in substance it was neither a political nor a religious settlement. By it the Italian Risorgimento was accepted and sanctioned as a movement for national and territorial unity in a single kingdom, leaving no area subject to another sovereign whether native or foreign, and with Rome as the capital of the kingdom notwithstanding the coexistence there of another sovereign authority, the Pope, with his special territory within the city. This did not mean that the Holy See

---

* Almost at the same time came the invention of the corporative state, which aroused enthusiasm among certain Catholics interested in social reform as if it were the fulfillment of the Catholic ideal. The measured criticism that Pius XI inserted in his encyclical, *Quadragesimo Anno,* of May 15, 1931, did not avail to make them understand the confusion into which they had fallen. Even today there are such ingenuous persons. See *Politics and Morality,* Chapter IX, "The Social Question," pp. 166–74.

intended to sanction the theoretical implications and legislative acts of the Risorgimento that were hostile to the Church. By the Lateran treaty the Church obtained through the fascist government a legalization both of the Pope's position in Rome and of the rights of the Church in the Italian kingdom. This did not imply that the Vatican approved the fascist theories and practice of government, or that it had made an alliance with fascism as was asserted by imprudent Catholics and ill-meaning anticlericals.

One may question the expediency of dealing with fascism in a question of such importance and delicacy, but after the event such a discussion is quite useless. At best one would only say that Pius XI was prudent or imprudent. The two assertions cancel each other. The truth is that the historical importance of the Lateran treaty transcends the will of its authors and their particular aims.

*   *   *

The war had again raised the question. Was the Lateran treaty really a satisfactory solution assuring the freedom and independence of the sovereign Pontiff? The Pope's position in regard to Italy was far more difficult in this war than in the last when the Law of Guarantees was in force. In fact the legal safeguarding of the Pope's independence by means of what is only a symbolical state counts for very little with a totalitarian government when such territory is defended only by some forty swiss guards armed with halberts and wearing uniforms designed by Michelangelo. If it had been to Mussolini's advantage to launch a religious persecution in Italy similar to that of his Teutonic ally, he would have had no difficulty. There was an inkling of it in the spring of 1931. But in a war as unpopular as that of 1940 on the side of Hitler, Mussolini needed the help of the clergy to keep up military and civilian morale. Religious persecution would have divided the people for and against the war, ranging on the side of the Church all who were against the war; that is, the majority of the country.

Mussolini had to tolerate all the speeches of Pius XII on peace, on a new world order, in defense of Poland and other occupied countries; the antinazi broadcasts of the Vatican radio, its denunciations of persecutions and deportations; the papal telegrams to the queen of Holland, the king of the Belgians, the grand duchess of Luxemburg; the visits to the Vatican of American envoys, Myron Taylor and Archbishop Spellman; and other things highly displeasing to fascism, including the pressure brought to bear on Pétain to prevent the persecution of the French Jews and even the reception of Jews in the Vatican or as members of the Pontifical Academy; above all the refusal of the Vatican to call for a crusade against Russia to support the arms of Hitler, the new antibolshevist Godfrey de Bouillon.

On several occasions Pius XII had emphasized his neutrality in the war. Such neutrality was solely political, and in no wise moral. The Pope could not be neutral on the moral issues of the war, nor fail to make a just distinction between the victims of aggression and the aggressor. More than once Pius XII made this plain in his allocutions, however cautious and confined to principles they were, and by his practical relations with the countries at war. On the other hand he was most careful to give the Axis countries no excuse for a conflict with the Holy See. In general the problem of how to remain in spiritual touch with the populations and the actual combatants was left to the discretion of the bishops in each country. Unfortunately there were, as there always will be, some nationalist excesses on the part of ecclesiastics who are deserving of censure, but no good can be done by exaggerated criticism of those who, in contact with the populations, had to use language above suspicion of hostility or incomprehension as regards the national situation at a given moment.

This does not mean that the Pope and the Italian bishops and clergy were fascists and should be treated as fascists when the hour of justice strikes for those who betrayed Italy. If some have incurred serious moral and political responsibility, let the evidence be quite clear. On the whole the clergy, apart from misguided rhetoric and patriotic appeals to nationalist sentiments, has at heart been antifascist and could not have been otherwise because of the eternal incompatibility between the Christian religion and the fascist ideal, between Catholic morality and the immorality of the fascist conception of life. The mansuetude of the Church in Italy has already been dearly paid for. God has seen to it that it has been paid for so dearly that there is no need for anticlerical Italians to foment a religious conflict in vindication of that purity of Catholicism which is altogether foreign to their own ideals.

In fact the controversy over the future relations of Church and State in Italy, which had been going on during the war among Italians by birth or origin who live or have taken refuge in Allied countries, has already shed much light upon the issue. Save for a few exceptions representing extreme and obsolete anticlericalism, there is general agreement that the position of the Pope as head of the Catholic Church must be respected, as must be his right to freedom and independence, his right to maintain the institutions of the Roman Curia, his right to appoint nuncios and receive foreign ambassadors. From this point of view the Lateran treaty is fundamental. There is much talk of internationalizing the Vatican city-state by agreement, so that the treaty shall no longer bear the ill-omened signature of Mussolini. Others have different views. There is time for discussion.

Most attacks are directed against the concordat. The prevailing idea is that of separation and liberty. There is a return to the slogan of Montalembert and Cavour: "A free Church in a free State." To those who adopt this attitude the author has objected: *

1. That the Italian concordat of 1929 settled or provided a basis for the legal and financial settlement of eccle-

* See Luigi Sturzo, "Italian Problems in Peace and War," *Review of Politics* (Notre Dame), January, 1943, and "Italy after Mussolini," *Foreign Affairs*, New York, April, 1943.

siastical matters that had been left in suspense ever since
the Risorgimento.

2. That it is one thing to enter into a concordat where
there is none (as in the United States, England, France
and Belgium), and another to denounce a concordat that
already exists.

3. That the financial obligations assumed by the Italian
state in various ecclesiastical laws from 1860 onward,
derived from the fact that the state liquidated a large
part of the property owned by local churches in Italy
in their own right.

4. That certain new provisions introduced in the concordat of 1929 because of fascism or for other reasons
can be revised.

5. That it should be possible for the future Italian government and the Holy See to reach agreement without pro-
voking a religious conflict which would be doubly in-
jurious after such a war.

This view is shared by all who, although of anticlerical
or rather lay tradition and as such opposed to the concordat,
recognize that a religious conflict in Italy must be avoided
at all costs. Naturally such men think it is the duty of the
Vatican to avert it by accepting in large measure their point
of view; on the other side it is assumed that those opposed
to a concordat will show greater understanding of the problems of the Church in Italy and not oblige the Church to
resist.

To the author it seems that these discussions among Italians abroad have not been useless and have placed the problem of Church and State on less thorny ground than might
have been expected, in view of the personalities of the chief
protagonists. One of the things upon which all seem to agree
is that the problem of the concordat will not have to be faced
at once; that the Italian people should express their own will
as to revision; that the government should approach the Vatican for a friendly solution of controversial issues; and that all

this can be put off till the new Italian regime is regularly established.

I have seen a curious suggestion* that the concordat should be maintained for a certain time and applied to bring about, in accordance with its provisions, a "purge" of those bishops and parish priests who have been fascists. Then when this delicate operation had been completed, the concordat could be abolished possibly in agreement with the Vatican and all the economic interests of the Church liquidated. The Church would then enjoy complete freedom, as do all religious and cultural institutions in the United States. By the logic of events, that is even stronger than the logic of ideas, such an ecclesiastical "purge" would be an intolerable interference in the life of the Church and would automatically arouse opposition and reaction. Once this were started no one could say where it would end. If really there are ecclesiastics who are notoriously fascist, either they themselves or their superiors will see to their removal. Canon tradition provides that a man *quem mala plebs odit* cannot be a pastor of souls, so how could those who have been infected with so grave a disease as fascism? Let us allow recovery to come through more natural and less odious forms, let us reject a policy such as that suggested, a policy that must be denounced as inimical to the Church. In the period that has elapsed since the fall of fascism as during a destructive war and an occupation, tyrannical on the part of the Germans and factious on the part of the fascists, the Italian clergy has shown abnegation, generosity and heroism worthy of respect, admiration and gratitude. There may have been some deplorable mistakes but on the whole the record is remarkably good.

Much of the hostility that is shown by antifascists to the Vatican comes from the old Ghibelline idea that the Papacy in Italy is a permanent political factor, creating rivalry in the heart of the country between national interests and Catholic interests. If this could be said with some show of reason dur-

---

* *What to Do with Italy,* Salvemini and La Piana, New York, 1943, p. 263.

ing the Risorgimento because of the question of the papal states, today such an assertion is groundless.

Today the fears of republicans spring from the supposition that the Pope will wish to side with the monarchy or that the clergy will be promonarchic. Others are afraid that the Vatican, fearful lest left-wing antifascists should adopt an anticlerical policy, or the socialist and communists gain the upper hand, will seek to support moderate ex-fascists, old-line nationalists and clerico-fascists for the future regime. But since we are on hypothetical and controversial ground we may reply that if the left-wing Italian democrats wish to foment an anti-Papacy and anti-Catholic movement, there will be many Catholics in Italy who, although democrats and indeed because they are democrats, will raise the banner of religious liberty and demand that Catholics be not treated as a class or race or sect to be discriminated against or persecuted, that the Pope and bishops be respected in their offices as well as in their persons as citizens.

It may be that there are bishops and priests who will lean toward monarchy as a guarantee of order and an institution friendly to the Church; there are deluded and reactionary men (if thus they are judged) among the clergy, just as among the laity. What then? Anybody may think as he likes about the monarchy as about any other political form of government. That the Vatican should wish to intervene in Italian political issues seems a gratuitous assertion. It is the right and duty of the Vatican to defend the interests of the Church, of religion and morality. It will be of more importance to the Pope to safeguard religious teaching, the Christian training of the young, the freedom of the school, the morality of families, than to support the monarchy against the will of the people or to support a republic if this is not desired by the majority in the country.

We have the example of France still before us. The mistake of the French clergy after 1871 was that of linking the fate of France to the monarchy and opposing the republic. But there is also—an historic act of ever actual importance—

the letter Leo XIII addressed to the French bishops in February, 1892, in which the great Pope exhorted them to rally to the republic and to work for good laws rather than in the interests of party politics or of a claimant to the throne.

It is the hope of the author that the Christian-democrats of Italy, who passed through the fascist adventure without being infected by the disease that contaminated the Italian soul and even affected certain circles in the clergy of Italy, may again be vouchsafed the strength and determination of the old Italian popular party to face an extremely delicate situation, to temper the two extremes with firmness, prudence and courage. But all Italians must share the responsibility of deciding the political fate of their country without violating the religious conscience of the nation.

8

Economic and Social Problems

FROM THE MOMENT when Allied armies began to occupy countries freed from the enemy, the day-to-day life of the people has presented a problem of extraordinary scope and complexity.

A psychological factor—a sense of liberation from restrictions, sacrifices, hunger, misery, bombs and death—rekindled ordinary human needs as though they had never been felt before. The intensity of these needs beclouded men's minds and prostrated their bodies. Expectation enhanced sensibility, I would even say produced nervous irritation. Incomprehension on the part of the Allied military and civil authorities seemed excessive. Divergent ways of approach made spiritual communication between the populations and their deliverers difficult. The disparity between needs and the means of satisfying them aroused even unjustified complaints.

The books, pamphlets and reports on future reconstruction are many; offices, research centers, and special agencies to meet immediate needs are already functioning; efforts are being made to provide food, clothing, medicine and other elementary necessities of life. What was done in Africa for the civilian population, both European and Arab, what was done in Sicily, southern Italy and Rome, has continued to be done elsewhere. The difficulties encountered will serve as experience for the future. In all affairs practical experience is worth a thousand times more than theoretical knowledge, and estimates of what has to be done are never more than partial and incomplete.

Apart, however, from what may be called "first aid" and

will depend more on organizing capacity and on available resources than on any preconceived program—economic and
social problems (including those of 'finance) is to be considered on broad lines, which must guide the policies of the
United Nations. Opinions are divided and the subject of
lively discussion. What form is the economy of the future to
take? Will it be liberal? Or controlled capitalism? Or planned
socialism?

For an adequate answer, the questions must be made precise. They are not purely theoretical, bearing on ideal pref-
erences, but mainly practical, concerned with possibilities and
usefulness in a given time and space. With this in mind, therefore, let us try to define the three systems.

Liberal economy is no longer today the pure laissez-faire of
the Manchester school, but the affirmation of freedom of enterprise. The word liberal recalls the economic system prevailing in the last century, when trade unions were either forbidden or merely tolerated (and in actual practice, attacked),
and thus the state only timidly and sporadically interfered in
the economic and social life of the country. But during the
past fifty years social legislation has been passed by nearly
every state; not only does the state no longer fear to intervene
in private economy, but because of the war this intervention
has perhaps been extended beyond what was necessary. Labor
unions have either been legally recognized or have been the
subject of special laws conveying implicit recognition. This
being the case in many countries considered to be democratic
(even if they are not actually so), it is better to speak not of
"liberal economy," but of an economy of predominant free
enterprise.

Controlled capitalist economy: This is that of the industrialized countries. The control is either in the hands of the capitalists themselves, within certain broad limits, as in Britain
and North America, or was in the hands of the state, that is,
of a party, as in the totalitarian countries, nazi Germany and
fascist Italy. The difference between the two cases is that in
the former free enterprise persists and the system partakes of

the so-called liberal type. In the latter, all initiative is either in the hands of the state or controlled by the state, and is always subordinated to the aims of the political class and its totalitarian system. During the two world wars, even in democratic countries, state intervention came to predominate, so that apart from the discreet use of political liberties, which allow the public a margin of control and criticism, their economies tend to resemble the totalitarian capitalist economy.

Socialist planned economy: This may be understood both as a progressive movement toward socialization of the means of production, and as the achievement of a socialist economy for various periods according to pre-established plans. Whether this comes about through direct action by the state, or the distinct activity of special agencies or economic or social groups, it implies that the supreme direction shall always remain in the hands of the political power. Soviet Russia has a mixed economy. Capital is in the hands of the state and socialization is actually a monopoly, save the exceptions where domestic agriculture is concerned.

It is a fact that during the present war the governments of the United Nations have, whether they wished it or not, continued in intensifying economic centralization and the trend toward economic planning as a means of obtaining a maximum output, exacting an evergrowing contribution from the country and if necessary even compulsory labor. Thus the freedom both of employer and worker has suffered economically, and competition has been in great part eliminated, all for one end: victory. The results of four or five years of this regime will be far-reaching, both psychologically in the face of economic and political possibilities after the war and the reactions of the various social classes, and economically in the adjustment of the positions of groups and nations.

No one any longer doubts but that war-time economy will be carried on into the postwar period, for how long cannot be foreseen, in view of the urgent necessities that will be created by crises of unemployment, impoverishment, transportation, insufficiency of goods and delays in the return from war industry to peace industry. The full intervention of the state, with the subordinate and disciplined co-operation of capital and labor, will thus be temporarily necessary till a certain normality has been attained. Such a postwar economy will not be liberal (it is obvious), nor capitalist (though capital will have an important role) nor socialist (though the trend toward socialization will be very marked). This notwithstanding, it will be precisely in this period that the conflicting ideologies, political and economic, will try to attain their maximum realization. Everyone will be dissatisfied with the work of the bureaucracies of Washington, London and Moscow, or even Ottawa or Paris or Prague or Rome or Rio de Janeiro or any other political center of the various continents; all will wish to apply their own, more or less vague or impracticable systems. Demagogic movements will find a wide scope.

On the other hand, there will be the absolute necessity for technical planning with approximative stages for the redistribution of labor as required by local demands and the formation of new institutions or centers able to direct efforts, so as to meet the needs of the populations. Which will be the trend that, in this common effort, will prevail over the conflicts of interests and needs? *Liberty? Capitalism? Socialization?*

We must start from firm ground. Where there is no fundamental economic liberty, political liberty is lost as well. On the other hand, every liberty of whatever nature has a limit beyond which it becomes license; this limit is provided by the respect of individual personality in the framework of social life. Thus every liberty is relative, not absolute.

The abolition of private property strikes a deathblow at individual liberty, at the same time as the monopoly of property (whether *de jure* or *de facto)* strikes a deathblow at the liberty of others. Between abolition and monopoly a middle way must be found, that of generalized property. The type of property depends on the prevailing type of economy; in Norway for many it is ships rather than land (though land, too); in Italy it is land rather than ships (though ships, too). Certain crops demand a common effort, either in a co-operative or a collective form. Certain industries are suited to home production, others to mass production. If in a country there are zones of very fertile land best cultivated as large units, it would be a mistake to cut them up into small fields; they should be kept as economic units either in the form of partnerships between capital and labor, or in that of co-operatives among those who directly work them.

In industry, in a general way, it is preferable for capital to be in the hands of private persons, so long as they are responsible for it and make their workers partners through special profit-sharing schemes, according to their grade and output. If, however, a given industry or trade is better run by the state or by a public body, like postal-services or railways, or even by the League of Nations, as perhaps tomorrow may be the case with airways, there must be no *a priori* refusal, but a study of possibilities.

All systems are good if they answer to the needs of the populations, are guided by the criterion of the minimum means for the maximum result, and in practice eliminate any political or economic monopoly of a class or even of the state. An economy either purely socialist or purely capitalist will be an economy of dictatorship and a rivival of totalitarianism. For where, even in economy, there is no possibility of legal changes, that only free individual initiative can bring about, there will be either war or concentration camps or both.

*   *   *

These premises are necessary to an understanding of where we are going today with all the bureaucratic centralization of war-economy, and where we may be going tomorrow if by chance there should be rapid economic demobilization under pressure for free industry, or an increase of controls and restraints under pressure of a demagogic bureaucracy. The present political uneasiness in America is precisely the result of this latent conflict between capitalism and the New Deal supported by the fluctuating mass of labor.

The principal aim of future economy should be the abolition of artificial trade barriers that have turned national economies into closed preserves, thus providing the widest range for monopoly whether capitalist or state controlled. This is also necessary in a very special manner for Europe, to prepare the way for a Union of European States.*

The world has been undone by two false principles: that of *exploiting capitalism* and that of *nationalistic autarchy*. Even those who think only of the material causes of human events will easily discern the influence during the last twenty years that these two factors of world economy have had in creating a war-atmosphere and in exciting the lust of dictators for world-wide political dominion. The sociologist who interprets economic facts in terms of personal activity sees in today's tragedy the conflict between liberty and slavery.

Here the word "slavery" is used in a general sense as the social system which by use of political power not only restricts but reduces and finally abolishes the free activity of one section of men for the benefit of another. Under this aspect we may say that slavery has never disappeared from the civilized world, even though legally the old personal slavery has been abolished. The present phase of such politico-economic slavery is bound up with two dominating facts of social activity: capitalism, which does not mean capital, and totalitarianism, which does not mean the authoritarianism of government. The former in democratic states has had to respect certain margins of freedom, such as universal suffrage, public opinion, and working-class organizations. In actual fact, capitalism has itself played an important part in organizing the political parties, has obtained control of the press, stifling free voices by monopolistic methods, has hampered or indirectly sought to control the free development of labor unions when it has not stirred up public opinion against them. This has not been difficult in countries and at times when the labor movement has assumed a revolutionary color.

Happily, in a democratic regime there are still safety valves. In such a regime all may attain either political command or

* See Chapter 11, p. 216.

economic command, and those who today are at the top may change their position without recourse being had either to civil wars or military *pronunciamentos* as in Spain, or to armed gangsters as in fascist Italy and in nazi Germany. Another safety valve is the recurrence of political and economic crises, which lead to a revision of the hostile positions taken up by political parties or economic agencies.

At the basis of the capitalist growth of modern society lies the materialist concept of life. A great part of education, training and culture, which may seem free to the individual, really tends instead to rivet the chains of the new slavery, for it makes of hedonism the foundation of the social edifice and abolishes those moral restraints without which human brotherhood cannot be achieved. When we speak of capitalism in modern society, we do not refer to the function of capital in productive activity. We mean, on the contrary, the phenomenon of the capitalist system that exploits economy in general, labor in particular, and even political activity—subordinating everything to profit for profit's sake.

To make our meaning clear, we may mention international cartels that were of such great advantage to totalitarian Germany and her war for world dominion; the rubber monopoly guaranteed by the British government and consented to, in spite of protests, by the United States government; capitalist insistence on trading with Japan up to the very eve of Pearl Harbor, falsifying facts and misleading public opinion that remained unaware of the imminent peril. All this presupposes political conditions in which free voices are reduced to impotence and economic dominion overemphasizing differences between labor and capital, racial discrimination and the exploitation of native labor.

A phenomenon of international capitalism in all countries, free or unfree, is the white slave traffic, bound up with vast organizations of houses of prostitution around which prosper the most shameful "industries" that man has ever invented. Who protects them, who subsidizes them, who enables them to create a nameless slavery, drawing therefrom fabulous profits? This capitalism, which finds no moral limits in its path and which often oversteps political limits, itself becoming political, is that which for so many years has bridged the chasm between the democratic countries and the totalitarian ones, not only in time of peace by creating an atmosphere of appeasement, but in time of war favoring the enemy. This capitalism, just as it has no morals, has no fatherland.

In totalitarian countries the enslavement of society has gone forward more widely and more rapidly than in the rest of the world because here the social forces of reaction or evasion, which fortunately are able to develop in the democracies, have been absent or unable to persist. The formation within the totalitarian state of a class privileged by virtue of political domination gave rise to a still more restricted and influential economic class, which deprived all others of political influence and personal safeguards. Autarchy results; a means of domination and exploitation. The theory that the individual exists for the state and not the state for the individual, that everything must be for the state, within the state and with the state, creates a clear-cut division between oppressors and oppressed, who in other words may be called *masters* and *slaves*.

The subsequent passage of the play of forces from within the ambit of the state to the international sphere can only come about in two ways: the threat of war and war. Hence the necessity in time of peace of directing the whole of the controlled economy to war purposes (or in the case of the threatened, to defense purposes). Thus the division between oppressors and oppressed within the country is reflected in the international division into victors and vanquished (granted that the victors were to be, by definition, totalitarian).

The old experiences of the ancient world, when the slavery of labor, the slavery of caste (or religion) and the slavery of war kept nine-tenths of mankind subject to the remaining tenth—or less—of arrogant, wealthy, dominating exploiters, are reappearing under another guise in the modern world. And this after two thousand years of Christianity! The main fact is the enslavement of the world, whether for racial reasons: Aryans against non-Aryans, and all against the Jews; or for labor reasons: the exploitation of nonorganized labor, of labor regimented by the state, or whole nations deported for forced labor. Finally enslavement resulting from wars, not only by prepared and deliberate subjugation of vanquished countries in an inhuman form of exploitation, but also by mass deportations, the devastation of populous centers, and the impoverishment of the world in a mad and titanic effort to dominate.

That these have been and are the prevailing aims and methods of the Axis countries is clear from their theories and statements and from their very acts. But what is astounding is that such ideas have crept into democratic countries where they circulate with impunity, finding a soil in the materialist conception of life professed by positivist sociologists, "realistic" politicians, economists and planners of the capitalism of the future. When reading certain much publicized books and reports, and looking at the substance of many plans for the future, one is almost tempted to ask why the present war is being fought because—to enslave the world to the forces of wealth and power—their authors have already adopted the ideas and methods of the fascists and nazis, with less clamor perhaps but with a precision that might be called scientific.

The defense of capitalism put up by certain writers in the name of individual liberty rings false when they admit the other capitalism, the state capitalism of the totalitarian countries. In such countries capital has not been abolished—as those infatuated by what they do not know, believe to be the case in Russia—but capital has passed in most cases from the hands of private interests into those of the state, that is of a class holding all the powers of the state, combining in itself (no matter whether for individual profit or for that of a ruling class) wealth and power. This cumulation abolishes first of all the play of forces limiting wealth in regard to power and power in regard to wealth, and facilitates the collapse of the moral barriers which in every society should render power and wealth less harmful in the hands of their possessors.*

Workers dying by thousands on certain public works in Russia in inhuman conditions, forced labor of political prisoners, purges and exploitation (even if the information that reaches us has been distorted or mutilated because of a secrecy that is part of the method of tyranny), characterize the not yet completed phases of state capitalism.

We do not believe for a moment that the new world order will be a terrestrial paradise unmarred by pride or greed. These two terrible demons will claw at the hearts of men as long as the world lasts. But there must also be the antidotes; social liberties must be sufficiently effective to set moral and political limits to power and wealth. In no other way can the specter of slavery, which has reappeared in the civilized world as a return to pre-Christian times, and in some ways under worse conditions, be again banished, along with political totalitarianism and the capitalism of exploitation.

*   *   *

One of the most difficult problems that has already appeared as part of the postwar setting is the monetary problem; not only from the strictly technical standpoint, but in all its political implications. The experience of the past, after the last war, should be enough to prevent a repetition of very grave mistakes which certainly had an influence on subsequent events. There must be no monopoly of a rich country at the expense of the rest, no indirect starving-out of the less fortunate after such a war as this.

We know that gold has become the privilege of America, with a few other countries in second and third place. The Morgenthau plan in America and the Keynes plan in Britain for an international currency, toward which each state would contribute according to its resources, had the merit of starting a discussion that led to the Bretton Woods Conference. The

* See *Politics and Morality*, by Luigi Sturzo, Chapter I, London, 1938.

two draft conventions signed there by forty-four nations,* July 22, 1944, regarded one, the establishment of an International Monetary Fund, the other, the statute of an International Bank for Reconstruction and Development. The public reception of such proposals was not enthusiastic. The main objections were against the establishment of the International Monetary Fund, in spite of the very fact that without such a Fund the reconstruction of Europe will hardly be possible. All the more so as one of the initial problems to be examined ought to be that of the currency stabilization in the occupied countries where to the inflation of local governments and the German armies have been added the inflations of Allied armies and administration.

The case of Italy is typical and serious, because of the sudden emission of Allied occupation currency, and because of continued inflation due largely to Allied expenditures, added to the already enormous inflation caused by the fascist government. The lack of merchandise on the local market, the disproportion between the amount of money in circulation and its purchasing power, the inadequacy (in certain cases impossible) of private incomes, salaries and wages in view of increasing currency devaluation, have made general living conditions unbearable.

The passage of each national currency from a similar state of chaos to a system which, although purely temporary, will gradually tend toward a slow stabilization, depends on the measures to be adopted by the two capitalist nations principally interested in the future economic order, the American republic and the British commonwealth. The other nations, poor in gold and not industrialized, even neutrals who have not suffered any war destruction, will have to subordinate their entire economic system to the general system that will be controlled by the United States, in agreement with London —I do not say by Wall Street in agreement with the City. Russia, after the war, will be obliged to depart from her

---

* There is no clear reason (save a purely political one) why the Italian Government was not invited to send its representatives to this conference.

economic isolation and her closed monetary system. In such a case she will have an important word to say when her internal conditions are normalized, her industrial development has been resumed, and her foreign trade freed from communistic handicaps and state interference.

The principal aim in setting up a future international currency must be to revive trade, and to do away with the isolation of peoples and economic conditions of inferiority brought about by war or through lack of industrial development or by other causes. The world cannot be changed overnight into an economic unit, because of the great variety of conditions in each state or group of states within the different continents. But between a closed system, with high tariff barriers, with political obstacles in the way of trade and exchange, and a single economic world unit, there are many gradations, as for instance, the formation of intermediate units, a process by which these could be increasingly widened, and other successive measures covering periods of various length, so that world unity may be brought nearer.

When Wendell L. Willkie spoke of "One World," he rightly declared that "political internationalism without economic internationalism is a house built upon sand" (p. 82). Further on in the same book he presented American prospects as follows: "America must choose one of three courses after this war: narrow nationalism, which inevitably means the ultimate loss of our own liberty; international imperialism, which means the sacrifice of some other nation's liberty; or the creation of a world in which there shall be an equality of opportunity for every race and every nation" (p. 84). He concluded that "economic freedom is as important as political freedom." He might have added that political freedom cannot be maintained intact unless there is economic freedom. It is plain that this requires first of all the instrument of freedom: an international currency, available to the whole world; then a lowering of such tariffs as are in fact trade prohibitions, gradually to arrive at a free-trade policy.

A postwar settlement in its human aspect cannot be

achieved by the deportation of peoples, according to the nazi system; or by inhuman considerations of military strategy;* or by the selfish interests of dominant groups; but by spontaneous attraction to the centers where there is most work, a greater capacity of economic absorption, and individual adaptability. These ebbs and flows of human tides must be helped and regulated, not left to individual impulse or to the exploiting initiative of labor contractors, as in the case of transoceanic emigration during the last century. On the other hand, the adjustment of production will not be achieved by monopolies and industries artificially swollen for national ends, concealing war industries under the mask of peace industry, but by methods of freedom so regulated that the various nations will co-operate and mutually complement one another.

With the removal of the nationalistic preoccupation of closed, overcrowded countries, organized as autarchies to prepare for war, and the conquest of lands, colonies, raw materials, for the subjection of other peoples and the exploitation of their labor to its own advantage, economic adjustment will come about more spontaneously and with fewer crises. At the same time, by removing the possibility of industrial monopoly on an international scale, for the advantage of big business at the expense of whole peoples; by giving labor the broadest protection, it will be possible to achieve a more humane economy, one which will tend toward stability, as far as possible spontaneous, overthrowing all artificial barriers raised by class, race and national egotism.

We must realize that the guarantee of world economic stability will have to be paid for. The American who fears a lowering of his standard of living must also remember that world wars every twenty years, and economic crises every ten

---

* Political or racial deportation was not initiated by Hitler; the Turkey of Ataturk was the first to oblige hundreds of thousands of Greeks in Asia to leave the land they had inhabited for *thousands of years*, not to mention those who perished at Smyrna. Now we are assisting with dismay the deportation (transfer is the used word) of millions in eastern Europe from one country to another.

years, have been and would continue to be too high a price
for the prosperity of a population of, let us say, some hundred
million, when set against the distress of a thousand million of
their fellows. I do not say that in a free system of world
economy there will be no crises. There will be many crises.
To bring into effect the new system will take decades: Germany and Japan will be bankrupt after this war; Russia will
have to effect the passage from a politically closed to a relatively free economy; China needs a long time in which to
reorganize, and so too will the other countries, before they
will be able to take their position in the economic community of the world.

*   *   *

The reader will think that I have lost sight of Italy. But
to realize that the foregoing applies in full to Italy, it suffices to say that she has never been self-sufficient as an economic unit, that fascism's made dream of adopting autarchy
to prepare for war proved doubly fatal, to the economic
structure of the country and to the war itself.

Those who have referred to the lack of morale among the
Italian troops on every front where they have fought side by
side with Germans have not only failed to take into account
that the Italian people never had their heart in this war,
never had anything to fight for, were never moved to sacrifice
by any ideal—nothing could be truer—but have failed to
consider the soldier equipment as effective military morale.
The truth is that except for certain classes of aircraft
and certain picked troops, Italian equipment was inadequate, old-fashioned, inferior and not to be compared
to that of the Germans, British and Americans. It is possible
to be a hero with the jawbone of an ass like Samson, or with
Hercules' club or David's sling, but armies must be on an
equal footing to stand comparison. The inefficiency of the
Italian army came from the inherent inadequacy of the autarchy that impoverished even the internal resources with
which the fascists wished to prepare for the conquest of the
world. They have left an Italy not only stripped of every-

thing and economically ruined, but also financially bankrupt so that a long and wise period of reconstruction will be needed to arrive at a minimum balance between the elementary needs of the population and the necessities of the country as a political state.

In the face of such a situation, imperative obligations will fall to the United Nations, and still graver duties on the Italian people itself and its responsible leaders. The United Nations have a clear line in the Atlantic Charter, Article 4, which provides for the access on equal terms of all states "great or small, victor or vanquished . . . to trade and to the raw materials of the world which are needed for their economic prosperity." They have prepared the necessary plans for aid to countries as they are conquered; aside from the great plans for the future, a special international agency, the UNRRA,* has been established for the rehabilitation of occupied countries so as to bring whole communities back to life in the soonest possible time. Italy, as an ex-enemy country, is not included among the nations represented in UNRRA but in the Montreal assembly of September 1944 there was established a fund of fifty million dollars as a first limited aid.

Unemployment is the evil that must be checked in time, to prevent a relapse into the conditions of the period after the First World War, when unemployment rapidly reached unprecedented levels, especially in Germany, Britain and the United States—industrial countries, and so more sensitive to the rhythms of production and trade.

Italy has always needed a fair-sized emigration both of industrial and agricultural workers. Lacking the capital necessary to exploit her own colonies, possessing colonies poor

---

* *The United Nations Relief and Rehabilitation Administration* represents forty-four United and Associated Nations. Organized on November 9, 1943, for the purpose of bringing immediate aid to the populations freed from Axis domination, it is a transitory agency whose scope is the facilitation of the resumption of economic life in the liberated countries. Uninvaded member countries contribute 1 per cent of their 1943 national income. The United States will thus be responsible for $1,350,000,000 out of a total sum of $2,500,000,000 of anticipated expenditures. Since then, many changes have been made to face the difficult problems. The UNRRA has been from time to time object of strong criticism.

in natural resources (Libya, Eritrea, Somaliland), and with
the United States closed to immigration, Italians have gone,
in recent years, to people the south and west of France, where
they found a suitable climate and environment, and were
becoming assimilated. From a sentimental point of view it
may be distressing that so many Italians should lose if not
their affection for their country of origin, certainly their
language and nationality. But if they are not to form a hostile element in the very countries giving them hospitality,
or to create nationalist resentment (as in Tunisia), or to
isolate themselves entirely from the rest of the community
(an attitude that ends by injuring them), it must be recognized that permanent emigrants are lost to the national cen-
sus; only the culture and traditions of the Italian family will
keep them in touch with their country of origin. So it is in
America; so it will be tomorrow in France and in Tunis, if,
as appears likely, such waves of emigration are renewed.

The fascist policy which wanted to transform Italian im-
migrants into militant fascists for its own advantage served
only to disturb the harmony of the various Italian communities abroad and to make them unwelcome to the other inhabitants, or to place those who did not rally to the fascist
regime in the position of traitors to Italy, or to drive them
to organize revolutionary movements. The emigration of
Italian workers should receive moral, religious, and social
assistance, but must constitute neither a disintegrating factor
in their own country, nor a cause of disturbance in the country receiving them. Assistance is a duty common to both
countries concerned.

Although free initiative and a free flow of emigration are
always preferable to those artificially induced, certain regula-
tions will be necessary both in the country of origin and the
country of destination. This problem must not be left until
it is too late; it needs to be solved with intelligence and
promptness during and immediately after the war, as little
by little opportunities and needs arise.

*   *   *

Italy faces a long period of economic and social reconstruction. The fascist political structure has collapsed; the so-called corporative system had already failed before the war and during the war was largely supplanted. As already evident, fascist pseudocorporation cannot hold together for a minute in conditions of liberty. There has already been a return to free and freely constituted labor unions. In fact, the tones of labor are canalized, through the socialist-communist group on one side, and the Christian-democratic on the other, and a certain reciprocal understanding has not been lacking from the first days. The problems of the organization of labor and of production, which are at the basis of a healthy modern social structure, will have to be solved with a minimum of intervention by the state and a maximum of reciprocal co-operation.*

The free municipality must rise again from the ashes, returning to the normal habits of the popular ballot. The region must be recognized as an administrative, economic and cultural entity. The error of bureaucratic centralization, fallen into for political reasons during the Risorgimento, must not be repeated today.

There can be no going back to the past. No one wants to repeat the past. Every generation must gain its own experience, even though it makes mistakes. The usual "guardians" of the people should not begin to cry out that there is disorder in this world. Disorder there will certainly be after so much alleged order. To restore order we shall inevitably pass through disorder. The bigots of order should recognize this self-evident fact. What is important is to fix the goal and to

---

* After the liberation of Rome in June, 1944, the communist, Christian-democrat, and socialist leaders of the working class agreed to maintain the vocational unity in one confederation called: *Confederazione Generale Italiana del Lavoro* (Italian General Confederation of Labor). The fundamental basis of such an agreement is to restrict the aim of the confederation to the economic and social needs of the workers, leaving each individual free to profess his religion and to follow his political party. In order to gain the confidence of all workers and their various organizations, the promoters agreed to give representatives of the communists, Christian-democrats, and socialists an equal share in the administration of the confederation. This experiment is now in its initial period. See: *People and Freedom*, London, March, 1945.

adopt the most suitable and rapid means of reaching it, in order to avoid unjustified delays, oppressive delusions, and corrosive mistrust.

I do not know if my words will be misinterpreted by those who, in the middle of the war, dreamed of a social revolution in Italy (and elsewhere it goes without saying), and used the word *revolutionary* in the name of their own party or group. In Italy we have heard that word since 1919 either from the so-called revolutionary socialist group or from fascism, which even after it had reached power, always boasted of the *revolution* it had accomplished, always promised a *revolution* yet to come. If after two world wars, in addition to colonial wars and wars of conquest (Abyssinia, Albania), or wars just for war's sake (Spain), after a revolution of twenty years and more like that of the fascists, the average Italian is told to begin another *Revolution* (with a capital R) either on behalf of the communists, or of the socialists of the Left, or of the extremists among the actionists, he will feel at once that his martyrdom is not over, and it will be goodness knows how long before he can begin to think of himself with a little peace and quiet. Let us therefore rule out not only street riots, which exasperate evils and incite reaction, but even those "revolutionary" initiatives that instead of helping the healing of existing wounds will make them more serious so that they will demand longer treatment.

Agrarian reform in the last war took the slogan: "The Land for the Peasants!" It suffices to mention, for those who do not know it, that it was the Italian popular party which presented the most complete (or the least incomplete) project for agrarian reform, and that, after the bill had passed the chamber of deputies in July, 1922, it was subsequently withdrawn by Mussolini in *odium auctoris*. But it is one thing to promote a great long-term reform, and another to impair or upset the structure of landed property, at a moment when agricultural production must be brought to a maximum to meet the urgent needs of the country. It would be folly to impoverish the country and bring about a dearth of produce by unsettling agitation and improvised demagogy, counting on getting corn from America or oil from Syria or wine from Tunisia.

This does not mean that the agrarian problem need not be faced. It means only that the new parties and their leaders must resist the temptation to make it a motive for political proselytizing or a means for revolutionary dreams, and must come to an agreement on gradual measures that will not impair the normal production of the country. This is the longer, but it is the surer way, albeit there will be much political and social impatience. There are those who say: "If we do not seize our opportunity, we shall never be able to obtain anything." They have not faith in democracy or in their own party; they seek to impose themselves on the rest with a fascist mentality, which unfortunately will survive for some time among the parties of the Right as well as among those of the Left.

If, however, socialists, liberal-democrats, Christian-democrats, and communists, already united during the period of war against the Germans, come to an agreement on a plan of agrarian reforms which does not carry the label of any party but is the outcome of sound technical and social studies, Italy will be better served than by the untimely declamations of revolutionary idealists. When it is necessary to create or to restore water courses, farmhouses, roads, schools, churches, reclamation-works so as to bring the land truly within the reach of the small farmer*, it is doubly necessary to undertake the task with practical and technical plans, the result of thorough study. The peasants on the whole want their "piece of land," their "family holding." In many cases this is a good thing, but in others, where the agricultural industrialization of big units is possible, either through co-operatives or by partnerships between owner and worker, it would mean the impoverishment of the community, or a detrimental transformation of production.

---

* Bonomi's government had already taken some good steps for the agrarian reform.

Italy has, or rather had, her own industry. Possibly it will
be found still in working order, or can be revived with little
difficulty. To start productive industries working again, even
during Allied occupation, and to direct their products toward Italy's natural outlets; to transform, once the war is
over, war industries into peace industries; to close down
those that are uneconomic (if any such exist), those which
were kept going only for nationalist purposes as part of the
autarchic system; to rebuild a merchant fleet like she used to
have, and even a better: here is an immediate program that
will cover several years of technical work and political
activity.

Everything that can raise the Italian's standard of living
and increase the productivity of our natural resources, and
the output of our traditional arts and crafts must be fostered
with special care and made efficient. When the greater part
of the budget no longer has to be spent on the armed forces,
munitions production, the making of guns, warships and
bombers and fighter planes, the period of economic-social
reconstruction can be faced with less anxiety.

Much will need to be done for what is now called "social
security." Before fascism old-age insurance, industrial insurance against accidents and so forth already existed. The
fascist government adopted other measures which should be
preserved and improved. A Beveridge plan for Italy will be
the necessary complement to what already exists or used to
exist before fascism.* It is true that the resources of the Italian
state will be miserably small, that the lira no longer has any
backing, and that everything will have to be done over from
the beginning. But we must not despair of the future. It is
the duty of the Allies to help Italy and Europe to recovery;
but we must not count on them; our first duty is to set in
order the finances of the state, making a clean sweep of all
parasites, professional in all governments; and to bring back

* The commissions of Study of the Party of Christian Democracy, Rome, have
published a very important brochure: Contributi alla Riforma della Previdenza
Sociale—SELI—Rome.

a sense of civic righteousness, the duty of everyone to participate in the rebirth of the country. This is not a technical book for the study of particular measures. It is true that Italy is poor in resources and has been terribly impoverished and despoiled by fascism. But just as she was made over a first time after the Risorgimento, she will be made over a second time by the labor, the thrift and the sacrifices of her sons. Great transformations, the real revolutions, are not those made in one day; they are those that bear the stamp of progressive development, decisive and of long range, those that reach the root of the evil to extirpate it without removing a little good that still exists and contributes to the resumption of the economic and social life of the country.

9

Education and Re-education

THE PROBLEM of the re-education of the Axis countries, during occupation and when the war is over, has been and is of chief concern and debate in England and the United States. The question is a serious one; not a few people are facing it with a sincerity equal to the immense confidence that exists in America, more than elsewhere, in schools, in books, in statistics for the education of the world. If we of an ancient culture smile a little, it is not that we do not appreciate American good will or seek to disparage their efforts. There is, in fact, a lack of understanding between the Old World and the New, such as may arise between a man old in experience and hence a little skeptical and mistrustful of the methods of others, and a man who has a long road to travel before attaining historical and worldly experience.

We do not refuse the hand stretched out to us; only we feel the futility of the pretension to refashion the soul of the Italians (or of the Germans) by means of lessons in social science, scientific psychology, positivist pedagogy and technology.* All education is a spiritual problem and is achieved

---

* Naturally some are reasonable. It is good to read what Dr. Howard Comfort of Haverford College wrote in the *Christian Science Monitor* (November, 1943), where after having referred to the ancient, medieval and Renaissance civilization of Italy, he continued:

"The Italians have done plenty else besides, but let these reminders suffice. The modern Italian passes daily the monuments of nearly a hundred generations. By comparison, the *Mayflower* is as yesterday.

"There is plenty which our young and vigorous American culture can and could contribute to the Italian, to the profit of both; but until we become more sure of our ground than we are, the most realistic American technique will be to dismiss the illusion that we are the divinely self-appointed missionaries of enlighten-

mainly from within each one of us, with our own experience in an environment of spontaneity and freedom. The quality and conditions of the environment are of primary importance. Where there is constriction, education will be artificial and give sophisticated results. Where there is freedom, the development of character proceeds more naturally; there is a speedy formation of spontaneous groups, the instinctive assimilations between those of the same kind; the clash of ideas leads to an active selection; with intellectual conviction, the spirit more readily becomes imbued with individual-social morality which will be the more deeply felt the less it is imposed from outside. A country's environment is formed by language, the family, the school, the town, the region to which people belong; by historical thought, quickened by tradition and the continuity of spiritual links with the past. Beyond the region, only through politics, university culture, the exchange of leading elites, can other more general values be introduced into the restricted environments of region or town; this comes about on a still wider scale and beyond the nation through the great social crises, like revolutions, wars or a transformation imposed by extraordinary events, rather than through normal causes.

The educational influence of environment must be aerated by broader ideas and cultural movements, not only national but international, not only technical but general; by local history and by universal history; by traditional law and comparative law; by the logic of ideas and by that of experience.

What is indispensable for a people is its own history as individual and collective life, lived in an uninterrupted process, with its crises, its gains and its achievements. In such a history that which lives is never material conquests, no matter how great, nor even military victories, but the virtues that men have sought to cultivate, the ideals by which they lived, the efforts to overcome evil and the moral benefits that

ment and democracy in a land which never heard of these desirable commodities; for actually some very substantial elements in our civilization and democracy are very well understood in Italy, perhaps better than here. That's where they were born."

have been won. By all this a people is what it is, and cannot be changed for better or for worse save by transforming its very environment, remaking its history, starting its course anew, as the exiles or colonists in America or Australia or Canada remade their collective life when, separated from Europe, they created a new environment in which to develop their own personality.

Education is always necessary. It must be readjusted to conditions of time and place in regard to technique, method, and particular aims. But the education of the spirit is always fundamental; it cannot be changed as can a technique or a method; it changes only in its spiritual directives, whether in philosophy of life or in religion. If we were Hindus, Chinese or Japanese, we should have a more or less pantheistic and pessimistic background, and from this conception of life the educators would draw a suitable method for molding the souls of their pupils. But we Europeans have as background Greco-Roman classicism, the Judeo-Christian religious outlook and the rationalism (both the sound and the distorted) that has developed ever since the Renaissance. Our background, our roots are there. If we are able to reach a unification of mind and will in a reappreciation of the treasures that this background contains, we shall have achieved a balance between optimism and pessimism, the two extremes of human thought. Otherwise we shall lean to one side or the other, preparing new crises more or less like that of today.

It must never be thought that on one side are angels and on the other are devils, and that it is the task of the angels to transform the devils or (how shall we say?) thrust them back into Hell. However, much as we, on the Allied side, are convinced of the justice of the cause for which we fight and of the injustice of the war waged by Germany and the other Axis countries, it must be recognized that on our side not a few are of fascist and nazi mentality, and on the other not a few whose hearts and minds are bound to the war aims of the United Nations. What is to be feared, on our side, is that military victory itself, as it is being won, may bring with it the bitter savor of pride, the thirst for dominion, the spirit of revenge, the scorn of the vanquished. If there is not a much higher tempering virtue, and a critical public opinion neither intoxicated by success nor warped by the outcries of capitalistic interests, there might be at the end of this war such a reversal of positions, between the totalitarian countries of yesterday and the democratic countries of today, as to show as many fascists and nazis on this side as were killed in the war.

That would be natural enough. The influence of events on the orientation of a people (even if only episodic and transient) is always considerable. After twenty years of war and triumph, the France of Napoleon was and felt humiliated, yet little by little instead of repudiating Napoleon and his methods France developed the cult of the hero. The episode of Napoleon III, defeated at Sedan, should have warned the French and made them follow a better method for the education of the young. This was attempted by men of the Left, with but little success in the educational field that was taken over by nationalists, monarchists and clericals (the latter, alas! largely nationalists and monarchists). The cult of Napoleon increased during the Third Republic. No one, indeed, can think of Paris without Napoleon's tomb and the Arc de Triomphe; the names of Rivoli, Marengo, Les Pyramides, Austerlitz, ring in the ears of all. Napoleon had merits above and beyond his wars; the code and the concordat count for more than the victories of Jena and Wagram. But, unfortunately, tomorrow the annals of the German army in the First and Second World Wars will stir the imagination and the heart of a defeated Germany, if there remains to her a name like that of Napoleon. The Kaiser and Hindenburg were not of his stature, and it is to be hoped that a Hitler-myth will not be created. What we have been saying of the defeated, under certain aspects holds good for the victors too, were they to lose human measure and make of their leaders either supermen or angels who have driven out the devils.

* * *

Italy has had so many historical cycles, so many historical and geographical units, that by natural consequence her people are very varied and complex. Although national unification was only recent, the sound and glorious particularism of her provinces was transcended by an ideal and higher unification which came about in language, art, culture and religion. In any case, each of her "hundred" cities was a world in itself, a world complete and often proud. That is why, from the political standpoint, the particular histories of Florence, Rome, Venice, Genoa, Naples, Milan, Turin, Ferrara, Palermo, Bologna Pisa, Brescia, Parma, Mantua, Modena and all the rest, have no common resonance except in moments of "national" or better, "universal" import: defense against the foreigner (the Sicilian Vespers, Balilla, Pietro Micca, the five days of Milan, the revolt of Brescia); or vindication of liberty (First and Second Lombard Leagues, Cola di Rienzo, the Siege of Florence, the Sicilian revolt against the Spaniards, the whole Risorgimento); or else in maritime expansion, artistic and cultural glories, historic universities, and geniuses that belong to mankind, such as St. Thomas Aquinas and Dante, Leonardo da Vinci and Michelangelo, Galileo and Vico and a hundred others, or Popes such as Leo the Great, Gregory the Great, Hildebrand, Alexander III, Innocent III, Innocent XI, Leo XIII.

To this historic background which has three periods of exceptional greatness—the Medieval Rebirth, the Renaissance, the Risorgimento—it is usual to add that of republican and imperial Rome (forgetting Etruscans and Greeks), to give it a political color that is unreal, because the greatness of Italy up to now has never been political, that of the Romans belongs to us only remotely, just as the ancient Greece of Leonidas and Pericles meant little to the Greeks liberated from the Turks in the nineteenth century. Civically and historically, we are of another stuff, political continuity was broken many centuries ago, in Greece with the Roman occupation, in Italy with the fall of the Western empire and the invasions of the barbarians.

The glory and the glamour of Rome have made Italians resentful of their political impotence, or overproud of their ancient nobility. Dante universalized Rome in his imperial concept, but Petrarch in singing the praises of Cola di Rienzo went bail for an impossible return to a greatness that history had washed away. Rome always served the minor poets who were capable only of flabby rhetoric; during the Risorgimento it was the theme of declamations against which the horse sense of Giuseppe Giusti protested with his mordant *"Grilli romani!"*

Could he have foreseen fascism with its "Lictorial Reds," who knows what witty poems he might have left us! Certain it is that this Roman legacy, of ideal and cultural value, politically (and worse still militarily) has been a bitter experience. Modern Italy, universal in spirit, refined in culture, critical by instinct, is no longer and cannot be the political and military center of the world. Let us remember the Rome of law, the Rome of human virtues, the Rome that was also materially grand and glorious, let us preserve its historic relics and its treasures of poetry and art: this is our task as the traditional trustees of a living heritage that belongs to mankind. All other feelings of vainglory or imitation which ancient Rome was made to inspire have supplied the antihistorical side of the education given to Italians (especially under fascism, but to some extent even before it); more deplorable even than the Napoleon cult of the French, because those ancestors of ours who dominated the world are historically and morally more remote.

When, at some more or less distant time, Great Britain is no longer at the center of the world, when the formation of her empire scattered over the oceans is an historic memory, because the dominions and colonies, having reached maturity, will have reordered themselves in accordance with new economic, geographic and political requirements, she will then seek another life. Her imperial past will mean to her what that of the fifth century meant to Italy, the preparation for a new destiny. In alluding to this possibility, I make no prophecy, nor say anything unpleasing to the English. Africa will have her federation or confederations; Canada, Australia and New Zealand, if they do not wish to be overpowered, will have to open their doors to wider immigration and soon become countries with fifty or a hundred million inhabitants, creating closer ties of interest in the Pacific and America. India will have political unification, even if she cannot find spiritual union. All will be England's daughters, just as Europe was the daughter of Rome. But we know that when sons and daughters set up house for themselves they take their own road; to the parents remains only the consolation of seeing them develop and prosper, the joy of caressing their children's children. If in the world in a hundred years' time there are more than five hundred millions speaking the English tongue and carrying on the tradition of British culture (as may well be foreseen unless birth control prevents one or two hundred million from coming into the world, vying with war in the decimation of progressive races), this will be the best England can hope for. She will not need to trouble the world as Mussolini did with a factitious and antihistoric empire.

Italy today must return, of herself and not through external coercion, to the sources of her moral and historical culture, to reshape her education after the fascist crisis and her military defeat, to raise herself up again from the inmost depths of her spirit and to place herself in the ranks of the civilized nations, from whom (voluntarily, out of pride and by misfortune) she set herself apart.

*   *   *

How, you ask, is our youth to be re-educated, our youth, who for twenty years received the imprint of fascism, beginning at the age of six when children were "baptized" Sons of the She-Wolf, later to become *Balilla*, with guns, and drums, uniforms, salutes, songs, lessons which, whether we like it or not, remain in the soul? Barely adolescent, some entered the fascist militia, others the army or navy or air force, all imbued with fascism and arrogance. The same spirit animated those in the schools and universities, in labor unions and the corporations, as well as those "decorated" with the honor of possessing the party ticket and still others with that of having been *squadristi*—armed gangsters—at the age of fourteen.

Even before the fall of fascism, and well before the present war, a section of studious youth, a section of the educated classes and many Catholics who had lost their enthusiasm of the days of the Lateran treaty, were going through a deep spiritual crisis, breaking away from all the falsehood that fascism had brought into the moral and social life of Italy, spontaneously seeking foundations on which to build a more natural and lasting concept of life. Propaganda in favor of nazism, the German alliance, the persecution of the Jews, the help given to Spain, the preparation of a world war, had ruined all the illusions of the first fascist youth, among those who, already in their thirties, measured with critical eyes the abyss into which they had fallen.

The Italian is critical by habit, even when he is illiterate. He is usually called skeptical, but the term is inexact. Skepticism is not an habitual state of mind, but only a pose of decadent intellectuals and the ultimate attitude of those defeated by life who are to be found everywhere and in all times. In Italy, the critical spirit is general, and this it is that often impedes spontaneous action. In a country with so long and varied a history, without true material satisfactions and without intoxicating successes, the critical spirit creates isolated and often powerful individualities, it impedes gregarious life and the psychology of the team. Because of this critical spirit, fascism has remained on the surface. It was the adventure following the postwar crisis, boosted abroad rather than at home, by journalists, rather than by thinkers, by demagogues rather than by statesmen. For the educated and thoughtful sections of Italian youth it has been an immense tragedy to see at firsthand the emptiness and immorality of fascism, and yet to see it taken seriously and imposing

itself on world opinion. Democratic and powerful governments like those of London, Paris and Washington, supporting fascism or enduring its impositions, rising up to denounce
it as in the case of the Abyssinian war and then failing to
carry out sanctions, indeed giving *de jure* recognition to the
conquest and to the imperial title. In the Spanish war, the
same democratic governments call the submarines Mussolini
sent to attack British shipping in the Mediterranean "unknown submarines" so as to continue the fiction of the nonintervention committee sitting in London. All this when
Hitler was not yet strong, when the nazi threat was not yet
visible on the horizon.

This unwholesome international atmosphere influenced the
youth of Italy, both educated and uneducated, more strongly
than what was happening in Germany. Italian youth, even
when it was fascist, could not unlearn the habit of criticism,
even when every school displayed in bold letters the slogan:
"Mussolini is always right." Indeed, from what we remember
of our own youth, criticism must have risen spontaneously
in the mind of every youth as soon as he read that inscription.
Criticism, even if incomplete and without the necessary guidance, was drawing many away from a facile credo, making
them take refuge either in Catholicism (the half-million
members of Catholic action) or in the philosophical idealism
of Croce or other masters, or in sentimental spiritualism or
stoical asceticism, which offset the orgies of words, parades,
speeches and threats that formed the daily life of spiritual
and intellectual wretchedness represented by fascism.

It is obvious that criticism was directed for years against
those who should have been fascism's natural enemies and
were not, or who were inconsistent with their principles, or
lacked courage and initiative, or yielded to blandishments
and intimidations. All were included in such criticism, men
of the past and new men, foreign governments and international journalists, priests, friars, bishops and popes, political
refugees and underground opponents. Criticism is not barren
when it rests on great and immortal principles; it is barren

when it is only resentment and defamation. Thus much of Italian youth was already redeemed even before the war came.

After having been in touch with some of these young men, and then talking to young Americans and Englishmen who seemed concerned only with sport or their jobs, utterly remote from the moral and political, national and international issues of the prewar period, I felt as if I were passing from reality to a dream. I remember a young English history master between twenty-five and thirty. This was in 1938 before Munich. I told him I expected that within two years England and France would be at war with Germany and Italy. He replied that no young man at Oxford or Cambridge would fight in such a war. "Then," I said, "you will see England reduced to the position of Denmark." He answered that he would prefer this, thus accepting defeat before the war had even begun. He was not alone; he seemed to me typical. Before the war the youth of England and the United States, educated by positivists and isolationists, were without the torment of thinking beyond their own world with which they were satisfied. These young men and women have experienced war, but have not had the experience of a social system that is loved or hated, or first loved and then hated with all the passion of those forced to live by it and in it.

That is why, when war broke out, all the resentment of the Allies was directed against Germany; Italy, fascism, Mussolini himself were spared. This was not a deliberately two-edged policy on the part of the Allies, as it was believed in Italy, with the intention of isolating the accomplices of the Axis who had already drawn up their pacts and fixed their tactics. It was a lack of imagination, which is not unusual in the political world, but also a lack of moral sensibility which is an obvious result of a materialistic and hedonistic positivism; in substance a lack of guiding ideas which should at the same time and with the same decisiveness have condemned both nazism and fascism.

Now this readjustment of ideas and of social morality has been made, under the pressure of events and in the harsh experience of war, but not to such an extent that traces of nazi and fascist contagion are not still discernible among the peoples and leaders of the United Nations. At the moment that the Anglo-Americans were presenting themselves at the gates of continental Europe not only as liberators by the force of arms, but as liberators of the spirit, it was hoped they would review their own spiritual, moral and political positions, so as to bridge the gulf that had come into being between some of the United Nations, and was unhappily very apparent between French and Anglo-Americans, and even between Anglo-Americans and Italians (not only because of the king or Badoglio).

At the meeting of the International Education Assembly held at Fredericksburg, Maryland, in June, 1944, before delegates of some twenty other states, Dr. Alexander Meiklejohn, representing the American Association for Adult Education, declared "absurd" and "childish arrogance" the belief that American instructors should be sent to Germany for the reform of the education system. He expressed the opinion that Americans need to re-educate themselves, adding that Americans could help Germany in her re-education only by making a reasonable world in which she could have a reasonable place. What was said for Germany could be said for Italy and other enemy countries.

President Roosevelt, in his talk of June 5, 1944, well represented the feeling of many toward Italy. He said, "The Italian people are capable of self-government. We do not lose sight of their virtues as a peace-loving nation. We remember the many centuries in which the Italians were leaders in the arts and sciences, enriching the lives of all mankind. Italy should go on as a great mother nation, contributing to the culture and the progress and the good will of all mankind—developing their special talents in the arts and crafts and sciences and preserving her historical heritage for the benefit of all people. We want and expect the help of the future Italy toward lasting peace."

Although there are strong feelings of resentment between

Italy and France (mainly through the fault of fascism, but also because many Frenchmen refuse to give credit to the Italian people, believing it congenitally fascist, which is an error),* it would be an absurdity if in the ethical and cultural revival of Europe, France were supplanted at the center of modern world thought by, I do not say Russia, but by the United States or even England. World education and re-education is a collective task in which all countries of Christian civilization must co-operate, with all the means they possess, even the vanquished, even the fascists and nazis, the isolationists and materialists of yesterday, if for them the war has been a catharsis that enables them to refashion their mentality and conscience.

This demands an ideal that will be like the star of the Magi, guiding to the center of salvation, and awakening the trust of the peoples. Up till now no word or gesture such as those of Wilson in 1918 has come. After Wilson's failure,† Roosevelt and Churchill were afraid of such a gesture. But the failure was not Wilson's fault, unless every generous idea is to be accused of being the reason for the failures of mankind. We ask the countries poisoned by the diabolical spirit of the Axis to cast out the poison of their theories, which brought on the Second World War. But we also expect the Americans and the British to reject the poison of their prewar tractations with the nazis and fascists. Catharsis is necessary for the victors and for the vanquished, for though the war was willed by Mussolini, Hitler and the Japanese militarists, the

---

* General de Gaulle is not one of them. After the fall of Mussolini he declared: "We do not hesitate to add that this close proximity, and in a measure this interdependence of the two great peoples of France and Italy, remains through the torment of humanity and, in spite of all present rancors, is an element on which the reason and the hope of Europe cannot fail to rest."

† Various American journalists, on the anniversary of the armistice of 1918, recalled the words of President Wilson, already ill and within a month or so of his death, to the crowd of admirers who had flocked to his home on November 11, 1923.

"Just one word more [he said, almost trembling], I cannot refrain from saying it. I am not one of those that have the least anxiety about the triumph of the principles I have stood for. I have seen fools resist Providence before and I have seen their destruction, as will come upon these again—utter destruction and contempt. That we shall prevail is as sure as that God reigns."

other countries did everything to make it possible. Britain's gesture of resistance in 1940 has redeemed her, but so far no British political leader has been able to make confessions of the errors that led to Munich. That is why today there is a fear of the peace. And without the "star of the East" there can be no going forward, neither in politics, nor in the education of one's own country nor even, alas, in that of the defeated countries.

*   *   *

The essential difference between totalitarian countries and democratic countries lies in liberty. This is a safety valve that lessens the instinct of dominion, nationalist spirit and racial egoism. Liberty, if well used, will also curb the pride of the victors, just as honest and measured criticism often serves to arouse remorse for evil acts that, alas, are not the monopoly of any one country or any one social class, but the heritage of all men.

That Italian youth should have forgotten or even despised the value of liberty during the fascist intoxication is nothing astonishing. But they felt the need for it reawaken, well before the fall of fascism, even before the occupation of Sicily, and southern Italy, before the liberation of Rome. For Anglo-American arms to conquer Sicily in thirty-eight days would have been a miracle, had the population been hostile; had Sicily felt that an enemy was approaching, as fascism sought to make out. Sicily had shown that she knew how to resist, like Russia, when in the Dark Ages the Mussulmans took fifty-seven years to conquer her. But without going back further than the Risorgimento, I would recall the courageous resistance of the people of Messina to the Bourbon of Naples in the rising and the following popular war of 1848. An English admiral had to intervene to prevent the massacre even of women and children on which the Neapolitan troops were engaged. It is well to recall that in 1848 the cry of *Liberty!* started from Palermo to shake all Europe, and from Palermo on April 4, 1860, came the signal for the Garibaldi epic which ended in the making of Italy.

Liberty will bring to the front not only the effects of past evils, but also the unrest of the people, the need of maintaining order and achieving a certain prosperity, the necessity of repressing disorder or riots, the duty of self-discipline, hard to attain after twenty years of constraint. Feelings, resentments, imaginary impressions, unjust criticisms, mistakes by leaders, charges of betrayal on the part of the people, and incomprehensions on the part of the Allies, are making the pangs of Italian rebirth harsh and painful. This does not matter. In spite of everything, this will be a salutary labor, it will be a practical re-education, it will be a great experience which will create the premises for a new life.

Youth must be guided, helped. Italians there are who, having remained immune from the fascist disease, paid for their dignity by twenty years of silence and meditation, perhaps stripped of all means of livelihood, perhaps relegated to the *"confino,"* or in prison or in exile—men deserving of respect if they do not adopt the attitude of martyrs or prophets, but return, as many have done, simply to fraternal communion with the others in a spirit of understanding and affectionate humility.

There will be those who have seen their errors; others who will be ashamed of their own weakness, those who will have paid dearly for their support of fascism, and others who will have drawn from it a deep understanding of mass-psychology. But there will also be those who will claim they were right in being fascists, and are right today in being so no longer.

New and generous directives will be needed if the spiritual crisis of the average Italian and especially of the young is to resolve itself into a higher activity, and not become a motive of prostration or of blindness. Those who think themselves superior to everything and everyone, those who have never been mistaken and are never mistaken, who despise those who think differently, and wish to justify all their own errors by condemning the errors of others, are faced by a melancholy temptation that will make all health-giving catharsis difficult.

Every country emerges from war in a state of spiritual crisis, both victor and vanquished, both the aggressor and the victims of aggression, since even the victims have faults, though they be indirect, with respect to the present war. The uprooting of whole populations, the habit of killing created by war, the sensual excesses felt as compelling physical needs, the psychological trauma caused by a thousand incidents of war, render necessary for all, a period of reorientation, of reconciliation with themselves and with others, a period for the revaluation of life.

Those, however, for whom war has been combined with tyranny, whether they have suffered it themselves or have made others suffer it, will require greater care for a real recovery. How can it be possible that officers and soldiers of the Italian army should have exercised so cruel a tyranny over Yugoslavs, Albanians and Greeks? To me, it is hard to believe. I think there must have been exceptions, for an imitation of nazi methods would have been unnatural even for fascists. The true and crude reality will be known. Those responsible must be judged and punished, and the others who carried out their orders will have to be re-educated, perhaps placed outside the social environment till they realize that they should have mutinied against their leaders sooner than show savagery to unarmed populations.

Another point in the re-education of the countries that have suffered totalitarian tyranny, and of Italy in the first line, must be the remolding of character. After twenty years in which lying, hypocrisy, adulation had become the habit of all, either as a defense for those in opposition or as a means of advancement and moneymaking, or as a social convention, the infection will remain for a very long period, even when all tyranny has disappeared. We have to deal with a sort of inferiority complex which having affected the soul and impregnated society can be cast off only by long efforts.

The lie is a stigma of inferiority for the individual and the collectivity. It may result from individual perversion, but often it is born of a widespread feeling of suspicion and fear which makes a lie seem the best defense. In consequence from the sociological point of view, lying is more widespread among the poorest and the richest classes, the poor as forming a kind of community cut off from the rest, the rich because they fear losses and do not want their businesses to be known. Politically, lying is common under tyrants, as are hypocrisy and flattery. Since the human community is founded on truth and on love, where the community spirit is vitiated by tyranny and by violence, terror and lying spread. For a return to human life, which is true life, the spirit must be made once more able to receive truth and to live by love. Then lying, hypocrisy and adulation will be seen for the ugly things they are, elements disintegrating the spirit of each of us and of society itself.

*　　*　　*

The freedom of the school is one of the great weapons in favor of truth and social love. Lies receive their deathblow from free minds. Italy never knew true freedom of the school, for a melancholy legacy of our Risorgimento was a state monopoly of education. Little by little, the state took over the elementary schools from the municipalities, opposed schools run by religious orders, and then under pretext of the Roman question, or "temporalism" as it was called, centralized and bureaucratized all the schools, often along positivist and rationalist lines with the set purpose of secularizing Italian education. The reaction against such centralization came from two quite opposite schools of thought, that of the traditional Christian, and that of Hegelian idealism, led then by Croce and Gentile. The two philosophers parted company. Croce's bill on the State Examination,* which was supported by the popular party, failed to pass owing to the opposition of the socialists and Giolitti's liberals; for a time the Gentile plan had better fortune when Gentile embraced fascism and became minister of education.

---

* By allowing pupils of all schools to take an open State Examination it would have removed the discrimination against those in private schools.

However, not even the slender and merely formal freedom of education contained in the Gentile scheme could exist under the fascist regime. Never was a state monopoly of teaching and general training so harsh and total. We have only to think of the nuns in teaching orders, compelled to give the fascist salute in the classrooms and gardens and corridors; to make their pupils sing *Giovinezza,* with all that it contains, and to sing hymns to the Duce; to alter history, geography (I could almost have said arithmetic), so as to make them conform to the fascist texts. Textbooks, illustrated copybooks, everything, even the air of the convent, had to breathe fascism.

Those among the antifascists who today, in 1945, speak of a single state school in Italy, do not realize the evil that they wish to perpetuate in the name of a future democratic state. To fix a legal minimum standard in order that education shall not be debased or placed in the hands of unworthy persons is a rightful safeguard, a prerequisite to any school system, but to impose restrictions in order to create fresh state monopolies would be to abjure the conquest of liberty.

Though saying this, I have to admit that the devastation caused by the materialism of the spiritual formation of the West has been truly tragic in the vastness of its extent. This materialism, presented under various aspects, now alluring, now useful, now as experimentalism, at other times as pragmatism, positivism, historicism, has cast off little by little the ethical principles of social life and created a hedonistic morality, limited only by the political power, holding a balance between the various social groups. It has come to be accepted as the normal and common system of society. But since man cannot live without moral ideals, materialism has disguised itself: for the masses it is the conquest of rights by class struggle; for the bourgeois elite it has become the national ideal; for the intellectuals, nationalism or pure naturalism.

The most materialistic of modern ideologies has been that of the race, yet the racial theory has won as wide and effectual support as any other; the race has been raised almost to the point of divinity for privileged members of "superior races." Theoretical explanations are sought for such phenomena; the Germans are masterly in finding a theory and a special name for every evil act. But this does not mean that Americans, Englishmen, Frenchmen, Italians, Spaniards, have no doctors in materialism. It is not the fault of science which as the quest for truth is a divine gift, it is the fault of those who do not know how to keep the various branches of science each in its proper place in the hierarchy of knowledge, leaving to philosophy and ethics the task of guiding human thought in the ways of universal and final truths.

We are fighting for a better world, but how are we to reshape it if we do not admit the responsibility and finality of our own actions? If we separate economics and politics from morals? If we do not give morals the solid basis of human reason, called also human personality or rational nature, that is, man himself as the true and fundamental subject of rights and duties?

If this man lacks the ontological and ethical unification in God, he will never be susceptible of true education and will never find the truth and love with which to imbue the new society. It is thus that freedom and democracy have become empty words for those who rest them on a materialistic pragmatism, defining them merely as modes of life with nothing more than a historic and social significance.

During the celebration of the two-hundredth anniversary of the birth of Thomas Jefferson, in 1943, various American writers asked whether the philosophical-religious ideal which inspired the founders of American democracy to write the Declaration of Independence were still such as to make it possible for us to repeat with them that "all men are . . . endowed by their Creator with certain inalienable rights, among them the right to life, liberty and the pursuit of happiness." Can such rights still remain without having them derive from a God? In fact, if God, natural rights, human personality, are the phraseology of myths of the past, it is still necessary to find something on which to base right (including the right to liberty), or to ask plainly whether any right exists among men, except the right of the strongest.

In Italy the same thing happened with those Mazzinians who have dropped the first part of the binomial *God and People,* thus raising up the people as a unique universal entity, without ethical or religious reference to God.

It may be, as it happens today, men are so preoccupied with the search of personal well-being that they forget its sources, confusing material reality with moral values. But at the bottom of our two-thousand-year-old civilization the religious, moral spirit of the Classical and Judeo-Christian tradition is never missing, even in theoretical and practical deviations. Men who have denied or fought the Christian religion (or have ignored it) when they speak of liberty, justice, and moral values, of public and private honesty, of the rights of the human personality, mean more or less the same things that we mean, even without actually referring them to God.

When, instead, they withdraw from such a natural concept of morality, then, even without denying God explicitly, they make a God of pseudovalues and personifications often expressed by well-known words (but in an equivocal sense): people, race, nation, class, empire, according to practical and immediate needs, they reproduce in iridescent colors the materialist substratum of modern collective life.

Benedetto Croce, in a famous article published in 1943 in *Critica,* spoke of Christianity as the greatest spiritual fact of history. He, who has always been critical of the Catholic Church, without abandoning his philosophical idealism, concluded his article by stating that the time had come to be good Christians, both *inside and outside the Church.* The testimony of Croce, who has up to now remained out of the Church, serves to take up once more the line of thought of Jefferson and Mazzini (both of them non-Catholics), in the sense that it links together moral and religious values, to refashion entirely the education of the peoples having a Christian tradition.

Liberty and democracy must today be reviewed in the light of Christianity even by those who are without religious faith; they cannot but recognize the incoherence of modern society as founded on scientific materialism, or pragmatistic positivism, or state, national or racial pantheism proclaimed as totalitarian.

Italy must be the first in Europe to return to her Christian tradition, and on this to renew and found anew the principles of freedom and democracy.

10

The Shape of New Europe

A S A STARTING POINT let us take the Moscow declaration of November 1, 1943, the communiqué of the
Cairo Conference and the Teheran declaration of December 1, 1943; and link these with the Atlantic Charter of
August, 1941,* the Washington declaration of January, 1942
and finally the report of the Crimea Conference at Yalta.
Although, politically speaking, they may be considered
under certain aspects as variants and corrections, taken as a
whole they provide valuable guidance; the later statements
being those that come closest to practical reality.

All these utterances had an immediate purpose: to
strengthen the determination of the United Nations, especially of the great powers, to carry on and win the war.
From this standpoint, each in its own time served to interpret
the urgent needs of the war and of maintaining or strengthening what is called morale among the Allies, and even
among neutrals and the people in enemy countries in favor
of the United Nations.

This was not always successful. Once the moment of
the declarations had passed (or even at the time they were
made), mistrust, public criticism, successive vacillations of
policy of the various governments, war difficulties in the
Pacific or in Europe, lessened their importance or revealed

* Although in the Moscow documents the Atlantic Charter was not mentioned,
there is a reference to the Washington declaration which in its preamble confirms
the Charter. In the declaration on Iran of December 1, 1943, Mr. Churchill, President Roosevelt and Marshal Stalin declared their intentions to be "in accordance
with the principles of the Atlantic Charter to which all four governments [the
Prime Minister of Iran was with them] have continued to subscribe." The last
reference to it was at Yalta.

their deficiency. The truth is that their promoters, successful as they were in the formation of the Atlantic Charter and the Washington declaration, found such difficulties in the way of realization that they became fearful of compromising the outcome of the war itself. In addition, the lack of a responsible international body, such as would have been provided by the League of Nations, made the co-operation of other nations with the three great powers spasmodic or ineffectual and for a certain time undesired.

Only at Moscow did permanent bodies begin to make an appearance—apart from the Mediterranean council which never functioned and was absorbed by the council for Italy. The first such body was the *European Advisory Commission* set up in London for the study of European questions affecting the three governments of London, Moscow and Washington (and, at the end of 1944, Paris) to make recommendations as to measures to be adopted during the progress of the war. A second was the *Advisory Council for Italian Affairs*, consisting of representatives of the three principal powers, with in addition those of the French National Committee in Algiers (now the provisional government) and later of the governments-in-exile of Greece and Yugoslavia. Although there has been much criticism of the inefficiency of these bodies, because they were merely advisory and powerless to follow the rhythm of events, or because of the divergent views of the three governments, they nevertheless seemed, when established, to be the beginning of true international political collaboration.

In addition to these measures, two undertakings were entered into by the four great powers (Great Britain, Russia and the United States, together with China). The first was that of establishing at the earliest practicable date a general international organization, based on the principle of the sovereign equality of all peace-loving states, and open to membership by all such states, large and small, for the maintenance of international peace and security." * The second

* We deal with such an organization in the next chapter.

provided that during the intervening period between then
and the creation of a new league of sovereign states "for
the purpose of maintaining international peace and security
. . . they [the four powers] will consult with one another
and as occasion requires with other members of the United
Nations with a view to joint action on behalf of the community of nations." This co-operation aimed in particular "to
bring about a practicable general agreement with respect to
the regulation of armaments in the postwar period."

The Moscow formula with regard to international organization was better than that of the Atlantic Charter, which
contemplated only "the establishment of a wider and permanent system of general security." However, in regard to
disarmament, Moscow exercised greater caution than the Atlantic Charter which held out hope of "all practicable measures which will lighten for peace-loving peoples the crushing
burden of armaments."

At Moscow was achieved a war agreement which, through
various political and military difficulties, seemed to have been
shaken by doubts and mistrust and not to have lasted long.
Its importance was enhanced by the Cairo and Teheran conferences, which, besides being held by the responsible leaders, achieved that measure of unity expressed in the words:
"We came here [to Teheran] with hope and determination.
We leave here friends in fact, in spirit and in purpose." The
war agreement of the three and four powers (according to the
sphere of action) was extended to the postwar period with
two principal aims: that of agreeing upon and insuring the
conditions of the surrender and disarmament of the defeated
countries; that of preparing the future organization of peace.
Only for the regulation of armaments was there any explicit
mention of consultation and co-operation. Unless the words
were not weighed as carefully as could be expected in such
a document, the principle "of the sovereign equality of all
peace-loving states" was suspended until the "United Nations
Organization."

It cannot be doubted that almost all the responsibility for

the conduct of the war has fallen, in varying degree, on the three or four, according to the points of view, and that first in Europe and in due course in Asia, on them will fall the responsibility for the maintenance of order and the rehabilitation of countries occupied by the enemy, of defeated countries themselves, and of others in a state of collapse. Finally, the political and economic burden of the new order will fall more heavily than ever on the United States and England. In view of this, it is clear that the three (I discard China, because she will be an area requiring aid rather than able to give it), and above all America and Great Britain feared to commit themselves to too much. But little by little they came to the happy phrases of Teheran, when the three declared: "We shall see the co-operation and active participation of all nations, large and small, whose people in heart and mind are dedicated, as are our own peoples, to the elimination of tyranny and slavery, oppression and intolerance. We will welcome them as they may choose to come into a world family of democratic nations." *

The public which hailed with enthusiasm the results of the Moscow Conference, and later those of Cairo and Teheran, was then little disposed to listen to the criticisms that appeared in the press, not only the part of impenitent "columnists" but also of serious writers—criticism that even appeared in carefully considered and authoritative documents.†

The promptness with which the American senate incorporated in the text of its resolution on postwar policy the passage in the Moscow document on the future international organization gave the signal of American support for the new

---

* It is no act of misplaced criticism if at this point we express the hope that Russia may become truly democratic and eliminate from the Soviet structure all totalitarian features repugnant to political and religious freedom.

† The American Catholic Episcopate in its statement on "Peace Essentials," of November 13, 1943, observed that: "They [the Moscow declarations] do not, however, dispel the fear that compromises on the ideals of the Atlantic Charter are in prospect. Some things these documents imply by statement and, more significant still, by omission, leave an uneasiness in minds intent on peace with justice to all." The allusion to Poland and the Baltic states held good, in spite of the reference to the Atlantic Charter in the Teheran statement.

policy of collaboration, and without any doubt strengthened international solidarity.*

According to Cordell Hull, not only is American isolationism ended (the support of the resolution by such an isolationist as Senator Norris who was a most significant symptom), but the cryptic isolationism of Russia was also nearing its end. Indeed, he went so far as to tell Congress that "as the provisions of the four-nations declaration are carried into effect there will no longer be need for spheres of influence, for alliances, for balances of power or any other of the special arrangements through which, in the unhappy past, the nations chose to safeguard their security or to promote their interests." Mr. Hull's vision seemed the subjective impression of one who thought he had realized all his old aspirations.

As a consolation, we reproduce the passage from the Teheran statement which, we believe, is intended to interpret the Moscow decision. It says: "We recognize fully the supreme responsibility resting upon us and all the United Nations to make a peace which will command the good will of overwhelming masses of the peoples of the world and banish the scourge and terror of war for many generations."

*   *   *

All the conferences and declarations of the big three have so far shed no light on the future of continental Europe, though this problem is primordial. Two people are and always will be pre-eminent in continental Europe: French and German. The solution of their inherent problems will dictate that of the problems of the Mediterranean and of eastern Europe. The resentment of the French National Committee (now the provisional government) at not having been repre-

---

* The American senate in approving the above-mentioned resolution added that even the treaties which would result from it would have to be approved by the usual two-thirds majority. This has aroused grave concern for the future, since one-third of the senate would be enough to make the country relapse into isolationism. The two-thirds system could be justified when America was made up of thirteen states and was about to take its first steps of international policy, with the specter of Europe behind her back. Now it is not so. That is why the motion to accept a simple majority vote of both houses of Congress even for the ratification of treaties was most opportune.

sented at Moscow, and at not taking a decisive part in inter-Allied political agreements (apart from the presence of France on the council for Italy) was not only natural but also legitimate. With the constitution of the Algiers committee the representative or personal value of General de Gaulle and General Giraud could be disputed, but after the occupation of the whole of France by Hitler, after the liberation of French Africa, after the formation of an army and the liberation of Corsica (Algeria and Corsica are part of metropolitan France), after the notable military participation of the French army on the Italian front, it was both impolitic and unjust to perpetuate the friction and misunderstanding between the Algiers committee and the governments of London and Washington.

It has been objected that the Algiers committee had no legal right to succeed to powers, and that it could not be said to represent the French people. Those who argued thus, hair-splitters or slaves of the constitution, saw a *legal* succession in Pétain, who forced Lebrun to resign the presidency under duress, in Pétain who deceived France by assurances that were never fulfilled, and sought ratification of his powers from a parliament summoned under the clouds of defeat and German invasion and, in violation of the fundamental laws of the republic and of the popular will. Unless we are to attribute to the entire French nation acts contrary to its own interests, such as the cession of Indo-China to Japan, the resistance to the Allies in Syria, in Madagascar, in North Africa, in Morocco and in Equatorial Africa, the acceptance of German occupation of the whole national territory, every act of the Vichy government was unconstitutional. Pétain could not even boast of Badoglio's merit of having declared war on Germany, when Hitler openly violated the very terms of the armistice. Indeed Pétain continued to appeal to the armistice to help the Germans push back the Anglo-American invasion of June, 1944.

Mr. Churchill, in his speech of November 9, 1943, at the lord mayor's luncheon in London, spoke words full of sympathy for France, and advanced the thesis we are defending when he said: "We hope that France will rise again to her true greatness and will play a worthy part in shaping the progress of Europe and the world." He spoke of the pleasure with which he had observed the increased military power of the Algiers committee, but he returned to the old theme that its members are not "owners but trustees of the title-deeds of France." To attribute the quality of ownership to a government is distasteful to us Latins, even in the most attenuated sense, that of claiming a title-deed as its own possession. But apart from the philological aspect of the question (we should say *legal title*), it does not seem that the Algiers committee made any pretense of being a *constitutional* government of France, but rather a provisional organ of government.

This is not the place to repeat the unfortunate story of the relations between the Allies and France from the time of the invasion of Algiers (November 7, 1942), until the invasion of France (June 6, 1944), a story of resentment and misunderstanding by the French, of incomprehensions and lack of suppleness of the Americans, and of waverings between the two of the English. Only later shall we know for certain the background of so many errors, which left a streak of inevitable acerbity, despite the fact that during the invasion of France satisfactory accords were reached, marked by de Gaulle's visit to Roosevelt and the reception accorded him in Washington and New York.

Before the invasion of Normandy, the three principal Allies should have been able to make the gesture of associating Fighting France with themselves as a fourth power, both for its effect on the war effort and on European reconstitution. All that would have been needed was to make it conditional upon the formation of an assembly and a government that would freely reflect all shades of French opinion (except the Vichy collaborationists). Such a gesture was considered undesirable or premature. Thus France's position was weakened, creating a moral cleavage between her and her British and American Allies, at the very time when the liberation of France was due to the valor of American and British troops.

No one could imagine or wish a France in political and economic subordination to the big three, nor a Europe in which France was weak, divided and segregated. For the good of Europe there must be a strong France, sanely reconstituted and politically open. Just as the Maginot Line has fallen forever, so too must fall forever Pétainism on one side and that species of de Gaullism which appears to a "man on horseback" or to a nationalist and lay Joan of Arc. De Gaulle had the merit of not surrendering at the time of the armistice, of holding fast to faith in France and her values, of defending her interest and her honor, even before the Allies did, and thus escaped becoming a puppet into the hands of Roosevelt and Churchill. He enjoys extraordinary popularity in France, even in the midst of violent dissensions and opposition, because he stood firm in the storm, because he symbolizes French resistance. He will remain the hero of the dark days and the symbol of liberation.

Events in France progressed differently than Washington and London believed they would. The almost entire liberation of France, except for the line from the Vosges to Lorraine, was achieved successfully in a little less than three months, although the Germans tried to retard the offensive by bombing London and adjacent regions by means of the so-called "Robot" bomb—serial bombs launched from the French and Belgian coasts at a tremendous speed. Damage, especially in London, was very severe, but not such as to interfere with the offensive or disorganize the services.

De Gaulle and his followers were able to overcome their difficulties because they set foot on France, even during the offensive, participated in the liberation of Paris (where the patriots of the *maquis* wrote many glorious pages), organized the provisional government of France, and finally obtained recognition. London and Washington, acting under pressure of public opinion, granted France a seat on the European Advisory Commission in London. When the Dumbarton Oaks

Conference (of which more later) met in Washington, the four interested powers (China, Great Britain, Russia and the United States) agreed that France should be one of the states having a permanent seat in the security council.

De Gaulle has been recognized as the actual head of the French state and government, until a general election can be held. This cannot take place until the European war is ended and French prisoners in Germany have been returned. Also he has rapidly reconstituted the government, with the participation of all parties that kept faith with the republican and democratic traditions of France, and fought in every possible way the occupying Germans as well as the Vichy government, that they rightly held to be illegal and to have betrayed French interests. A consultative assembly was created in November, 1944, which included representatives of all parties, old and new. The difficulties of party orientation, the demands of the guerrilla fighters and underground resistance forces, the communist infiltration from Moscow, are problems that beset not only France but all liberated countries. France however has been able, through her foreign policy, to reassume the place denied her in vain for several years. Now she has returned to her traditional policy: with England an *entente cordiale;* with Russia a treaty of alliance.

The final act of this long political odyssey of the new France was the signing of the Washington declaration concerning the coalition of the United Nations. This took place on January 1, 1945, on the third anniversary of such declaration and was executed in solemn form at Washington in the presence of the diplomatic corps. Unfortunately, France was not present at Yalta. She deeply resented it, and though General de Gaulle was asked to sign the invitation to the San Francisco Conference, he refused, not without reason, because he was not in full agreement with the big three on the decisions taken at Yalta. Events will show whether or not those who today have assumed the task of the reconstruction of France *

---

* Georges Bidault, foreign minister, whom this writer knew and admired in the dark days of *appeasement* is one of the most promising men of new France.

can replace the nationalist tradition by a sound European internationalism, and whether or not the big three will allow France to acquire such an international position. It is certain that in the reconstruction of Europe (and there will be a Europe whether or not the three great powers want it) France will have to play the role of leading nation.

*   *   *

Germany was the most complicated problem of Europe. Before Teheran, Cordell Hull in reply to a question asked at a press conference said that "unconditional surrender" and the disarmament of Germany agreed upon in Moscow had ended the significance of the Free Germany Committee. This committee had been set up in Moscow on July 12, 1943 (the day the great summer offensive began), in agreement with Stalin and in harmony with his Germany policy as defined in November, 1942. He had said then that he had no intentions of destroying "all military forces in Germany, for every literate person will understand that this is not only impossible . . . but it is also inadvisable from the point of view of the future. But Hitler's army can and must be destroyed."

To forestall a German collapse in the convulsion of mob uprisings, or the disintegration of her political and economic structure, the Free Germany Committee issued an appeal to the German people with the slogan: "Germany must not die!" It was clear that such a committee was to have followed the Russian armies in the invasion of Germany and directed the formation of a civil government.

At Teheran, one thing alone was revealed in regard to Germany: complete agreement on plans "for the destruction of the German forces." The German people were not included in the destruction, except insofar as military necessity demanded. The silence at Teheran on the future of Germany may have been due to reason of war secrecy of which we know nothing, or to a lack of agreement among the three. Yet the problem appeared urgent for three reasons: first, that the German people should know what awaits them when its military structure fails to meet the supreme test; secondly, to be prepared (as they were not in Italy) in the event of a sudden collapse; thirdly, to avoid disputes among the three (or four, with France) and ill-feeling among other nations more closely connected with Germany.

The general feeling among the United Nations regarding the future of Germany leads to the conclusion that Vansittartism had gained ground and the voice of reason was growing ever fainter. Even the Morgenthau plan to reduce Germany to an agricultural status seemed strange and against the course of nature. Nations cannot die. Germany cannot be wiped off the map; and even if this could be done, it would be monstrous. To reduce a people to impotence, to place it in servitude, to destroy its industry, to prevent its trade, to institute forced labor, are all unfeasible aberrations. At Versailles the Allies made the mistake of demanding indeterminate reparations. Almost at once these had to be fixed in figures, then reduced and finally abandoned, while in addition loans were made which were finally written off as losses, both capital and interest. A fine piece of business, let alone the war which came of it!

Be it not said that all this was the result of gullibility, ignorance, condescension or folly. It was imperative to help Germany to her feet. The Allies were unequal to their task, first because of wavering and delay, then because of their policy of appeasement. But the same and worse would befall tomorrow, with a so-called strong-arm policy that would be openly destructive. It is impossible to create a vacuum in a country of eighty million inhabitants without bringing down the economic and political structure of the whole of Europe and for that matter of America.

We have no choice but to reconstruct. Germany, defeated and prostrate, must gradually regain her moral and economic health, and remain one of the cornerstones of the political edifice of Europe. He who writes these words is one who today sees the destruction that Germany brought to his own beloved country; who could not read with dry eyes the news of cities and villages razed to the ground, the shooting of hostages, the decimating of populations, the looting or burning of precious documents, books and works of art, and a thousand other brutalities that awaken an instinctive demand for justice and vengeance. But leaving the just punishment of criminals to international or local justice (according to the Moscow decisions), we must not lose sight of the fact that the main concern—even above the question of just atonement—is how to bring Germany back to a human and Christian sense of civilization.

The disarmament to be imposed on Germany will have to be total and effective for a period of probation (apart from a police force for internal order). The industrial transformation from war to peace will have to be complete, without however depriving Germany of means of production adequate for her needs and her subsequent development. Finally, educational reform will have to be as far-reaching as possible, facilitated but never imposed from abroad, for then it could bear no fruits and only hasten reaction. On the contrary, it must be promoted from within by civil and religious groups whose experience and convictions will necessarily fit them for such a task. For a period of some length the Allies will exercise a supervision over the new Germany that will be reborn out of defeat, until such time as she is able to regain possession of the rights of "sovereign equality" and become part of the "general international organization," or better, of the "family of democratic nations."

This optimistic vision of the future of Germany is founded on the principles of faith and on the methods of liberty. The Moscow Conference declared that democracy must be restored in Italy. Mr. Cordell Hull has stated that the lines laid down for Italy will also apply to other nations. The same must be said of Germany, unless Europe is to be thrust back into chaos.

No one can think of establishing in Germany, a dictatorial or military or capitalist or communist regime. A monarchy? A Hohenzollern to be sought among the many descendants of

William? It would be ridiculous to imagine that Moscow would want such a neighbor. There remains only a sound democracy, that will not fall into the hands of Junkers, of nationalists, of crypto-nazis or of makers of guns.

It is vain to think that by arms and oppression the victorious countries can impose a political system from without. Such a system must be born of popular conviction as circumstances dictate.* The policy of the Congress of Vienna, directed against the liberal movement of the nineteenth century, failed utterly. It would be the same thing today if the Allies sought to impose, either in Germany or any other country, a political system that was not really desired by the European peoples.

Some have suggested that Germany be split up into various areas—the Rhineland, Prussia, Bavaria and so on. Mr. Hambro, the well-known Norwegian statesman, has warned the American public against such a mistake.† It is essential to avoid in the defeated countries the resentment that would be aroused by enforced and unjust territorial provisions. In a post-war Europe we shall have a flaring up of nationalism, indeed it it already on its way. Let us hope that Britain and America, after all their sacrifices, will not have to face a wave of acrimony and dissatisfaction that is already beginning to be felt everywhere.

There is no need to divide Germany in order to keep her in her place. When Hitler began to manufacture tanks and airplanes, London and Paris could have fallen upon him within twenty-four hours. They did not do so. Let it not now be said that the fault lay with the Teutonic knights or Bismarck.

---

* At Teheran a phrase was coined which could apply to Russia (when she ceases to be totalitarian), but which is also suited to a Germany purged of nazis. The communiqué speaks of the day "when all people of the world may live free lives . . . *according to their varying desires and their own consciences."*

† Austria claims Berchtesgaden, which was taken from her during the Napoleonic period, wishing to prevent its remaining in Bavaria as a symbol of nazism; this can pass. Danzig will be expected by Poland, who demands rectifications in Silesia. The Sudeten will return to Czechoslovakia; this is to be foreseen from the cautious declarations by Mr. Eden to the House of Commons. These and other rectifications may be legitimate or useful: they have nothing to do with the dismemberment of Germany.

This is as absurd as it would be to deny that the France of Louis XIV and Napoleon, with the resources of their time, did to Europe more or less what was done by the Germany of Bismarck or of William II.

The Allied Advisory Commission in London had not revealed its plans. For purposes of military occupation, Germany has been divided into four zones: the east going to Russia, the west to England, the south to America; a special zone to France. A mixed commission has been formed at Berlin, but each zone will be autonomous from the military point of view. This, in the opinion of the author, is a very grave mistake, which can now no longer be remedied. The second point more or less agreed upon is that East Prussia will be divided between Russia, who will take Koenigsberg, and Poland, who will extend as far as the Oder, and a distance of two hundred miles along the Baltic with Danzig, of course, included. There is some idea, neither human nor Christian, of deporting the German population from these areas, to make way for new occupants. Prime Minister Churchill estimates that about ten million persons would have to transmigrate.* Lastly it is said that France although unwilling to annex German territory will insist on the separation of the

---

* As a first reaction to the speech of Winston Churchill to the House of Commons on December 15, 1944, on the Polish question, the author sent the following letter to the magazine *America* in New York (published in the issue of January 6, 1945):

EDITOR—Four "kind" words were repeated with great frequency by Winston Churchill in his House of Commons speech on the Soviet-Polish Frontier (December 15)— "Disentanglement," "transfers," "expulsion," "deportation" of populations. He predicts that, if Poland receives the western and southern part of East Prussia (the rest is reserved for Russia) in compensation for the loss of the zones east of the Curzon Line, there will be a need to "disentangle" the mixed populations, to "transfer" peoples of foreign nationality (foreign in respect to the acquiring state), to "expel" the conquered peoples and to "deport" them, even by force, into the appointed zone. According to Mr. Churchill's calculation, this would involve about ten million persons.

In order to convince public opinion that this was the question of an operation not only legitimate but useful, he recalled the expulsion from Anatolia and the deportation into Greece of about a million persons, referring to it as "an affair" that turned out very well. In truth, Mr. Churchill does not take account of the indisputable fact that these undesirable Greeks had been in Asia Minor since before Homer, that they had prospered under the Romans, later under the By-left bank of the Rhine from Germany, either as a French protectorate or as an international zone—it is not known which.

zantians, and that, good or bad, they had lived on their land in that region for five hundred years under the Crescent.

To say that such an action—which cost tears and blood, suffering and conflict—turned out well for the friendship of the Turkish and the Greek peoples has the same flavor as saying that a man who has committed suicide has done well because he has freed himself from melancholy and his wife from the worries he caused her.

Concerning the well-being of the people achieved by "creating" a single "race" (aside from the error of believing that he is actually dealing with a race), history contradicts Churchill—even the history of his own country. The value derived from ethnic diversity has been of great importance for the development of Great Britain: English, Scotch, Britons, Irish (not to mention the Latins, Danes and Normans) and other alien races have created the historic greatness, the language, the culture, the morale and political activity of that country. Nor can it be said that all is going smoothly even today between the "races" which have survived the ancient strifes: Ireland is not yet assimilated. Is Churchill perhaps thinking of the "kind" act of deporting the rebellious Irish?

The United States of America is the greatest argument against the theory of unity of "race." Here there have come together peoples of all the European countries, as well as of the Latin American, Asiatic and African countries. The system of religious, social, linguistic, ethnographic discrimination has been largely overcome by liberty, by the granting of equality and the rule of tolerance. And that discrimination which still remains will not be abolished by "transferring" thirteen million Negroes to Africa or to some island of the Pacific (and the same for all the other ethnic groups) but by *adapting them* to American civilization and *adopting them* as brothers.

Switzerland is the center of the European continent, and it gives visible proof of how three races and three different languages (four if we include Latin) can live together in equality and liberty.

The central point of criticism against Churchill (and even Stettinius, who, in the name of the American government, has promised to help Poland in such a "gentle" operation), is that forced deportation of peoples is against the laws of nature, offends the rights of the human personality, and constitutes not only an act of barbarism but an actual and undeniable *crime;* it is unworthy of those who impose it and those who profit by it.

If I were Polish, I would cry out to the people not to accept so evil a gift. If Poland has the right to claim a part of western Prussia in order to avoid the inconveniences of the old Corridor; if, as seems just to me, Danzig should go to Poland as an integral part of the state; the native population should remain where they are found—free, if they wish, to move away, subject, always, to the laws of the new state and with the necessary guarantee concerning the rights of ethnic and religious minorities.

I hope that the Polish people, who today must feel their tragedy as the gravest of all tragedies in the world, will see it as a Divine punishment for the mistreatment of the ethnic minorities in their territory during the twenty years of their rebirth as a state.

Poland's future must be prosperous and glorious; for this reason the new period cannot be begun with a crime (willed by others but agreed to by the Polish people themselves) of "expelling" and "deporting" the conquered peoples.

The big three after the Yalta Conference declared "we have agreed on common policies and plans for enforcing the unconditional surrender terms, which we shall impose together on nazi Germany after German armed resistance has been finally crushed. These terms will not be made known until the final defeat of Germany has been accomplished." The declaration made it clear that the purpose of the United Nations is to destroy nazidom and its evils. "It is not our purpose [they said] to destroy the people of Germany, but only when nazism and militarism have been exterminated will there be hope for a decent life for Germans and a place for them in the comity of Nations." This purpose was reaffirmed by Mr. Churchill and the late President Roosevelt in their following parliamentary addresses.

The unconditional surrender which was demanded of Germany (as imposed on the other already-conquered countries) cannot have any moral or political significance if it is not accompanied by a plan of European reconstruction including Germany itself. Up to now, no such plan exists, while it seems that plans are being made for the partition not only of Germany, but of all continental Europe, under the principle of spheres of influence.

*   *   *

Immediately after the Moscow Conference in 1943, Cordell Hull declared that all questions of frontiers for the European states would be faced and solved after the war, as any attempt to do so today would cause unrest. He also said that the Atlantic Charter still holds good, and this was more authoritatively repeated at Teheran, where it was clear that the so-called "Iranian question" was solved in such a way as to assure the territorial integrity and independence of Iran (Persia), against claims attributed to Russia and arising from the occupation by Allied troops. The idea was then that there would be no territorial aggrandizement on the part of the nations that signed the Atlantic Charter, and that territorial questions of rectification of frontiers or other details (excluding aggrandizement) would be amicably discussed between the countries concerned, subject, of course, to arbitration in cases of disagreement. The war has altered the boundaries fixed in 1919, has stirred up old interests and old wrongs, has created new ones, so that from this point of view Europe faces the ugly prospect of prolonged controversy and nationalist ebullition.*

Moreover the procedure outlined by Cordell Hull has failed completely, not through any fault of the small nations concerned but because of the very decisions of the three big nations, whether together or unilaterally. First things should always come first; this has not been done. Not having decided in time what to do with Germany, no one can tell what the situation of Europe will be, and so no clear solution has been reached concerning the problems of the smaller European states and their reciprocal rights and interests.

The first repercussion from this initial error has been in eastern Europe, because Stalin has refused to discuss his gains made during the period of neutrality, following the Soviet-German pact of August 23, 1939. By this agreement Russia obtained half of Poland, evacuated the population of German origin (almost eighty thousand of whom were property own-

---

* Apropos of this, the author published in the *New York Times* of November 15, 1943, the following letter, with the intention of avoiding newspaper controversy concerning the boundaries between Yugoslavia and Italy:

I cannot deny the Yugoslavs' right and interest in asking for the revision of the treaty of Rapallo, signed in 1920 by Italy and Yugoslavia, which fixes the present boundaries between them. For there is no doubt that the unhappy war between the two countries has called forth a wave of hatred and recrimination. But in order to denounce the treaty of Rapallo it is necessary to find a judicial basis to obtain what is asked for. This basis cannot be provided by the rights of the victors which are merely the rights of the stronger, nor by that of investiture of the three great powers to dispose of the boundaries of European states, a right which would bear an unfortunate resemblance to nazi practice.

The basis is given in the Atlantic Charter, which provides under Article 1 that the signatory powers "seek no aggrandizement, territorial or other," and under Article 2 that "they desire to see no territorial changes that do not accord with freely expressed wishes of the peoples concerned." "They" refers to the thirty nations signatories of the Atlantic Charter, among them Yugoslavia.

Let us wait until Yugoslavs and Italians have succeeded in throwing out the Germans and in establishing governments of their own choice. Then, in a friendly spirit, let us discuss boundary problems.

ers and men of business) from the Baltic states, and finally, by the plebiscites of 1940, incorporated these states in the Soviet Union. After Hitler attacked Russia and obliged in self-defense to accept American and British help and to sign the Washington declaration and the Atlantic Charter, Stalin always made reservations (explicit or implicit, one does not know which) concerning his *"acquired"* holdings. Roosevelt and Churchill were perhaps not in a position to clarify this point or else believed it better to leave the matter to time. Churchill went even further: on one hand he gave his open support to the Polish government formed at London after the Russo-German occupation of 1939, and on the other he entered into the Anglo-Russian pact which, in the eyes of the author, gave a first inkling that spheres of influence would be the fate of Europe. Stalin has always been firm on this point, in the difficult periods of the war as in most favorable periods. Not only has he not given way to a single inch, but he has maneuvered so skillfully that part of public opinion in Allied countries favors his claims; thus making his two conferees, Churchill and Roosevelt, powerless to oppose him.

Whether the Russian troops remained outside Warsaw, from early in August to the end of 1944, for military or political reasons cannot be said with certainty. It seems probable that Stalin did not want to enter Poland without an assurance that he would meet with no opposition from the Polish government-in-exile in London and the Poles who followed its instructions, and that in the meanwhile he set up a rival government to which he granted his recognition and support. This government was finally created at the end of 1944, when the national Polish committee representing the resistance movement and the socialist and peasant parties met at Lublin and attempted to organize themselves politically. They appointed Boleslaw Bernst as president of the Republic and as prime minister and minister of foreign affairs, Osubka Morawski. Conflict among the various Polish parties and differences among the Allies continued till the Crimea Conference at Yalta, where they agreed "that the eastern frontier of Poland should follow the Curzon line, with digression from it in some regions of five to eight kilometers in favor of Poland," and "that Poland must receive substantial accession of territory in the North and West." The accord reached at Yalta for the establishment of the role of government was not implemented before the Conference of San Francisco.*

Considering the affair of Poland from its inception, from the time when Russia occupied half of it (dividing the booty with Germany) until the Crimea Conference at Yalta, it must be recorded that the Poles have lacked diplomacy and statesmanship; America has lacked clarity and force; but England has lacked understanding of the European problem of which the Polish problem is an integral part.

Now Poland is caught upon the horns of a dilemma: either to accept the Yalta solution, the Curzon line and German territories in compensation, and to set up a government friendly to Moscow—or to undergo Russian occupation and face civil war between the Polish factions, without any possibility of real help either from England or from America.

People never lose hope in their rebirth, nor do they ever abandon their own national rights nor their own development. The day will come when Poland will find her way again. That way is locked in the mystery of the future. As we see it, the fundamental duty of the Polish people is not to accept the fatal gift of that German territory which is not absolutely necessary for an outlet to the sea, but Poland must also, in annexing Danzig and other lands, respect the native populations. She must treat them fairly, to assure the integrity of Poland and to guarantee to ethnic minorities their natural, civil and religious rights; finally she must seek to create friendships in the east and in the west, with Russia and with Germany; careful at the same time to maintain her own sovereignty in the future international organization.

Having said this about Poland, we cannot remain silent on our convictions concerning the rights of the Baltic states, of which London and Washington have made no more mention

* See Appendix VI.

than if they had never existed, although until 1940 they were members of the League of Nations and had diplomatic representatives in all the capitals of the United Nations. The silent suppression by diplomatic and political means of these three states lies on the conscience of the public men of England and America. It is in line with many things done before this war such as the partition and later the occupation of Czechoslovakia, the occupation of Austria and its incorporation in the Reich, the occupation of Albania—all acts which were not opposed but actually tolerated or favored, or passed over in silence by London, Paris and Washington. An encouraging sign was the awakening of public opinion, after its long quiescence lasting from June, 1942 (when there was an outburst of indignation at the rumor that the Anglo-Russian treaty had sold out the Baltic states), till the eve of the Moscow Conference. Thereafter, public opinion was agitated only by the Polish government in London, and by Americans of Polish origin. The voice of Baltic exiles or Baltic groups in America had almost always been weak and there were few reactions in the press and none in Congress.

The author has elsewhere expressed his opinion that the Baltic states have a right to political independence.* Certainly, Russia must protect herself for the future; but it seems clear that no one of the great powers is inclined to trust entirely to the "general organization." This is the worm at the root of the whole "security" question. Yet, just as Britain and France will never be threatened by Belgium, Holland and Luxemburg, Russia and Germany will never be threatened by the Baltic states or by Poland herself. Therefore, to apply the principles of the Atlantic Charter to them also, can do no wrong to Russia.

The plebiscites in the Baltic states, held during the period of Russian occupation and in wartime, must be considered null and void as held under duress. Cordell Hull once said that future plebiscites will have to be completely free. If the

* See *America*, August 28, 1943 (New York); *Il Mondo*, October, 1943 (New York); *People and Freedom*, November, 1943 (London).

Baltic states are to have a plebiscite on their incorporation in the Soviet Union, it should be asked for by the citizens of the states concerned, in conditions of complete freedom, without armies of occupation. Neither Russia, nor England, nor any other country has the right to impose a plebiscite on any nation in possession of its rights. But, unhappily, the alleged rights of victory fall more heavily on the weak than on the strong.

*   *   *

At the Moscow Conference, Italy received special attention,* and it was pleasing then to hear from the three foreign

---

* It is worth while to reproduce the whole text of the agreement regarding Italy, as follows:

"The foreign secretaries of the United States, the United Kingdom and the Soviet Union have established that their three governments are in complete agreement that Allied policy toward Italy must be based upon the fundamental principle that fascism and its evil influence and configuration shall be completely destroyed and that the Italian people shall be given every opportunity to establish governmental and other institutions based upon democratic principles.

"The foreign secretaries of the United States and United Kingdom declare that the action of the governments from the inception of the invasion of Italian territory, insofar as paramount military requirements have permitted, has been based upon this policy.

"In furtherance of this policy in the future the foreign secretaries of the three governments are agreed that the following measures are important and should be put into effect:

"1. It is essential that the Italian government should be made more democratic by inclusion of representatives of those sections of the Italian people who have always opposed fascism.

"2. Freedom of speech, of religious worship, of political belief, of press and of public meeting shall be restored in full measure to the Italian people, who shall also be entitled to form antifascist political groups.

"3. All institutions and organizations created by the fascist regime shall be suppressed.

"4. All fascist or profascist elements shall be removed from the administration and from institutions and organizations of a public character.

"5. All political prisoners of the fascist regime shall be released and accorded full amnesty.

"6. Democratic organs of local government shall be created.

"7. Fascist chiefs and army generals known or suspected to be war criminals shall be arrested and handed over to justice.

"In making this declaration the three foreign secretaries recognize that so long as active military operations continue in Italy the time at which it is possible to give full effect to the principles stated above will be determined by the commander in chief on the basis of instructions received through the combined chiefs of war.

"The three governments, parties to this declaration, will, at the request of any

secretaries at Moscow what antifascists have always said and repeated for more than twenty years, and what the Italian people themselves loudly demanded on the very day fascism fell, when from Milan to Palermo democratic parties (among them the Christian-democrats—formerly the popular party) made their voices heard. This proclamation of Italian democracy made at Moscow (where democracy has yet to be born) may have seemed curious. Likewise, the special plea placed on the lips of Anthony Eden and Cordell Hull, that "the action of their governments . . . has been based upon this policy," when we and all the world know what the Allies have done to hold back the democratic elements and to reach understanding with the reactionaries and ex-fascists, sounded like an excuse to justify what cannot be justified in the eyes of the Italian people. We note that so as not to appear simpleminded, but we attach little weight to it. We note likewise that democracy arrived in Italy in the guise of protection for certain antidemocratic or militarist factions and especially to defend not only the monarchy, but also King Victor Emmanuel, whose responsibility for twenty-one years of fascist domination cannot be transferred to people or unloaded upon a really democratic government.

But every cloud has a silver lining. The determination of the Italian people to have a democratic government, even during the war fought on its own soil, has prevailed over the intrigues of the lees of fascism, over the unjustified fears of Allied military commanders and over the incomprehension of the political leaders of England and the United States. First there was the compromise with the king and Badoglio, through which representatives of the six parties could participate, in the government (April 21, 1944), then when Rome was liberated, the king retired to private life conveying his powers to his son Humbert as lieutenant, and the new cabinet, headed by Ivanoe Bonomi, was formed as the expression

one of them, consult on this matter. It is further understood that nothing in this resolution is to operate against the right of the Italian people ultimately to choose their own form of government."

of the popular will to set up a new democracy and prepare the ground for a Constituent Assembly.

Thus, not from Moscow but from Rome, not by the suggestion of foreign powers as something imposed from without but spontaneously and from the people itself, democracy was born and reborn in Italy. The road to a complete realization of democratic ideals is long and full of difficulties in Italy, as in all the other European countries; but it is not without significance (and the merit belongs to the events of war and the Allied victories) that the first democracy to be reborn on European soil has been Italian democracy. This spontaneous revival has been stifled, from its very inception, by the Allies' belief that the Italian people were all fascist, and by the policy adopted by the AMG (Allied Military Government) of retaining the political police and economic structure of fascism and using its men.

This first phase was partly overcome by the passage of the southern provinces and later of the islands and the central provinces under the control of the Italian government. But at the same time the Allies placed so many political, financial and economic shackles on the government and on its administration that the rebirth of the country was made impossible. In many cases the needs of war were a valid and effective reason for this, in other cases they were simply a pretext.*

None of the desired changes were realized during the year and ten months of war fought on Italian soil against the Germans supported by the fascist faction. The armistice imposed on Italy in September, 1943, was still in force; the conditions added to this armistice on September 29 following were still secret; the political and economic control of the Allies was still operating though the word control has been dropped. All this in striking contrast to the promises and declarations

---

* The revelation made by the American press in January, 1945, of the secret report of Lord Halifax to the State Department, by which he made known the intention of the British government not to favor the economic reconstruction of Italy, gives the belief that the "exigencies of war" can be a pretext for cloaking so inhuman a policy toward the Italian people. It is said that Mr. Churchill has changed his mind on that subject.

of the Allied leaders, from the Moscow Conference down to
the most solemn joint declaration of President Roosevelt and
Prime Minister Churchill following the agreements reached
at the Quebec Conference held in the same month, on September 26, 1944.

It is no mystery to anyone that Italy was regarded by the
British government as in its particular sphere of interest, and
that it wished to have a decisive voice in Italian affairs. The
United States agreed to this. Stalin gave Churchill a free hand
in Italy and in Greece, so that he himself might have a free
hand in Poland, Yugoslavia and Bulgaria. All this is being
brought about more by the sequence of events than through
declarations of governments and debates in parliament.

Apart from spheres of influence (with which we shall deal
later) it is true that British influence is felt in Italy more than
that of America or Russia. Admitting that England has vital
interests in the Mediterranean, interests greater than those of
Russia or America, she cannot be allowed to become the arbi-
ter of the fate of peoples who live in peninsulas bathed by
that sea. Italy was not conquered. It surrendered unconditionally to the English and Americans after the declaration
of Roosevelt and Churchill, speaking for the United States
and the British commonwealth, that they had come as liberators. Liberators they have been, but not politically or morally
since the secret armistice terms have been maintained. Co-belligerency was a first step taken to overcome the status of ex-
enemy; after the contribution of its army, its navy, its air
force, and of Patriots in the struggle against the Germans and
against the fascists, Italy demanded a revision of her status.

President Roosevelt and Mr. Churchill often praised the
Italian military contribution, often promised to support the
democratic rebirth of Italy, recognized (in the declaration of
September 26, 1944) the urgent need of reconstructing its
power system, railroads, bridges and roads in the military
interest of the Allies.

In July, 1944, there was hope that some sort of provisional
peace would be signed with Italy. But, for some unknown

reason that has remained secret, the proposal which came from London never reached its conclusion.*

The extraordinary Italian situation derives from the fact that—although the British government is now officially in agreement with the American government in wishing to alleviate the deplorable economic conditions of the Italian people and to contribute to the rebirth of the country—the attitude of British representatives in Italy, the attitude of certain British journalists and public men, the statements of Eden and even Churchill himself, reflect an animosity that springs more from resentment against Italy than against fascism. This attitude seems premeditated. This opinion is already widespread in America and was expressed in a typical sentence by Myron Taylor, President Roosevelt's personal representative at the Vatican, with the rank of ambassador, that the British thesis is that Italy must pay and pay for her faults. †

At the end of September, 1943, Churchill declared that Italy had lost her colonies—and Eden repeated this in August, 1944. Their statement was unilateral and, to this very day, has never been endorsed by the American or the Russian governments. ‡

Up to the present, nothing specific is known about British or American ideas concerning Italy's boundaries with Yugoslavia and Austria. Recently it was disclosed in Washington that the State Department was in favor of giving Trieste to Italy, but not the rest of Istria with Fiume, nor the southern Tyrol.

It has often been stated that Sicilian separatism has been fostered by English agents. Opportunely, although somewhat delayed, came a statement by Foreign Minister Eden denying any special British aims in Sicily, and one by the American Office of War Information that the State Department in Wash-

---

* See in Appendix III, an article by Luigi Sturzo, published in *Il Mondo*, New York, November, 1944.

† This remark was contained in a U.P. dispatch from Rome on December 11 by Eleanor Packard.

‡ On the subject of the colonies, see in Appendix IV, an article by the author, published by *Il Mondo*, New York, October, 1944.

ington does not favor any Italian separation, particularly Sicilian.*

In substance, a rumor that has received wide credence is that the British government (perhaps till before the Churchill visit to the Italian front) wanted a weak Italy that could never regain its economic and political strength, so as not to constitute a threat in the Mediterranean. Such a policy would be diametrically opposed to that pursued at the time of the Risorgimento, when England supported Italian unity to counterbalance French influence. The author is not in Italy, nor has he any direct confirmation of such a rumor, but he is concerned over the concurrence of opinion on this point of the Americans returning from Italy. If this were so, the mistake of the British government will have most serious effects on the future of the Mediterranean and of Europe.

There may be some exaggeration on the part of Americans, in view of the secondary position the representatives of the United States hold in Italy. The divergence of the two policies in Europe do not concern Italy only. This is one of the weaknesses of the Allies. It has often been urged that America publicly define her foreign policy and state clearly up to what point she can or will commit herself in Europe. It is to be hoped that the Seventy-ninth Congress will give a clear answer, so that the president of the United States can make the full weight of American influence felt in Europe.

Italy awaits justice and understanding from the Allies, so that she may resume in Europe that place which rightly belongs to her as a free and democratic country.

*   *   *

* On September 18, 1944, the leader of the separatist movement in Sicily, Andrea Finocchiaro Aprile, in defense of one of his followers accused of having edited and circulated an underground manifesto against the Italian government, declared:

"We shall publish this manifesto without asking anyone's permission, because in Sicily we do not recognize the authority of any constituted Italian body. I am making public the fact that when Bonomi sought my arrest the Allied authorities laughed. And if I am here today, it is by the very will of the Allies."

May the Allies have promised Signor Finocchiaro Aprile immunity if he should commit acts against the public order? And for what purpose? It appears, as a matter of fact, that there are two policies in Italy: that which is announced in communications and in parliamentary speeches, and that which is practiced by Allied officials who are stationed in Italy.

Since the day the Allies invaded the continent of Europe, from the south, from the east and finally from the west, the differences of viewpoint between the three leading powers have increased, because of the lack of a clear policy and of an agreed policy. What happened in Algiers, first with Darlan, then with Giraud and finally with de Gaulle, happened in Italy with the monarchy and Badoglio, with the six parties and Bonomi; happened in Greece with King George and the different leftist and rightist factions (to the point where the British government believed it right to intervene with armed force to suppress armed revolt); happened in Yugoslavia with Tito and the Serbian military chiefs; happened in Belgium with the Pierlot government and the patriots—not to mention Rumania, Hungary and Bulgaria, where Stalin has not allowed British and American representatives to remain, and has not spared any of his real or supposed enemies.

At the end of 1944, notwithstanding the openly monarchist policy of London, all the Mediterranean kings were dethroned. Victor Emmanuel, the Savoy King of Italy, had had to hand over his powers to his son Humbert, as his lieutenant; George II of Greece (of Schleswig-Holstein-Sondeburg) had been forced to accept the regency of Archbishop Damaskinos of Athens; Peter of Serbia had been forced to accept a provisional regency for Yugoslavia; and Russia has its protégés in Rumania, Bulgaria and Hungary, so that the various kings of the houses of Saxe-Coburg-Gotha and Hohenzollern-Sigmaringen, and regent-for-life Horthy may look forward to prolonged exile. For that matter, Mediterranean and Balkan kings have not shone in history to the advantage of their peoples, and one is at a loss to understand why, after the passage of one hundred and thirty-two years, Churchill should wish to play the role of Metternich, notwithstanding that in the Atlantic Charter he proclaimed that the people should be left free to have the government which they believe most suitable for themselves. The friction that has arisen between the Allied leaders and the liberated peoples have been an indication of the inconsistent Allied policy in Europe, which has been alike devoid of sound principles, stable views and concurrent policies.

During the first days of 1945 there appeared in the *New York Times* two Cairo dispatches from C. L. Sulzberger, in which the views of the State Department of Washington on the territorial questions of eastern and southern Europe were explained.*

According to this correspondent "the plan has three parts. It provides for frontier rectifications by direct negotiations of the states concerned; it seeks to sponsor the idea of regional groupings, and it wishes to encourage the economic rehabilitation of these lands after their selection of a popular government." Concerning "frontier rectifications," the State Department, although it does not intend to interfere and will leave the interested states to settle their own differences, approves the granting by Italy to Greece of the Dodecanese Islands (from among which the island of Castellorizo is to go to Turkey) and favors the granting of Cyprus to Greece by England. America considers excessive the other Greek demands concerning the boundaries of Albania, Macedonia and Bulgaria, although regarding some rectifications as timely; she concedes it as right that Bulgaria and Yugoslavia should have access to the part of Salonika; for the Turkish Straits (the Dardanelles), she thinks that the existing provisions agreed upon at Montreux should continue. For Albania she proposes an exchange of territory with Yugoslavia, probably giving Scutari to the latter. Italy would give up to Albania the island of Saseno, and to Yugoslavia she would give Zara, certain Adriatic islands, Fiume and other Istrian regions, except Trieste and Gorizia to be left to Italy,† Bulgaria would withdraw to the 1939 boundaries, although retaining the southern part of Dobruja granted her in 1940 by Rumania. Rumania would cede Bessarabia and northern Bucovina to Russia, and

---

* The *New York Times* (January 1 and 2 of 1945): The Department of State is in the habit of confiding to certain journalists its proposals and the lines of its policy of the moment, and these bits of information are sent up as trial balloons, in order to determine the reaction of public opinion.

† See *Il Mondo* (New York). Some articles on Trieste question.

have all the northern part of Transylvania taken from Hungary, except for small changes in the Avad region. Concerning Poland, although disagreeing with the unilateral policy of Russia, the State Department would accept the Curzon Line as the Russian boundary but would leave Lwow and Bialystok to Poland; it would favor also compensating Poland by part of East Prussia and Silesia as far as the western bank of the River Oder. Poland would have to return the Teschen region to Czechoslovakia. Concerning the Baltic states. the opinion is that there is nothing more that can be done. Finally, concerning Austria (which at the Moscow Conference of 1943 was recognized as a political entity in its own right, distinct from Germany) the prevailing opinion is that it should regain the south Tyrol (or Upper Adige) which Italy received at the 1919 Peace Conference.*

Secretary of State Cordell Hull as well as his successor, Edward R. Stettinius, has always insisted that territorial problems should be deferred until after the war, unless settled directly by the parties involved. This reservation, however, did not hold, because, until the war was over, it was impossible to have in countries on the continent of Europe responsible government and free expression of the peoples' will, uninfluenced by the great powers whose prevailing interest was the winning of the war. What government is there for Poland, which can deal with Russia? What government for Greece, for Bulgaria, for Czechoslovakia, for Hungary, for Rumania, for Albania, even for Italy?

The very tests of public opinion the government of the United States is trying to make can only serve to increase the apprehension and the resentment of the various peoples concerned, and to favor the intrigues of nationalist parties and group interests, which seek to foment the rebirth of fascism or the spread of communism.

There is also the problem of Spain where it seems impossible that Franco and the Falange can long survive. The pro-

---

* After the agreement between Hitler and Mussolini, the majority of the German population in the south Tyrol (Alto Adige) accepted the transfer to Austria.

posal of a monarchist restoration is opposed not only by the republicans in exile, but also by a large body of people within the country. There is no Spaniard who wishes to have his country relapse into civil war, but so far there is no plan acceptable by all. Even in Spain, the people must walk blindly toward an unknown future, just as in all of Europe.

The big three at Yalta jointly expressed "their mutual agreement to concert during the temporary period of instability in liberated Europe the policy of their three governments in assisting the peoples liberated from the domination of nazi Germany and the peoples of the former Axis satellite states of Europe to solve by democratic means their pressing political and economic problems." The principle reaffirmed at Yalta for this purpose was that of the Atlantic Charter in order "a) to establish conditions of internal peace; b) to form interim governmental authorities broadly representative of all democratic elements of the population; c) to facilitate where necessary popular elections." Ensuing events have shown how difficult it is to implement such a policy for each case.*

* See Appendix VI on San Francisco.

11

United Nations Organization

ON OCTOBER 9, 1944, the text of the Dumbarton Oaks Conference proposals was published. This conference was held at Washington in two parts: the first conference included the delegations of Great Britain, Russia and the United States; the second the delegations of China, Great Britain and the United States. Russia, as is known, avoided at that time any meetings with China, because of the war with Japan, but met freely with the United States and Great Britain, also at war with Japan. Diplomatic protocol is much more complicated than it used to be.

The Dumbarton Oaks Conference proposals for a new international organization did not immediately arouse the enthusiasm of the American people, who remembered Wilson's fourteen points. Little by little, through discussions by scholars, statements by clergymen, political influence and newspaper controversy, a considered and favorable opinion has been formed, apparently capable of prevailing over America's instinctive and traditional repugnance to specific commitments in foreign policy.

The change in the orientation of the United States from isolation in 1920 to intervention in 1944 was one of the effects of the present war. After the enormous sacrifices of men and money to win the war, it would be stupid not to pledge the will and the energies of the people toward winning and maintaining peace. The United States emerges from the war as one of the powers most responsible for world order: for Americans to hold aloof would not only show a lack of sense and responsibility toward themselves and toward others, not only moral cowardice, but would be a sort of political suicide. The United States, however, is acquiring a sense of its task and its mission. The Dumbarton Oaks Conference was the first attempt to arrive at a future international organization.

It is obvious that public opinion in America (as also in other countries) is divided between those I would call *democratic internationalists* and *authoritarian realists*. The former insisted that the general assembly of states, as proposed at Dumbarton Oaks, would be reduced to more or less decorative functions. Under the provisions of the Chapter Five, this assembly may *consider* general principles of co-operation for the maintenance of peace and international security; it may *discuss* all questions related hereto; it may make *recommendations* in this connection; but that is all it can do. Whenever it is necessary to *decide* and to *execute* (in connection with any of the purposes of the "organization") the security council must be resorted to; the assembly can never have a voice nor interfere in what is the exclusive and absolute concern of the security council.

Moreover, only on the *recommendation* of the council can new member-states be admitted to the assembly. They can also, upon such *recommendation*, be suspended from the rights and privileges of the organization as member-states, having presumably failed to live up to their obligations.

Even in economic, social or other nonpolitical matters, the assembly might limit itself *to making recommendations*. Thus, from a legislative assembly, paralyzed by the rule of unanimity in political or otherwise important affairs, as was the case in Geneva, we pass to a consultative, powerless assembly, indeed a sort of minor child under a guardian.

The old assembly was antidemocratic, because every state, no matter how small, under the rule of unanimity, could affirm its independent sovereignty, and was thus able to veto the decisions of all the other states. The new assembly would also be undemocratic, because under the constitution the individual states will have renounced in advance all power of decision, with which they will have invested the security council.

So, the Catholic bishops of America, in their serious, well-balanced and on the whole favorable declaration on the international organization, have very properly asserted that this organization "must try to include, with due regard for the basic equality of rights, all the large and small, strong and weak nations" and that "its constitution must be democratic."

Opposed to this democratic conception were those who feared the weakening of the security council, which would be at the mercy of the assembly and its majorities that might vary considerably according to the fluctuating interests of the various states. They asserted (and it seems that their opinion is becoming the prevailing one in America) that the direction of the international peace might be the concern of the three great powers, because on them has fallen and will fall in the future, the responsibility for every world war.

I said three, because China (which is one of the great powers with a right to a permanent seat in the council) has not yet surmounted the crises of war and internal order, and because France, admitted at the eleventh hour, has not yet been given complete parity with the first three. Actually, the United States, Great Britain and Russia feel that they hold all power in their own hands. The other two associates may eventually succeed in asserting themselves, but it seems natural that for the time being, the *yes* or *no* of the United States or Russia, and relatively of Great Britain, will have greater weight than that of France or China. Whether we like it or not, the pentarchy is already established and its power will dominate the world.

In the Dumbarton Oaks plan no precise method is provided for voting in the security council, because agreement was not reached on this point before Yalta. The most debated points at the conference was the Russian proposal to assure the right to vote to the state interested in the question to be decided. This proposal was made in opposition to another, formulated in the course of the discussion, that although to validate the deliberations of the council, in addition to the prescribed majority the unanimous vote of the five states with permanent seats would be necessary, an exception was made in case one or more members of the council (even though holding permanent seats) were interested parties. The solution reached at Yalta was that decisions on procedural matters should be made by a simple majority of seven; on other matters by an affirmative vote of seven members including the concurring votes of the permanent members. A party to a dispute should abstain from voting only in preparatory or judicial decisions, not in definitive and practical decisions.

This required unanimity of the five permanent members seems perilous to many, because it gives any one of them a veto right, that would stall the international machinery. Those who defend this rule assume that peace can be maintained in the world only if the great powers, which alone have means and armies at their disposal, remained united, even in their deliberations, and find, in permanent co-operation, the road that will lead them to rise above their particular points of view and their national interests. To us it seems that this veto privilege, agreed upon beforehand, will always make the stronger of the five prevail over the weaker, whether they are states with permanent seats or elective seats or states not belonging to the council. The best way to achieve a necessary, although limited, functional dynamism of this council would be to require a minimum of three votes of states with permanent seats in secondary questions, or four in principal questions; and a minimum of three and four, respectively, of states with elective seats. Thus the rights of the minority would not be suppressed by maneuvers, nor subject to domination by others, as by a veto.*

* The precedent of the assembly of the UNRRA is excellent since the majority-system of votes was adopted, equal as between great, medium and small powers. Naturally, the administration of UNRRA is in Anglo-American hands, and no objection is to be made to this as a beginning. The papers spoke of a "Geneva of New Jersey," which will have pleased the friends of the "Geneva on Lac Leman." In the first conference of UNRRA at Atlantic City, the small European powers and those of Latin America took a good part. They made their voices and

The most dangerous of the measures proposed at Dumbar ton Oaks concerning the privileges of the five great powers affects the very constitution of the international organization In fact, any possible and even necessary amendments (since there can be no perfect constitution, once and for all) will have to be adopted by two-thirds of the assembly and ratified by each individual state in accordance with its own procedure; but they will not go into effect unless ratification is obtained from all the five states with permanent seats, plus the majority of the other states.

This measure tends to block from this very moment, all really interesting modifications; as any one of the five states can defeat any attempt at amendment, while all the other states, large and small, if they believe their rights have been infringed (and up to now very few of their rights have been recognized) will have to form a coalition of half plus one (at least thirty or more of them) to obtain the desired change.*

There is even more: the weapon of the veto may even be used by the parliamentary minorities of each state called upon to ratify the proposal. If, for instance, the United States of America retains the rule of a two-thirds majority of the senate for the ratification of the international constitution, the hostile vote of one-third plus one in the senate would be enough to defeat the proposed amendment, despite the favor-

feelings heard, even in the face of the delegates from London, Washington and Moscow. I do not say that they were always right. In the question of help to the Axis countries, the delegate of Great Britain upheld the right thesis: he did not prevail. Yet the method, which seemed lost forever, has been rediscovered.

I should like here to recall the precedent of the United States of America. When the confederation of the thirteen states was formed in 1776, each remained a sovereign state, with "freedom and independence and every power, jurisdiction and right which is not by this confederation expressly delegated to the United States." What was bound to happen, happened. The poor confederation remained without powers, without sufficient funds to guarantee its public debt, without authority and without an army to face movements of rebellion in each separate state. After about ten years, the Founding Fathers met in Philadelphia "for the sole and express purpose of amending the articles of confederation." The rights of sovereignty of the separate states, in regard to foreign affairs, defense, tariffs and interstate questions or those between states and the central government, were passed to the competent federal organs; thus the United States of America received its permanent form, even its life.

* See Appendix VI on San Francisco.

able vote of all the member-states. What may be said of the United States may also be said of Russia or China, of Great Britain or France, according to their present or future constitutions and parliamentary rules of procedure.

Another much debated point, in connection with the Dumbarton Oaks proposals, was the lack of any stated principles, to guide and regulate the activity of the security council for the maintenance of peace. The provisions of the Atlantic Charter, which today bear the signature of all the United Nations, was not incorporated nor mentioned in the proposals, nor was the assembly granted any directive power, nor was there any mention of traditional international law and of agreements previously established, not even as rules to be kept in mind by the international court in its decisions.

We agree with those who say that all this is presupposed so as not to hamper the action of the security council, and to permit the spontaneous adaptation of facts to principles, and not in pre-established form. It is necessary indeed to avoid too rigid rules and too precise pledges, but not to go to extremes, in which the lack of rules and laws will facilitate arbitrary measures and opportunism.*

One of the points that will necessarily have to be established in constitutional form is the definition of an aggressor, so that all the nations may know, even those nations who will eventually be outside the organization, under what conditions they may be subject to international sanctions. Not only should a nation which resorts to arms and attacks another nation be considered an aggressor; but also any nation which oversteps the armaments limitations to be agreed upon in common or imposed by decision will also have to be considered and treated as an aggressor; as also a nation which, having received the mandate from the security council for some measure necessary to the maintenance of peace and fails to comply with it, will have to be considered and treated as an aggressor. That they are in the right must not serve as a justification, because, if they have a right to assert against

* See Appendix VI on San Francisco.

another nation or against the international organization itself, they will have to resort to friendly mediation or arbitration, or they will have to seek a decision of the competent court, but never to make use of force, breaking pacts and violating collective discipline.

The nation that does not belong to the international organization, that is not a neutral nation, and has not made agreements with the security council, may also have to be considered a *potential* aggressor. I say a nation that is not *neutral*, because in this case, as in the case of Switzerland, it would cease to be a threat to the peace of the other nations. But in all other cases, it can be a threat, present or future, and should be treated as such, until it has been induced either to enter the organization and submit to its laws, or to enter into undertakings not to disturb the peace and therefore settle all eventual questions peacefully.

There remains the case of resistance to the aggressor. It is clear that one can resist an armed assault and in certain cases one must resist, though *"cum moderamine inculpatae tutelae,"* as the ancients used to say. At the same time, the nation assailed will have to appeal to the security council and the case brought up for its decision. Eventual resistance to aggression cannot be classified as war, any more than the armed intervention of the nations called by the security council to the defense. It would only be a question, in the first case, of opposing force to an act of violence, and in the second of police intervention.

It is true that a war between rebellious nations and the international organization could occur in the future, just as it did in America when the southern states seceded. This would not be a legitimate war, but one of those revolts against a central authority which, as those by partisan factions within a nation, can also occur, for various motives in an organization of nations. It would be imprudent not to foresee and prevent them in time, but it would also be foolish to feed the resentment of small nations and minority groups through the injustice of the big nations and majority groups, and to reduce an organization which is of a moral and juridical nature to an oligarchy of a few well-armed nations. The new organization will have to be so strong as not to fear the freedom of its members, and so democratic as not to fear the tyranny of its leaders.

The new and most interesting point of the international organization is Section B of Part VIII, relative to military sanctions for the maintenance of peace. Unlike that which had been established in the covenant of the League of Nations, the decisions in this matter do not concern the assembly of nations but the security council. This simplifies the procedure, gives a greater sense of responsibility and makes possible a timely intervention to prevent an aggravation of the situations. Moreover, the council is authorized in advance to use armed force, when necessary. To this end, a series of agreements is foreseen, either regionally among the states or between the states and the international organization, concerning the military contribution that may be required of them according to circumstances.

Special mention is made of the air force at the disposal of the security council, because with this force a rebellious state can more directly be obliged to fall back into line. Moreover, a military directive committee is proposed, to give advice to the security council. The various provisions of the three sections of this chapter, including Section C on regional arrangements, were well delineated, but all were of the opinion that they might undergo changes in the revision to be made by the assembly of the United Nations, hoping that both monopoly by the five powers with permanent seats in the matter of military sanctions and the dictatorship of the security council over the whole world would be avoided. This shadow which hangs over Dumbarton Oaks caused perplexity among the other nations which feared a strong decrease in their international status. At any rate, a revision of the proposals of this chapter will suffice to give common consent to the collective responsibility of all the nations.

The late President Roosevelt, in one of his election speeches, said that if war could be prevented for another ten or twenty years, keeping firm the international organization

(even if it were not perfect), we could overcome the danger
of a third general war. This is the idea that prevailed in the
political world, in establishing the international organization
which would be able to function and to intervene authoritatively at the opportune moment in quarrels among the nations, rather than to establish an ideally perfect organization
which in practice might be ineffective. It is for this reason
that much has been conceded to the promoters of Dumbarton Oaks, given the responsibility they must assume. Provided, however, that the way is left open for the necessary
amendments to the constitution when it is clear that it is not
functioning satisfactorily, and also provided that postwar
economic reconstruction will be undertaken with breadth of
view and generosity of impulse.

One of the mistakes of the past was precisely that of en-
closing world economy within customs barriers, anti-emigra-
tion laws, monopolist egoisms and international cartels. That
is why the proposers of the Dumbarton Oaks plan have
thought proper to leave to the new organization the task of
facilitating the solution of the economic, social and humanitarian problems of the United Nations. Unfortunately, the
phraseology of Chapter IX is too vague and general, the
duties of the assembly in this matter are merely advisory; *
there is no mention of the economic pledges, presumed in
the Atlantic Charter, nor is any mention made of the international labor office which still exists and is functioning. As
for the rest of the proposals, neither courage, nor breadth
of view was lacking. All peoples expect the general economic,
social and humanitarian affairs to be an integral and necessary part of the future organization for world peace.†

* The amendments to Chapter IX approved at San Francisco fulfilled the wishes
of all delegates and the public. See Appendix VI.

† One of the European problems which has not been foreseen by the conference
and which cannot be deferred since it is an integral part of the economic reconstruction of the coming world, and which must, therefore, be solved precisely in the
transition period, is that of tariffs. If we leave the separate states free to keep up
the prewar customs barriers or worse to raise them, for the sake of immediate
advantages or in order to protect parisitic industries, a circle of capitalistic interest
will be formed which it will be impossible to break.

It was not the task of the United Nations Conference at San Francisco to deal with the post-war questions. In spite of this, the first question that rises in everyone's mind is: What is to be done with Europe? Will it form a federation? Various confederated federations? An assembly of individual states brought together in a League of Nations? A continent divided into spheres of influence between London and Moscow?

A federation of the states of continental Europe, without Great Britain and without Russia (a plan that has met with a certain approval in the United States) would entail strange consequences. Either Russia and Great Britain would be its jealous custodians from outside, or the federation would gravitate now toward Germany, now toward France, creating an intolerable dualism, or else Germany would be reduced to impotence, thus creating within Europe itself a permanent hotbed of agitation and intrigues.*

Various federations are suggested: Latin; Scandinavian, including Finland; Russo-Polish, with the Baltic states; German, consisting of the states of Germany remade more or less along traditional lines; Danubian; Balkan; British, with

When the very life of the occupied countries is already compromised, and will be even more through the collapse of Germany and the effects of war, only the combined effort of all the states will be able to face the problems of reconstruction. Therefore, customs barriers should remain only as indicative of frontiers and not for the elimination of eventual imports, especially where neutral countries are concerned. There is an urgent need of agreements not to introduce new tariffs nor to raise existing ones to set up barriers where they do not already exist, and at the same time to promote understandings between neighbors for their gradual elimination. There can be no hope for a European confederation if a tariff policy is not fixed in the terms of the armistice. We do not ask that Europe should turn free trade overnight, or that the healthy countries (if there are any) should assume the burdens of the bankrupt countries: it is a case of taking measures in time to avoid the creation of a *de facto* situation that would prevent all reasonable understanding between the states for a real international organization.

Mr. Paul van Zeeland, who was prime minister of Belgium and was in charge of international economy, has supported the idea of an economic league and of free trade between Great Britain, France, Belgium and Holland, with a view finally to a single monetary standard—or at least a stable exchange—as the first seed of European understanding.

* Several times it has been stated in the press that Marshal Stalin is opposed to a European federation. If this were to exclude Russia, Stalin would be right in opposing it.

Holland, Belgium and Luxemburg; and finally Switzerland, as she is already. It should be noted that federations cannot be constructed *a priori* on paper * but must come into being through moral and material interests, according to the historical background of each. Standardization cannot apply here.

Of all the above-mentioned federations, apart from that of Germany (which could form a kind of United States instead of an artificially centralized *Reich*), the most natural would be the Danubian, Balkan and Scandinavian. Geography, tradition, ways of life and economy, would promote life in common. The others are merely literary combinations, chance political convergencies, or geographical curiosities.

The idea of an Italy united with France may have pleasing aspects, despite the resentment with which the Algiers press greeted the Sforza proposal in this connection.† But politically, it would be meaningless, unless to counterbalance British or German influence in Latin Europe; this cannot be an *a priori* aim, but can be sought only in the event that one or the other power were really to exercise undue interference, whereas there is a dawning awareness of the British interest to keep Great Britain united with the Latin countries.

Europe must move toward the unification of all states, including Great Britain and Russia.‡ It is hard to understand why so many Americans insist on considering Great Britain as an extra-European power. The fact that she is at the head of the British commonwealth and has in addition a colonial empire is no reason for cutting her off from Europe. France too has an empire scattered over the world, and, what is more, this empire had direct representation in the French parlia-

---

* Like those of Ely Culbertson and the Geopoliticians.

† Count Sforza in *Foreign Affairs* of New York (October, 1943), developing the thesis of Italy's good neighborship with the Mediterranean countries, outlined the idea of closer ties with France, to be extended, also, if possible, to Spain, Portugal and Belgium, as a kind of Latin federation to be brought into being without blueprints and following a line of practical steps as suggested by time and expediency.

‡ Naturally, Ireland, Iceland and Greenland, too, are in Europe and European.

ment. Russia herself must be considered in part a European power. What makes Europe is not geography reflected by different colors on the map, but tradition, history, culture and economic interests. The Europeanization of Russia has been going on for centuries. First Byzantium, to Christianize the Slavs, pushed as far as Moscow; then the emperors sought the northern and southern seas as outlets for trade; finally the intellectual and aristocratic elite felt the influence of France and Italy. For political reasons, the Muscovite empire drew toward Germany and Austria, annexed part of Poland, or fought against Sweden, and during the Napoleonic wars brought Russia into the European coalition, with Finland as a reward. If all this is unknown, merely because for twenty-two or twenty-five years Soviet Russia closed her frontiers, cutting herself off from the capitalist world, we can only conclude that for certain people the range of political knowledge is limited to what appears daily in the press, to be hastily read and as quickly forgotten.

Unified Europe is a historical necessity, especially now that Europe is passing through the gravest crisis she has known since the fall of the Roman empire. At first this unity will be in the League and through the League, in view of the fact that the problems of the defeated countries and of the countries occupied by the nazis will take no short time to solve. When the defeated countries are able to become part of the League of Nations, having passed whatever period of probation is considered necessary, then the European states will have to seek a general settlement, which today cannot be fixed as a blueprint since we do not know what tomorrow's world will be like.

Jan Christiaan Smuts, in his important address of December 3, 1943, at a private meeting of the United Kingdom branch of the Empire Parliamentary Association, gave the warning that in the "Trinity of Nations" (the three great powers) there is no perfect equilibrium and that Great Britain will be the weakest. His remark was opportune from many points of view that have been indicated more than once in this book. But he suggested a dubious remedy when he talked of reinforcing Great Britain, "apart from her position as center of the great empire and commonwealth, outside Europe, by working closely together with those smaller democracies in western Europe which are of our way of thinking, which are entirely with us in their outlook and their way of life, and in all their ideals. . . ." Such smaller democracies may be assumed to be Belgium, Luxemburg, Holland, Denmark, Norway, Sweden, so as to form a kind of crest to continental Europe. That this crest would be a reinforcement of Great Britain in Europe is most doubtful, but it is certain that it would be nothing but a similar pendant around Russia. Between the two groups there will always be such an enormous difference that England will never be able to make a solid bloc of it. Instead, Russia will dominate the eastern states with no counterbalance whatsoever. The rest of Europe will be influenced by the two groups, and form a zone that can be used not only for economic ends but for a policy that will certainly lead to a third world war.

Apart from this last remark (which may be taken as a presage of ill omen), the fact is that Russia is already working for her group of states in eastern Europe. The pact with Czechoslovakia, signed in Moscow twelve days after Teheran, though it had been in the air for a long time, gave the idea that in the co-operation of the big three, there was something lacking on Stalin's part. He was too quick to give the lie to Mr. Hull's declarations that in the future there would no longer be any spheres of influence or single alliances.

The protocol added to the Russo-Czechoslovak pact provides for the adherence of third parties if the two signatories are in agreement. The allusion to Poland was clear. The Balkan states are already under the influence of Russia, except Greece which is still (for how long?) under British control. Hungary and Austria are in the hands of Russia by right of conquest. In Italy also, Russian influence divides the political and social field with Britain.

These facts, with their lights and shadows, have developed

so rapidly that public opinion has not been able to keep pace with them and remains bewildered. Stalin and the chiefs of the Moscow government have given to the Soviet republics some degree of internal autonomy (which without political liberties will remain a potential scheme only), with the accent upon military formations and diplomatic representations. Among the sixteen republics are the three Baltic states: Esthonia, Latvia and Lithuania (which perhaps will reach as far as Koenigsberg). There is no need to speculate on Stalin's hidden motives. He is the Napoleon of the Russian revolution. He has begun to widen the narrow limits of communist economy, introducing private enterprise. He has attenuated the antireligious campaign, allowing an Orthodox Church, benevolent to the regime, to exist in Russia, tolerated and even favored. He has created a new and powerful national army which for more than three years endured the blows of the Germans on its native soil, drove them back over the Russian boundaries beyond the Elbe. Today the new Napoleon, with the title of marshal, has entered into an imperial phase; Russia is reorganizing internally to expand externally and assure for herself a zone of influence over friendly satellite countries.

Politics is never the result of a blueprint; it is at once tradition, invention, creation. . . . It may be that Stalin arrived at this point because of the delay in opening a second front; it may be that the enormous sacrifice of human lives that four years of war has entailed on the Russian front has created in Stalin's mind his right to expand in Europe as a guarantee against any future eventuality, including even a war with Great Britain. What hypotheses are not possible when stability in Europe is lacking? While Washington and London have been faithful to the pacts with Russia concerning armaments and provisions, they have not been able to furnish certain and secure plans for the future of Europe. So Stalin, notwithstanding the conferences in Moscow, Teheran, and Yalta has retained the political initiative and has played his cards.

Today one sees the error of seeking to restrict the responsibility of the war to the three big powers, of having sought the elimination of France, of having ignored the smaller states, of not having created during the war at least an embryo of the new League of United Nations; of having allowed the Atlantic Charter almost to collapse. Last, but not least, a little error with serious consequences, the mistake of having taken away diplomatic representation from the three Baltic states, leaving only diplomatic immunity to their former representatives.

Notwithstanding all this, we must not be distrustful of Russian policy; we must try to understand it and help it in its inevitable evolution. The changes desired by us of the West in the internal policy of Russia, as well as in the economic field, cannot be obtained in a day or by the will of one man alone. Maturity brought by the experience of war and the difficulties of peace is needed here.

We of the West also must change some of our ideas and orientations. If England pursues a "balance of power" policy in western Europe, Russia will pursue it in eastern Europe. But if England and America insist on solidarity not only of the three great powers but of the League of Nations, Russia could agree, did she not fear vacillations in the future. Stalin for his part is right in not feeling sure, because up to the present he does not see that America and England have any stable and firm long-range policy either in Europe or in Asia. After the speech of Smuts, came that of Lord Halifax at Toronto in January, 1944, in which he gave the impression of a policy to defend England's interests in the world, to reinforce her imperial basis. The Canadians resented it, fearing the specter of power politics.

English intervention in November and December, 1944, in Italy, Belgium and Greece, served to show that such a policy of spheres of influence was then openly pursued by the Churchill Cabinet, a thing that aroused the resentment of America and of the countries involved. Churchill has clearly stated that he does not intend to liquidate the British empire, and in this he is within his right, but with the policy of spheres of influence he liquidates Europe. America, it is said, has not yet stated definitely what she desires, and it would seem that she is not anxious to make definite and long-range commitments. England, on the other hand, in her desire to safeguard her interests, finds herself for the first time faced by two powers that have become more powerful than she is, each of which, in its own sphere, tends to become a hegemony. England fears for her future and, as everyone knows, fear in politics inevitably precipitates a serious crisis. England now finds herself in a serious crisis, although in this war she has been the courageous and indomitable standard bearer.

If England could have faith in the future international organization, she could overcome the crisis with which she struggles. However, with a Russia shrouding her policy a mystery—a Russia which, although one of the three powers, reveals herself foreign and opposed to the other two, and moreover is not very tractable (the Polish affair is one instance of this, but it is not the only one)—England has not the courage to stake everything on the international organization unless she can first arrive at agreement with the United States and, I think, with France.

The late President Roosevelt in his message to the seventy-ninth Congress reaffirmed world co-operation, the Atlantic Charter, the policy of rehabilitation of the liberated countries, the recognition of their right freely to establish for themselves the governments of their choice, freedom of commerce, and the plan for the international organization; and he called for unity for victory and peace. So far as generalities are concerned, the declaration of Roosevelt, made in the name of the United States, certainly answered the common feeling of all peoples. Mr. Harry S. Truman has pledged himself to follow the international policy of his great predecessor.

The principal doubt under which the United States rests is whether she will again delude the world by a suspicious, not to say isolationist, policy that will deter her from binding herself too closely with England and Russia on the question of European affairs. It is to be hoped that the memory of the error of 1920 (and the consequent Second World War) will spur her to assume her rightful responsibilities. The speech of Arthur H. Vandenberg, republican senator from Michigan, delivered in the senate on January 20, 1945, in answer to President Roosevelt's message was epochal, because it marked a change in the trend of the republican party. He voiced the prevailing American opinion and formulated constructive proposals which the federal administration at Washington as well as the London and Moscow governments would do well to take into serious consideration if they wish to avoid an aggravation of the present state of affairs. His fundamental proposal is for a tripartite pact to guarantee the world against the rearmament of Germany and of Japan; and the United States in agreeing to such a pact would consent, once and for all, that its president might act without any further authorization of Congress. Once the fear of a third world war by Germany or Japan is eliminated, it would be possible to have faith in the international organization of which the three or four great powers, or even five, with France, would be the fulcrum.

Senator Vandenberg further made an interesting point that once such a pact is concluded, the various changes made in Europe or elsewhere during the war should be revised by the new organization, because the American people do not wish to guarantee the wrongs that have been done to small and medium states by unilateral actions as in the case of Poland. Finally, he assumed (a thing not contained in the text of the Dumbarton Oaks proposal) that the new international organization would revise treaties and pacts become inapplicable thus following the spirit and the letter of Article 19 of the covenant of the old League of Nations.

American public opinion was almost unanimous in its approval of the stand taken by Senator Vandenberg, which effectively contributed to strengthen the vacillating foreign policy of the administration. From the strictly American view-

point, the level of the debate was raised, because the big three
must be on a par and the United States must not be treated
as "the American Uncle" (as they say in Italy) who pays,
grumbles, and follows the way the others have traced.

The conclusion to which one arrives is the same as our
point of departure: the alternative is either a real League
of Nations with its own legal and political powers, with its
own international police force, and the respective contribution of armaments by each state; or else the imperialist predominance (to call it by its real name) of the great powers
who would assume the responsibility for world order and
the protection (jointly or by spheres of influence) of the other
states. Any combination that could be worked out between
these two extremes, with the prospect of a third world war,
can only result in making one or the other predominant.*

It is possible to avoid the second alternative only if public
opinion will arise against the policy of spheres of influence
over the smaller states. It is ridiculous to insist that the
small countries are to blame for the disorder in Europe. The
crises of the old League of Nations were caused by the constant disagreement of the big five of that time. Now again
we have the big five (though not the same five as before).
In spite of this all nations in the coming organization will be
able to raise their voices, state their rights, seek to make the
new League more elastic and strive to show that great powers
have as much need for small powers as small powers have for
great, and that the new organization can flourish only if there
is solidarity, balance and mutual respect among all peoples
and states.

*   *   *

We cannot conclude this chapter without reference to the
Cairo Conference and the various Asiatic and African prob-

* In the Appendix will be found my treatise on the new League of Nations
which appeared in *The Contemporary Review* of February, 1943, and was reissued
as a pamphlet by the People and Freedom Group of London. It has been included,
also, in the *Reference Shelf*. Col. 16, No. 7 ("Reconstituting the League of Nations"), compiled by Julia E. Johnson, The H. W. Wilson Company, New York,
1943.

lems which the international organization will have to solve.

The importance of the Cairo communiqué lies in the fact that where China is concerned the period of uncertainty, suspicion and doubts was left behind and she took her place as fourth among the great powers. It is true that she did not sign the Moscow protocol, and she has yet to win recognition of her right to greater China. At Cairo her right to Manchuria, Formosa and the Pescadores was recognized. Thus the China of Marshal Chiang Kai-shek is in a position to over-come if possible the disintegrating forces within her borders and refashion the weak structure of her political system. The China that will emerge from the war will have the merit of the constancy with which she fought the Japanese when London and Washington had abandoned her to her fate.

The "Pacific Charter"—for so the Cairo communiqué may be called—after proclaiming that Japan must restore all she has gained by all her wars during the past fifty years (including Korea, whose right to independence has been recognized in principle)* does not say what will be the lot of the Japanese. A people of eighty millions cannot be enclosed on a group of islands as on a convict settlement, without infringing upon their human rights and creating a focal point of intrigues and constant disturbances. Just as Germany must come back pacified into Europe, so must Japan come back into Asia. Let us remember that Japan would never have undertaken so many wars if she had not been aided, encouraged and urged so to do by the world policy of the last half century. Just as Germany could have been checked in 1936 when she occupied the demilitarized zone of the Rhineland, so Japan could have been checked in 1931, and again in 1937. On the other hand, if a people has an excess population

---

* The independence of Korea, mentioned in the Cario communiqué, is a problem apart, but one connected with the general situation of China. The Korean provisional government at Chungking has made remonstrances against the not-too-happy phraseology of the Cairo communiqué in this connection, but the Koreans of the United States are jubilant. (Not so the Balts of the United States.) It is not clear whether Stalin has any intention to intervene in the future of Korea.

and a limited territory it is authorized by nature herself to seek outlets and to extend its activities.

Asia has other problems. That of India takes first place. It will be impossible to have a China in the forefront of the nations of the world and leave India for any length of time as a "colony." In spite of differences of race and civilization, and other difficulties in the way of giving autonomy to India, they will have to be overcome in one way or another before the war ends. To have a revolt in India when the war is over would put England in the wrong and arouse public opinion even more than it was aroused in 1919 by the revolt in Ireland.

Other Pacific problems arise out of the Asiatic colonies of France, Holland and Great Britain; out of the interests—in varying degrees conflicting—of the great nations, especially of the United States, which will claim its share of new possessions or mandates. All this will be matter for the international organization. The prevailing opinion in America is that an understanding should be sought between the interested parties, but who are they? The first would be the native peoples, secondly, adjacent countries, including Australia, New Zealand, India, Indo-China, Burma, Siam, China, the Philippines, and so on. We do not deny the interests of the United States and Great Britain, France and Russia too, but we ask ourselves whether at one and the same time they can be interested parties and trustees.

Asia now has her "Charter" (a first draft of it). Africa must have hers. For Africa, too, a first draft to do away with exploitation in the colonies, the position of the natives as inferior races, the backward conditions of life in the villages and inhabited centers, and to promoting civic and political education more adequate for local needs. The lines of a colonial program in Asia and Africa were given to the House of Commons in a few words by Herbert Morrison in January, 1943, when he spoke of "politics which can combine progressive policies of education with opportunities for native people to take an increasing part in the forms of self-government." The rest will develop of itself within the framework of the international organization where such peoples should have a voice distinct from that of the colonizing countries. The Arab world is in a ferment for its rehabilitation, and its great importance in Africa and in the Near East. Africa is still largely a geographical expression; with time it will necessarily become an economic and political continent on its own, with an important part to play between two oceans.*

A British cabinet minister, Richard K. Law, defined the Moscow agreement as "the first step and only the first step toward an articulated international society." Cairo and Teheran have been further "first steps." Dumbarton Oaks and Yalta other steps; finally the Conference of San Francisco, just at the very moment when nazidom was collapsing and the victorious Allied armies were crushing the last resistance.†

* Stalin is showing interest in Mohammedan populations; Mussolini did so in the past.
† See Appendix VI on San Francisco.

12

The Difficulties of Rebirth

ALTHOUGH IN OUR HEARTS we may have foreseen the worst, it was impossible to imagine the break-up of economic and civil life, the political disintegration of Italy, that followed as quickly as lightning upon the announcement of the armistice (September 8, 1943). We must go back to the period of the barbarian invasions to find such a breakdown. We must turn to the occupation of Sicily by the Modammedans to imagine what nazi occupation of beautiful Italian cities has cost, or to the Black Death to find so entire a collapse of a people's activity. But in addition to civil war, fascism gave us a demagogic and anti-capitalist republic to allure the masses who, fortunately, resisted seduction, threats and vengeance.

It was not inevitable that this should happen, but the Italian people were dragged by fascism into the European crisis and the ensuing war and have been forced to experience the tribulations of other European countries occupied by the nazis, so as to realize the gratuitous evil done by the fascist government to Greek and Slav brothers and to the French, not only in actual warfare but by a terroristic system of occupation. It is with deep grief that I write these lines. I hope my Italian readers will not resent my referring to Italy's share of responsibility for the war. Assuredly the majority of Italians never wanted the war; still less did the active minority that was fighting for freedom. It is unhappily true that the faults of political groups (especially of oligarchies) overflow upon subject peoples, who thus learn by experience how much better a mediocre regime of liberty is than absolutism with a façade of national greatness and economic prosperity. As soon as Naples had been taken (October 1, 1943) President Roosevelt raised the moral tone of the enterprise when he said, "The objective of Allied forces in Italy was to free Rome, the Vatican and the Pope, much in the manner of a crusade, while at the same time avoiding all possible destruction." After nine months Rome was freed, in great part undamaged, but on the road to Rome only smoking ruins were left, typical among them being those of Cassino and Montecassino.* After the capture of Rome Allied progress was considerable but the Germans awaited the Allied troops on the Gothic Line, from Pisa to Bologna. The stand there was long, but the end of the war on the Italian front has been so glorious for the Allied armies and for the Italian patriots and so rapid that many of the great cities of Northern Italy have almost been saved from destruction and miseries. The armistice was signed by the German plenipotentiaries at Caserta on April 29.

The wars fought by Italy after 1848 were all for unity and liberty. The war of 1848–49 against Austria, waged by little Piedmont, with the support of the Italian people (then divided into various states) was an audacious epic in spite of the political and military errors inevitable in such an undertaking. The achievements of Milan, Brescia, Venice, remain imperishable glories. Venice wiped out the dishonor of having fallen without a fight when she was occupied by Napoleon, bringing her republic back to life for a brief spell and heroically resisting Austria in 1849. Piedmont was defeated. Charles Albert abdicated and was succeeded by Victor Emmanuel II. In the bitter conflict a "No" (it matters not whether implicit or explicit) was enough to raise the moral and political fortunes of Italy. It was said that the new king and his government, given the alternative of a favorable peace if the constitution were abolished, or a harsh peace if

---

* That the destruction of these might have been avoided is now common conviction among English and Americans as it is common conviction that not a few bombardments of Italian cities were not necessary from a military viewpoint.

the constitution were maintained, chose the second out of respect for the will of the people.*

The second war, also against Austria, was fought by Piedmont in alliance with Napoleon III in 1859. It is not for us here to judge the military phases of this war which had its triumphs and disasters. What concerns us is the national spirit behind it, seeking the liberation of the Italian provinces from the foreigner and with national unity as its ultimate aim. The first was but half completed, for Napoleon III, fearing intervention by Prussia, stopped short halfway in spite of his treaties with the Turin government and made peace with Austria, winning only Lombardy for his ally. It was impossible for Venice to remain longer under Austria. Her position was unnatural and unjust, in view of her geographical location, her history, her wholly Italian culture. Hence a new war. Italy, already constituted as a united kingdom, allied herself with Prussia and fought again. In spite of local victories and the heroism of her soldiers, military fortune did not favor her; but Vienna understood it was her interest to give way, and Venice was redeemed. The Trentino and Trieste remained, however, under Austria, and were only won in the World War of 1914–18.

In none of these wars was Italy's national life compromised. Never was the government disintegrated, never did the country lose its political and administrative structure, never did parliament cease to function, never did the people remain aloof and hostile, never was civil war proclaimed by an illegal and spurious government, never did the foreigner occupy the country from end to end, never were the Italian army and navy, although then in their infancy, subjected to foreign command, disbanded or handed over to the enemy,

* The American historian McGaw Smyth published in *Modern History* (Chicago, 1935) a study on the armistice of Novara discrediting the legend of this No attributed to the young king (who was anything but liberal). But the facts which cannot be denied are the following: 1, the armistice conditions imposed by Austria on Piedmont were very heavy; 2, the constitution of 1848 was maintained in vigor, in spite of Austria's protests; 3, Piedmont directed all her policy toward revenge and thus came to an agreement with Napoleon III for the War of 1859.

never did foreign powers fight in Italy a war of their own and without our full consent.

Now all this had come about. History will tell us the worst of what is even now happening. Just as the depths of evil are not reached without sin, redemption cannot be achieved, even in the human natural sense, without sacrifice. Italian soldiers and the very people themselves, who ever since the day of the armistice have fought till the armistice of Caserta in areas occupied by the Germans, in Yugoslavia and on the French frontiers, showed not only that the Italian knows how to die for a noble cause, but also how sacrifice can ennoble a people that had reached the edge of the abyss.

The armistice signed in September, 1943, by the representatives of General Eisenhower and Marshal Badoglio was the official act that closed the past and opened the future of Italy. It might be said that the first act had been the fall of fascism on July 25, yet this was but the premise; only a complete breach with Germany could create the new status of Italy in her internal and international life.

The text of the armistice contained provisions obviously intended for a country that had admitted defeat and others, especially Articles 6, 7 and 8, which we can now say failed to take into sufficient account—even in the interests of the Allies—the danger of German occupation of almost the whole peninsula, including Rome. Consequently in the Balkans and in France, the Italian soldiers were surrounded and disarmed by the Germans or fled or were taken prisoner or resisted or took to guerrilla warfare as opportunity offered and according to the means and spirit of initiative of each unit or each man. In northern and central Italy, where the troops could unite with the citizens and make a stand against the Germans, they did so with promptness and courage. Some were overpowered, some betrayed, as in Milan. In Sardinia the troops and population were able to drive out the Germans, saving the Allies much fighting. So in the early days did the troops stationed in Corsica, and they would have continued had not the French on landing despised their company in the field and even kept silence as to their presence.*

Another point raised by the armistice was that of the AMG or AMGOT (Allied Military Government for Occupied Territories). This organization was set up to take the place of the legal governments of the defeated countries, as little by little enemy territory was occupied. It operated first in Sicily. But a government, when it surrenders and signs an armistice, does not lose its political, civil and administrative status, or even under certain aspects its military status, merely by having to submit to the conditions imposed. It is a contracting party, not an *evictus*. Thus, in France, Pétain remained head of the state with his own government and administration in spite of the fact that two-thirds and later the whole of French territory was occupied. On the contrary, Belgium, Norway, Holland and Luxemburg, which signed no armistices, had governments imposed on them by the occupiers. The question of the government of Italy was not raised in the armistice. It was stated in Article 10 that: "In particular, the commander in chief will establish an Allied military government over such parts of Italian territory as he may deem necessary in the military interests of the Allied nations." This formula was so broad that it could apply to the whole of Italian territory and, under pretext of the military interests of the Allied nations, result in *de facto* eviction.†

* Mr. Churchill bore witness to this in his speech of September 21 when he said that "the French have landed in Corsica and added to the Italian garrison there are actively attacking the Germans." And a little later: "At one site in Bastia harbor the batteries were manned by Italian and French patriots whom the Italians had been sent to put down. The fight was conducted by Italian destroyers and a British submarine." It appears that General de Gaulle resented the behavior of the French leaders in Corsica toward the Italians.

† That this was not a far-fetched interpretation could be deduced from the news given by an Associated Press correspondent (Edward Kennedy) writing on September 21 from "Somewhere in Italy" (published on September 27th). Above all he reproduces an article from the *Eighth Army News* (the official newspaper of that army) in its "Mainland edition in Italy," where it strongly objected to the possibility of having Italian soldiers as allies in the fight against the Germans. It said, *inter alia:* "The Italians, who sincerely cheer our troops today when they enter a new city, also cheered Mussolini. Now they find they backed the wrong horse. . . ." And it concludes: "We would then be doing Italy two good turns: Firstly, we would be getting the Germans out quicker than would otherwise be the case; sec-

Mr. Churchill, in the speech I have quoted, declared that it was necessary for the Italian people to rally round their own government to drive nazis and fascists from the soil of Italy. At the same time Victor Emmanuel was proclaiming, in a broadcast message, that the Italian flag still flew over the Italian fleet.

But even before the appeals of Badoglio, Victor Emmanuel or others, the Italian people had shown by strikes, sabotage and underground movements that they wanted to hear no more of either the Germans or the fascists. A few hints in the press show what such Italians were doing in Savoy and Yugoslavia long before the fall of fascism. If the Sicilian people had been truly fascist, the Allies could not have taken the island in thirty-eight days, with a loss of only 35,000 men. If the Allied troops had been Bourbon troops, they would have found the men and women of the villages fighting them desperately in the streets, instead of greeting them with flowers and fruit, kisses and cheer.

To write, as did the *Eighth Army News,* that the Italian people cheered the Allied troops just as they had cheered Mussolini was nonsense and revealed an utter ignorance of twenty years of Italian tragedy.

There were those who recommended a favorable policy toward Italy to save human lives among the Allies and obtain swifter and surer results by making use of her military forces. It was right that this should be taken into account, but why not take into account also the sympathies of a whole popula-

ondly, by making the Italians pay the price of their folly in believing in Mussolini, they will learn not to be foolish again." Such swashbuckling language is deplorable when used by the official paper of so valiant a corps as the Eighth Army. It certainly does not conform to sound policy or to the line followed by London and Washington.

Very different was the tone of President Roosevelt, in his message to Congress, when he said: "The unmistakably sincere welcome given to the Allied troops by the Italian people has proved conclusively that, even in a country which had lived for a generation under a complete dictatorship—with all of its propaganda, censorship and suppression of free speech and discussion—the love of liberty was unconquerable. It has also proved conclusively that this war was not waged by the people of Italy of their own choice. All of Mussolini's propaganda machine could not make them love Hitler or hate us. The less said about the feelings toward Mussolini, the better."

tion in the very country in which the battle was engaged?
These were of immense political value, not only in respect to
Italy but also in respect to the Balkans. Such an attitude
would have been at once a foretaste of European pacification
and the outward sign of the spiritual return of a people to
its liberty-loving past.

Both President Roosevelt and Mr. Churchill stated in
their official speeches that the heart of the Italian people
was undoubtedly with the Allies. I have already quoted President Roosevelt's message to Congress of September 17. Mr.
Churchill on September 21 expressed himself to the House
of Commons as follows:

"I will, however, emphasize some main points which stand
out. The first is that the Italian forces and the Italian population have everywhere shown themselves unfriendly or actively hostile to the Germans and everywhere have endeav-
ored to obey, as far as possible, the order of the king of Italy's
new government. The second is that every effort has been
made both by that government and its forces to comply with
the armistice conditions. Fighting is taking place at many
points between Italians and the German intruders and there
is no doubt whatever on which side the sympathy, hopes and
efforts of the Italian nation now lie.

"In Sardinia, for instance, which until lately was considered a major prize in itself, four Italian divisions have driven
out the German garrison. American forces have now landed
in their support."

His testimony carries all the more weight in that he had
doubted both the Italians (for him either fascists or revolutionaries) and Badoglio, uncertain of the latter's good faith
although, from the very beginning of August, he had let Mr.
Churchill know of his wish to surrender and at the same time
emphasized the German peril. The serious consequences of
this incomprehension with regard to men and affairs in Italy
were understood in the spring of 1944 when Churchill admitted to the House of Commons that military and political
errors had been committed in Italy. Among those errors he

perhaps did not place the fact that when he was appealing to the Italians to drive out the Germans and fascists, he added that "their empire has been lost, irretrievably lost." *

It is superfluous to repeat our view: the Allies must aim at the pacification of peoples rather than at their punishment. The oft-repeated expression "guilty people" in regard to Italy deserves no other reply than that which was given to the London *Times* by *People and Freedom* † when the editor wrote: "Let us clear our minds of cant . . . guilt is to be attributed only where there is actual responsibility, to those who deliberately accepted and furthered the fascist ethics, and to those, whether in Italy or abroad, who consolidated it by their approval and support."

Moreover, things immediately grew worse. Rome was occupied by the Germans, as were Naples, Salerno, Benevento, Foggia. The king, his son and Badoglio fled to Brindisi, without a government, without ministers, without a treasury, without archives. Under such conditions Badoglio was obliged by the Allies to sign, on September 29, the conditions added to the armistice—conditions which were described as most harsh and Badoglio asked to have kept secret so as not to give a forceful propaganda weapon to the enemy, and also perhaps to safeguard the king and himself, who had committed this act without any consent of the government or of the six parties, the moral representatives of the country. The secret has been maintained by the Allies in spite of the request made by the Bonomi cabinet and the leaders of the six parties to let the Italian people know the terms‡

*   *   *

On October 13th, in the name of the king, Marshal Badoglio declared war on Germany, denouncing the German atrocities on Italian soil, especially at Catania, Salerno and Naples, and proclaiming that "there will be no peace in Italy as long

* See Appendix IV, "The Italian Colonies."
† See "Guilty Peoples" in *People and Freedom*, September 15, 1943.
‡ See Appendix III on *"Provisional Peace."*

as a single German remains upon our soil." In a joint statement Mr. Churchill, President Roosevelt and Marshal Stalin
accepted "the active co-operation of the Italian nation and
armed forces as a cobelligerent in the war against Germany."
The word "ally" was avoided, for obvious political reasons
and to lessen the resentment of the troops who were ill-dis-
posed to accept as comrades in arms the very men against
whom they had been fighting the day before.

So we may discount the recriminations echoed in the press
of the United Nations and the references by nearly all the
war correspondents, news writers, columnists and politicians,
to the "guilty nation that must pay for its misdeeds" or worse,
to the "faithless nation that passes readily from one side to
the other." It is human that such things should be said, even
if their authors do not remember the Atlantic Charter or the
invitations of Mr. Churchill, President Roosevelt and General Eisenhower to the Italian people to rebel against fascism,
in order that "Italy may regain an honorable place in the
family of nations," and other like expressions.

The suffering and heroism of a people that is finding its
soul again may not be sufficiently appreciated by the Allies
(just as normally there is little appreciation of Italy's contribution to the last war, and the part she played in preventing
the collapse of France). On the contrary, all those who until
yesterday were praising fascism and fascist Italy, naturally
treat the Italy of today and the Italian people with lofty disdain. There are moments in the life of peoples as of individuals, when a sacrifice made in silence and humility is worth
a thousand times more than worldly success (such as fascism
had for twenty years) and recognition on the part of others.
Italy, in the misery of defeat and while her soil was still occupied by the Germans, raised herself morally to a higher
position than she held before fascism, even if in the future
she does not receive the place that is her due.

Mr. Churchill, President Roosevelt and Marshal Stalin
hastened to declare that the armistice and the other secret conditions remain in force despite Italy's entry into the war,

save for such modifications as it will be possible to make "in the light of the assistance which the Italian government may be able to afford to the United Nations cause." The measure of the help that Italy could give had already been discounted from several points of view, for it is well known that the chief contribution is that of the fleet. The army did not have adequate weapons and depended entirely on the will of the American and English military leaders, but the moral contribution that Italy gave had a value in itself, above and beyond the hundred thousand troops, more or less, that were put into action. Nobody can minimize the enormous help given to the United Nations cause by Italian patriots since the day of the armistice, and the glorious days of the Naples revolt against the Germans. If France had made the same gestures as did Italy, and with the Germans in the house (as they were in Italy) had declared war on Germany, she would not only have redeemed herself (as has Italy) for the betrayal of her Ally Britain in 1940, in the darkest moment of the war, but she would have given the death blow to the nazi reign, even if she could not raise a hundred or two hundred thousand men and even if Pétain himself had been compelled to flee to Spain or had been made prisoner. Moral values always count more than material ones, but they are of special worth in certain moments of crisis in the life of a people.

In 1940 de Gaulle's gesture counted for France. If de Gaulle had not existed, it would have been necessary to invent him. Would that there had been an Italian de Gaulle! But who would then have accepted him? The idea of an Italian legion, though belated, did not fail to occur to the Italian refugees in America, and received much support and encouragement. But the American and British governments, which even then had in mind another policy for Italy, never gave their approval. Hence the absence of the lead-line that from outside could have connected the Italian people with the Allies in the war without incurring the charge of having betrayed the ally of yesterday or the suspicion of wishing to profit by the ally of today.

That is why, apart from any other consideration, it would have been better if the declaration of war on Germany had not been signed by Victor Emmanuel III, who in May, 1939, had approved the treaty of alliance with Germany, or by men like Badoglio, who had made war against the Allies. It should. have been left to. the true representatives of the Italian people, who never wanted the war, to raise the banner of the liberation of Italy from the foreigner.

Fortunately, in their declaration, Churchill, Roosevelt and Stalin, after taking account of the Badoglio government's pledge "to submit to the will of the Italian people after the Germans have been driven from Italy," added their guarantee with the words: "It is understood that nothing can detract from the absolute and untrammeled right of the people of Italy by constitutional means to decide on the democratic form of government they will eventually have." This pledge was reaffirmed at Moscow and after Moscow, as many times as opportunity presented, during the ensuing political crisis and parliamentary debates.

From the moment freely formed parties with an open democratic tendency were able to express the popular will, to the extent permitted by the difficulties of war, there has come to the surface a strong and clear determination to break with the fascist past and with the men who were responsible for it. Among those singled out in the first place were the King and Badoglio, and at the same time those officials and army commanders who had a fascist past.

It is not necessary to re-examine here the political crises that, at the end of January, 1944, led to the Bari congress, where the six parties of the committee of liberation unanimously called for the abdication of the king and the formation of a popular government. The king's refusal was followed by the formation of a cabinet to dispatch current affairs, still under the presidency of Marshal Badoglio, but without the co-operation of the political parties. That government, remaining however under control of the Allied Commission, had the direct administration of part of the liberated South (Naples excluded) and of the islands of Sicily and Sardinia. The seat of the government passed from Brindisi to Salerno.

Because of the hostile attitude of the parties reunited in the committees of liberation, negotiations were resumed through De Nicola, president of the chamber of deputies before fascism, who secured the king's promise to retire from the exercise of his royal powers and name his son Humbert as lieutenant. At this point reference must be made to two notable facts due to the initiative of Stalin: the exchange of ambassadors between Moscow and Salerno, and the consent of Badoglio and of the Allied military authorities to the return to Italy of Togliatti, a communist refugee in Russia under the name of Ercoli. The latter persuaded the communist party to drop its opposition to the king and to participate in a government presided over by Badoglio. Some of the liberal leaders and Christian-democrats had already supported a similar policy, but the weight of the communists was decisive in inducing the other parties of the Left to accept the proposal. The Allied Control Commission consented, making it evident that the king and Badoglio were to be kept in power until the capture of Rome. So on April 21, 1944, a new compromise government under the presidency of Badoglio was constituted with the participation of all six parties.

When Rome was liberated, the king yielded his powers to the lieutenant, his son, who accepted the proposal of the Rome committee of liberation and named Bonomi prime minister (although he had previously sent for Badoglio). Bonomi succeeded in forming a ministry composed of civilian elements (except the ministers of the navy and of air), democratic in faith and opposed to fascism. The exclusion of Badoglio and the decision not to take the oath of allegiance to the crown disquieted the Allies, especially England; they found even more disturbing the increasing concern of the Italians in regard to the secret conditions of the armistice. Naturally as a condition for the recognition of the Bonomi government the Allied Control Commission had insisted upon the observation of these conditions and their secrecy. Concerning the oath of allegiance the government held fast to the new formula.* At the same time, having decided to postpone the monarchial question until Italy had been liberated from the enemy, it pledged itself to abstain from any act whatsoever that might prejudice its solution until the convocation of the Constituent Assembly.

The story of the fundamental disagreement between the Italian people and their political groups on one hand and the Allied representatives in Italy on the other hand will be told in its own time, after Italy has been liberated from her enemies and is once more completely her own mistress and free from any further control by her friends. But at this time it is necessary to be frank: the enthusiasm with which the Allied troops were greeted, from their first landing in Sicily until the liberation of Rome and Florence, has been decreasing little by little, as the physical sufferings and moral humiliations of the people have increased—people who believed that the Allies had from the first distinguished clearly between fascism and Italy, between the fascist criminals and the Italian people. Such a distinction has been almost entirely lacking, to the point where Allied officials have, for many months, made use of fascist leaders for public administration under the pretext that they are unable to find capable persons to take their places, and have guaranteed fascists and others equally responsible against dismissal from their posts, or against incrimination for their past deeds (especially in the case of military leaders for "reasons of war"). But when it was a question of using harsh and arbitrary methods against the people, then the answer to the complaints and the protests was ready enough: they were dealing with ex-enemies, who deserved this and more for not having prevented Mussolini's declaring war on the Allies. They seem to have been unaware that that war

* The members of the government swear on their honor "to exercise their functions in the supreme interest of the nation and until the convocation of a Constituent Assembly not to engage in any acts that may in any way prejudice the solution of the institutional question."

was declared by Victor Emmanuel and waged by Badoglio (as chief of the military staff), the very men with whom they had established contact and had imposed upon the country.

There is nothing worse for a people than to be humiliated by its "friends" and "liberators," to hear them justifying their broken promises by blaming faults that are not personal faults although pressed down, like a crown of thorns, upon the brows of all the people. This is all the worse when those faults, like that of having left Mussolini in power, are shared by the same Allies, who until 1940 supported Mussolini and paid no heed to the anti-fascists.

The psychological ill effect can be traced to a number of reasons: first, that while for Italy the distinction between fascism and the Italian people is denied in word and deed, for France the distinction between the people and Vichy was accepted without discussion, not so much on account of the merit of de Gaulle and the French patriots (who for a long time were ignored and opposed) as in accordance with a more intelligent and realistic policy. Italian resentment rose even more after Russia published the armistice terms signed with Rumania, with Finland and Bulgaria, while those with Italy imposed by England and the United States were maintained secret.

If we add to this the material damage done, the cities and villages destroyed, the artistic patrimony damaged and lost, the misery of the people without food, clothing, housing, left a prey to devastating inflation and largely without work, together with the fact that there were millions of prisoners and deportees in enemy and friendly countries alike, no one can deny that Italy has paid a high price for her liberation, undergoing suffering far beyond her strength.

All this notwithstanding, our gratitude still lives for those soldiers who died on our soil, giving their lives so generously; our faith still remains firm in the justice of the cause for which the Allies fought. There was no weakening of our determination to fight side by side with the Allies, which, in relation to the part played, was always underestimated and at times scarcely noticed. The atmosphere seemed to change after the visit of Churchill to Italy, in August, 1944, although his message was padded by a little lecture on democracy to the Italian people and a little sermon on the lynching of Carretta.*

* * *

There was even greater hope when President Roosevelt multiplied his promises to Italy, which culminated in the famous communication of September 16, 1944,† signed also

* The crime of the exasperated Roman mob which, through tragic misfortune, lynched an innocent, is among those things which arouse feelings of reproof and horror, even taking into consideration all the attenuating circumstances. (It can be assumed that there were provocative agents; certain the authorities on the spot lacked foresight and courage.) All this taken into consideration, we do not seek to justify either the pharisaic resentment of foreign correspondents, who forgot that lynching is indigenous to certain of their countries, or the fact that they did not attach the same importance to the lynchings which (according to report) occurred in France and Belgium, showing that mass pathology during the war is not exclusively an Italian disease.

† The joint statement of President Roosevelt and Prime Minister Churchill on postwar Europe (*New York Times*, Washington, September 26th):

The president and the prime minister had further discussions Monday and Tuesday, September 18 and 19 at Hyde Park, on subjects dealing with postwar policies in Europe. The result of these discussions cannot be disclosed at this time for strategic military reasons, and pending their consideration by our other Allies.

The present problems in Italy also came under discussion, and on this subject the president and the prime minister issued the following statement:

"The Italian people, freed of their fascist and nazi overlordship, have in these last twelve months demonstrated their will to be free, to fight on the side of the democracies, and to take a place among the United Nations devoted to principles of peace and justice.

"We believe we should give encouragement to those Italians who are standing for a political rebirth in Italy and are completing the destruction of the evil fascist system. We wish to afford the Italians a greater opportunity to aid in the defeat of our common enemies.

"The American and the British people are of course horrified by the recent mob action in Rome, but feel that a greater responsibility placed on the Italian people and on their own government will most readily prevent a recurrence of such acts.

"An increasing measure of control will be gradually handed over to the Italian administration, subject of course to that administration's proving that it can maintain law and order and the regular administration of justice. To mark this change the Allied Control Commission will be renamed 'the Allied Commission.'

"The British high commissioner in Italy will assume the additional title of ambassador. The United States representative in Rome already holds that rank. The Italian government will be invited to appoint direct representatives to Washington and London.

"First and immediate considerations in Italy are the relief of hunger and sick-

by Churchill, who added other declarations on Italy in his speech made two days later to the House of Commons.

But things grew worse again: the promised measures including the most important from a moral point of view, the gradual elimination of political and economic controls, were delayed, the situation became more critical; political suspicions of maneuvers between foreign agents and monarchist and neofascist groups increased; dissension among the six coalition parties became serious and for a while insurmountable, giving rise to the government crisis at the end of November. This lasted until December 11th, because the English ambassador, Sir Charles Noel, made it known that London would not consent to Count Sforza either as prime minister or as foreign minister. The intrusion of London was so inopportune and mismanaged that the Department of State at Washington took exception to it, declaring that Washington had no objections on its part to the nomination of Sforza and to allowing Italy to establish for herself whatever government she chose; while in London Foreign Minister Eden and Churchill himself persisted in their attitude, using rather immoderate language against Sforza and the six coalition parties.

The crisis was overcome by the formation of a second Bonomi cabinet based on four of the six liberation parties (the

ness and fear. To this end we instructed our representatives at the UNRRA (United Nations Relief and Rehabilitation Administration) conference to declare for the sending of medical aids and other essential supplies to Italy. We are happy to know that this view commended itself to other members of the UNRRA Council.

"At the same time, first steps should be taken toward the reconstruction of an Italian economy—an economy laid low under the years of the misrule of Mussolini and ravished by the German policy of vengeful destruction.

"These steps should be taken primarily as military aims to put the full resources of Italy and the Italian people into the struggle to defeat Germany and Japan. For military reasons we should assist the Italians in the restoration of such power systems, their railways, motor transport, roads and other communications, as enter into the war situation, and for a short time send engineers, technicians and industrial experts into Italy to help them in their own rehabilitation.

"The application to Italy of the Trading with the Enemy Acts should be modified so as to enable business contacts between Italy and the outside world to be resumed for the benefit of the Italian people.

"We all wish to speed the day when the last vestiges of fascism in Italy will have left Italian soil, and when there will be no need of any Allied troops to remain—the day when free elections can be held throughout Italy, and when Italy can earn her proper place in the great family of free nations."

socialist and action parties remained aloof) and without the participation of Count Sforza.* The Allied Commission gave its approval, under the same conditions as were laid down in June after the liberation of Rome concerning the secret conditions of the armistice and the oath of office.

The international aspect of the government crisis in Italy was of great importance, not only because it revealed that the Department of State in Washington was not in agreement with British policy on Italy as well as in Europe, but also because it gave Mr. Churchill an opportunity to explain to the Commons his policy and his reaction to the criticism in England and abroad of his actions in Italy and Belgium, and especially in Greece and Poland.

A London correspondent noted that the exaggerated resentment of Eden and Churchill against Sforza was not entirely due to "the intrigues [of Sforza] which ended in the expulsion of Marshal Badoglio from office" (as Mr. Churchill told the House of Commons, with little regard for historical accuracy), but because Sforza had never been enthusiastic over the terms of the armistice (perhaps Badoglio was retained for this purpose as *persona grata* to the British) and because Sforza resented Eden's declaration about the future of the Italian colonies and opposed giving Great Britain some Italian bases for her navy. If so, would it be impertinent to say that Churchill and Eden can never expect any Italian prime or foreign minister to accept such a hard and humiliating policy? Is it extraordinary that Italian statesmen seek to protect their country by appealing to the United Nations for justice and liberty? For that very reason whatever Mr. Churchill has said and done or will say and do in favor of Marshal Badoglio and the Italian monarchy will certainly be detrimental to both, because the people will have the impression that they have not firmly and fully defended Italian rights and interests.

---

* Count Sforza withdrew from public office and refused the post of ambassador to Washington through a sense of responsibility toward the country and of dignity toward himself, after the personal attacks of the British prime minister.

In this picture, the British veto on Sforza has had no personal effect: the man, the diplomat, the antifascist, the exile, the statesman will be judged without reference to a not disinterested animosity. Sforza's answer to Churchill is notable for its calmness and clarity. Mr. Churchill pictured his veto as an opinion expressed by the British ambassador in Rome to someone who made an inquiry. In my opinion this was a diplomatic retreat because of the statement Mr. Stettinius made about the American policy of noninterference in Italy. But saying, as Mr. Churchill did after those violent attacks in the House of Commons, that Italy was free to put Sforza in charge as prime minister or foreign minister seemed insincere. But Mr. Churchill went further: he declared that the six parties of the committee of liberation in Italy were acting "in their personal and political interests." This charge is usually made against all parties, even about British and American parties, but not as a specific accusation made in a foreign parliament against parties and their leaders who fought hard against Germany and the fascists and for the common cause of liberty inside and outside their country.*

The improper interference of the British government in Italian internal affairs had this result: Signor Togliatti, head of the communist party and an envoy of Moscow, the man who made possible the second cabinet of Badoglio in April, 1944, also made possible the second cabinet of Bonomi in December, 1944.

The discussion on British policy continued during December and the first half of January, 1945, so that Mr. Churchill thought it necessary to restate his position. His address of January 19 was most important. With some reference to President Roosevelt's message, he clarified four interesting points for the future of Europe. First, although the British have sacrificed everything, they ask nothing in return except that consideration and respect which (as he said) "are our

* I personally know the chiefs of the Christian-democratic party; for twenty years their sacrifices for a free and democratic Italy have been constant and valorous. The other parties too have men of unusual morality, dignity and self-sacrifice. I hope that Mr. Churchill will be able to find men of the same quality in the British House of Commons.

due and if that were denied we would still have a good conscience." Second, that "enforcement of unconditional surrender in no way relieves the victorious powers of all their
obligations to humanity or their duties as civilized and Christian nations." Third, that the application to liberated countries, or repentant satellite countries, "of the principle of a
government *of*, *by* and *for* the people must be set up on the
basis of free universal suffrage, elections with secrecy of ballot
and no intimidation." Fourth, that in the forthcoming conference of the big three "a demand will be made for the creation of machinery with power to deal quickly and jointly with
international political problems," as Mr. Eden declared in
winding up the debate.

These four points met with general acceptance as the basis
for a better policy in Europe, great importance being attached to the proposed machinery with which, it is to be
hoped, no more unilaterial moves and decisions will be possible. A new European policy must be a concerted policy
with the full responsibility of all three (or better four, with
France) great powers.

In such a symphony, Mr. Churchill's harsh note toward
Italy (with reference to Spain) was out of tune.* It seemed
to give evidence of a plan in contradiction to his four points.

Italy has never asked to be a partner of England in a "political combination in Europe." Italy had asked only for a revision of the unnatural and illogical status of ex-enemy cobelligerent, and for full participation in the war side by side with
the Allies. Spiritually and in fact such participation began
before the armistice itself. It was accepted by the big three
with the declaration of cobelligerency on October 13, 1943.
Since then our navy has been fighting side by side with the
British fleet; our air force, our soldiers, our patriots were in
the field, fighting with courage, determination, ability and
sacrifice. It was a strange coincidence that at the very time

* Churchill said: "Let me say once and for all that we have no political combination in Europe and elsewhere in respect of which we need Italy as a party.
We need Italy no more than we need Spain, because we have no designs which
requires the support of such powers." I do not know if Mr. Attlee could say the
same words.

when Churchill was making such unpleasant references to Italy, Stalin laid down the conditions of an armistice with Hungary and immediately published them (January 21), showing more understanding, political psychology and fairness than his other two democratic partners.

In spite of all obstacles Italy must look calmly at the situation with a firm decision to improve it by all means in her power. The "fragile" nature (using Mr. Churchill's own adjective) of the government was a matter of concern to all Italians. But, for the time being, it is not possible to have in Europe a government constitutionally based upon the popular will; it is sufficient that it be representative of the popular will. The basis of the Italian government has been and must be the six-party coalition, in spite of occasional cleavages. Italy will certainly meet with new refusals, incomprehensions and miseries; that is the way to remake her destiny. The help and friendship of the United Nations are asked and offered. It is neither useful nor generous to add humiliations on the one side and resentments on the other side.

The new provisions announced in Rome on February 24, 1945, by Sir Harold MacMillan were another step made in the name of the Allied governments. Mr. Churchill declared three days later in the House of Commons that he had brought about these provisions in fulfillment of the promises made on September 26, 1944. Five months of waiting do count. Moreover, the Allies allowed Italy to have diplomatic representatives in friendly and neutral countries and empowered them to carry on diplomatic correspondence freely. They stated that the Italian government should no longer be subordinated to the Allied Control Commission which was transformed into the Allied Commission with consultative duties.

The main obstacle in the rebirth of Italy was that the secret terms of the armistice were obstructing the effect of each provision, of each concession, putting the country in a humiliating position and preventing the reconciliation of Italy and the United Nations. At Yalta no mention was made of Italy and consequently there was no place for her at the San Francisco Conference. The rebirth of Italy is hard in itself, but it is harder because of the incomprehension of the Allies and their uncertain and incoherent policy.

Finally, the end of the war and the liberation of all Italian provinces came the last week of April, 1945. The Italian patriots showed their complete mastery of the situation and liberated the main cities like Bologna, Genova, Turin, Milan, Venice even before the Allied armies had made contact with the German commands on the spot. The Committee of the Liberation reorganized the civil life of the towns and villages very quickly so that collaboration with the Allied authorities was made easier and mutually more confiding.

The armistice with the German forces was signed at Caserta, April 29. On the same day Mr. Churchill sent to President Bonomi the following telegram: "I look forward to the time which cannot long be delayed when Italy whose forces have co-operated in the war with those of the United Nations will work with the United Nations in the more fruitful labor of peace."

The end of Mussolini, executed by some patriots marked the inglorious liquidation of the fascist republic and the end of civil war among Italians. Though objectionable from a judicial viewpoint, it was an act of popular justice. The ensuing scene at the Piazza Loreto in Milan was disgusting and against Christian respect for the bodies of the dead.*

* * *

* The author, asked by the Press Service of the National Catholic Welfare Conference in Washington, made the following statement:

"The name of Mussolini will always be linked to the worst tragedy that has befallen Italy through the centuries. But though he has been the main factor of that tragedy, he was not the 'only man,' as Mr. Churchill once said. He was helped at home by those politicians and capitalists who feared the participation of the working class in the political life of the country, and abroad by those conservative leaders in England, France, and elsewhere who in their dealings with Mussolini began to apply the policy of appeasement, from Corfu and Fiume to the Abyssinian war and the intervention in Spain. Without Mussolini we would hardly have had Hitler and the present war.

"Mussolini was obsessed with the idea of an Italian fascist empire, but because

There has been and will be in Italy much discussion of the future Constituent Assembly. The fear that such an Assembly might be revolutionary was soon overcome. In a State that has just undergone an anticonstitutional, arbitrary and tyrannical revolution, such an Assembly is a return to constitutional ways.*

The Albertine statute given in 1848 to Piedmont and Sardinia was of paternalistic origin, and was based on feudal right. It was the king who gave the charter to the people and swore to it; the people, through their representatives, accepted it and swore fealty to the king. This corresponded to the historical period of the Holy Alliance on the one hand and of constitutional agitation with a liberal tinge on the other. The result was a compromise adopted, with shocks and revolts, in more than half of Europe. By plebiscites the Albertine statute was accepted by the other Italian provinces, as one by one they became united to Piedmont and so it became the constitutional law of the new kingdom of Italy.

From the time of the unification onward, the statute of 1848 was a symbol of liberty and remained intangible in the law, although it underwent theoretical or practical interpretations adapted to the spirit of the liberal state, well on its way toward democracy. The periods of the states of siege, anticonstitutional in spirit though not in form, were corrected by successive enlargements of political participation by the people, and in the very use of the rights of the crown. The march on Rome was an anticonstitutional revolt rather than a revo-

he was mainly a demagogue and not a warrior he had never entered a war without the apparent certainty that victory would be on his side. Thus, in the present war he was hesitant to commit himself until he saw France knocked down and believed England was gasping to death. Otherwise, he preferred this usual method of playing with two decks of cards, a method in which he showed special ability and in which he persisted to the last.

"Now he is a terrible ghost for all Italians, even for those who in past times, and in good faith, believed him to be a new Constantine. Even some of the good achievements realized through twenty-one years of dictatorship were infected with fascist poison and have perished with fascism.

"Fascism must not survive its author, for the rebirth of Italy must be brought about in the name of Christian morality and democratic liberty."

* As one of its first acts, the Bonomi Ministry issued in June, 1944, a decree-law on the Constituent Assembly.

lution; the king failed in his duties as custodian of the constitution when he accepted the accomplished fact of armed revolt by a group of citizens bent on seizing power by force and imposing their will upon the country. The fascists damaged the spirit and the letter of the Statute even to the extent of suppressing every political liberty and every civil guarantee.

It is a mistake to think that with the fall of fascism and the abolition of fascist laws, the Albertine statute has automatically returned to vigor. The two sources of authority that from 1848 to 1870 gave it life, the monarchial concession and the popular plebiscites, no longer have the same juridical relation. The monarchy of that time was based on the triple tradition of feudal right from which it drew its origin, of the divine right of absolute monarchs of the sixteenth to the eighteenth centuries, and of the historical right affirmed at the Congress of Vienna. Only a minority participated in the plebiscites which expressed the popular will, but for lack of better this minority believed itself to be the interpreter of the populations of the various provinces that were being annexed to Piedmont by virtue of arms. The ulterior process of the constitutional adaptation to democracy finally resolved the dual basis of the statute into the more natural, more modern and more sound foundation: the will of the people. For this reason the monarchy (or the presidency in case of a republic) is nothing but an institutional authority endowed with faculties and subject to duties, responsible like all the other institutional authorities (and never irresponsible); and can, therefore, be dismissed like the feudal kings of antiquity or the king of England in 1934.

This was the inner meaning of the gesture made by the ministers of the Bonomi cabinet in refusing to swear the traditional oath of allegiance. Whatever the compromise for immediate adoption under the power of an alien will—that of the Allied governments—the gesture retains its full worth for the future.

The net result is that the people have reassumed the right to adopt a new constitution, without any relation to the stat-

ute of 1848. If the representatives of the people in the future
Constituent Assembly wish to retain the monarchy, it will not
be the same monarchy as of old, for it is not the monarchy
that will grant the charter to the people, it is the people that
will decide the rights and duties of the monarchy. The king
will no longer be the guarantor of the constitution; the people
will control the king in the exercise of his high function and
see to it that he maintains himself within the assigned limits.
In substance, the king would be a president of the republic
for life (save for removal), while the president would be a
constitutional king for a limited number of years and with
the possibility of re-election, as the case might be. In fact,
apart from the ecclesiastical appanage that still belongs to the
kings of England, the king may be called in the constitutional
evolution of that kingdom a president for life who wears a
crown.

Having made this clear, and without taking into account
the well-known leanings of the author, the problem of monarchy or republic ought to be well defined before the Constituent Assembly to spare Italy the sad sequence of events
that poisoned the political and religious life of France after
1870. Even if the members of the Constituent Assembly vote
for a republic, by a majority of one or by the same majority
for a monarchy, the country, after the decision has been
reached, should not be so profoundly divided between monarchists and republicans as to perpetuate for generations a
bitter and tempestuous struggle. There ought to be a moral
understanding among the parties, by which the minority is
content to abide by the vote of the majority and to accept
either the republic or the monarchy in the new and constitutional spirit of true democracy. Otherwise, the sad result will
be a perennial political division at the very time when the
country must be reconstituted, protected from external harm
and reintegrated in its international position.

The same is true with regard to the religious question. The
relations between Church and State can well be omitted in

the provisions of the new constitution, where two fundamental clauses would suffice, liberty of conscience and respect of the rights and position of the Supreme Pontiff as head of the Catholic Church, leaving its practical application to the legislative and executive organs of the state. But aside from the problems of the Lateran treaty and the related concordat, which we have dealt with in Chapter 7, there will surely arise the question of Article I of the Albertine statute, concerning the state religion with discussions pro and con that will disturb the mind of peoples and render difficult the understanding among the parties. It is the opinion of the author that this article was a relic of the period of the Reformation and Counter-Reformation, when the prince adopted his own religion and imposed it upon the states, giving to religious minorities the choice either of emigrating in search of a benevolent prince or of submitting to the civil and religious disabilities of the epoch. So it was in France for the Huguenots after the abrogation of the Edict of Nantes, so in Ireland for the Catholics (the majority in the island, but the minority in Great Britain) prior to emancipation. Since the nineteenth century, Catholic countries bound by a concordat have preserved this policy with various dispositions concerning other cults, while in the spirit of the modern state (as in the United States, France, Holland, Belgium and other countries) equality of religious rights and the freedom of worship have prevailed.

Italy today has a concordat: every change that the state may wish to introduce must, according to the author, be negotiated in a friendly way with the Holy See. Certainly it is right and desirable that in the fundamental law of the state there should be a reference to God as the author of human rights such as that made by the founders of American democracy as well as the recognition of the right of public divine worship according to the traditions of the country.

I do not pretend to solve the problem; I hope as a Catholic and as a priest that a formula may be found which will calm the consciences of all, the great Catholic majority as well as the Protestant and Jewish minorities.*

One or two chambers? I am for the bicameral system: it is surer, it integrates legislative power and creates a tradition of stability. The chamber of deputies is to be elected directly, with the system of universal male and female suffrage of all citizens who have reached the age of twenty-one. The electoral system does not form part of the constitution: the author prefers the system of proportional representation, with individual choice, in districts of two or more provinces united together. The number of representatives should never exceed six hundred. A five-year periodic renewal seems preferable, save in the case of the dissolution of the chamber before the end of its term, for the purpose of ascertaining public opinion on most serious issues, or when there is no other means of resolving a conflict of views either between the two chambers, or between parliament and the government, or the head of the state himself. For the dissolution of the chamber the opinion of the council of ministers suffices, but the head of the state should have the privilege of asking the opinion of the council of state † before taking a definitive decision either one way or the other.

There is no longer any doubt that the senate will be elected: the popular party in its program of 1919 proposed a second-degree election, by representatives of provinces and communes, universities and academic bodies, professional unions of employers and workers. Today I find nothing better, unless it be to include representatives of the judiciary, the state officials and of the Church. These latter representatives ought to be co-opted by the senate itself, in limited number, say one-

---

* Gaetano Salvemini has taken upon himself to prove to Americans that practicing Catholics in Italy are only a minority of about 20 or 25 per cent and that many of them are true idolaters who adore images and statues of the saints. Basing his proof on the statistics for the Easter Communion and on the lamentations of the bishops, he concludes that Italy cannot be called a Catholic country. He himself agrees, however, than when it is a question of baptized people who marry in church and have a religious burial, the Catholic percentage is above 90 per cent. Let us keep this last figure as the legal reckoning, leaving to the Church the task of caring for her flock.

† In Italy the council of state is the high administration court (see next page).

tenth. Three hundred senators seem quite adequate a number for purposes of control. The senate should not have the initiative in financial matters.

There should also be a third body, the council of state, composed of state officials by virtue of their office, of senators elected in part by the senate, among its own members, and appointed by the government. This council should pass upon the constitutionality of any law whatsoever, on appeal by a number of citizens or communal councils or other public bodies, or even by the government itself.

The election of the president (in the case of a republican regime) may well be made for a seven-year term by the two chambers in congress assembled, under two-thirds rule for the first and second polls and a majority vote on the third poll. The same system could be adopted for amending the constitution. It is the opinion of the author that the right of referendum should be introduced as a method of legislation when a given number of electors ask for it, or if the government should consider it an opportune method to decide important issues under debate, to avoid the dissolution of the chamber and at the same time acquaint itself better with the opinion of the country.

The establishment of regional divisions should be effected by the constitution and not left to legislative fluctuations. According to the author, each region should have civic administrative and economic powers as an autonomous entity and be an organ of state decentralization. Once this has been laid down in the constitution, all other provisions should be left to parliament, in matters concerning the state, and to local initiative in matters concerning the self-organization of the individual region. It is understood that the council of state could intervene in case the constitution was violated.*

There is no need here to insist on matters that no one to-day discusses, on matters that come under the head of a bill

* Since August, 1943, there has been in Sicily a strong group that maintains the thesis of separation from the kingdom of Italy and the constitution of a Sicilian republic. The author expressed his opinion in a motto, accepted by the Christian-democrats of Sicily: *"Autonomy, Yes; Separatism, No."*

of rights. Probably some groups will wish to revise property rights and inheritance. On this point one ought to be precise and leave no opportunity for doubts. We must reconcile property and inheritance rights with state intervention, not only for fiscal reasons or reasons of public utility as in the past, but also for social reasons. These rights will have to be well defined so as to remedy injustice and avoid the insecurity of individual and family inheritance, which would be harmful to the very increment of productivity and utilization of sources of wealth.*

One cannot turn back, but in the need and under the impulse of progress it is necessary to move gradually and allow time for the maturation of the problems. Italy today is an ailing and not a healthy body. After twenty years of totalitarianism, it is first of all necessary to breathe liberty, to have it and to carry it into effect. The author does not fear far-reaching political and economic reforms; he fears chaos and demagogy of the Right or of the Left, and especially he fears a relapse into totalitarianism.

* The cabinet formed at the end of June 1945 under the presidency of Prof. F. Parri with the participation of all six parties of the Liberation is making the necessary steps for the Constituent Assembly.

Conclusion

THE PREAMBLE of the new constitution ought to contain a clear rejection of fascist theories and methods, repugnant to an elementary concept of civilization, the affirmation of those principles of political life that are the achievement of true democracy and of the Christian tradition, and the premises for an international order based upon human solidarity.

It is the duty of the Italian people, who at first fell into the toils of an exaggerated nationalism (to use the definition of Pius XI) and of a totalitarianism masked by respect toward the Church, to repudiate fascism, not only for the evils it has caused us, but also because it has altered the spirit of the triple universality of Roman law, Christian faith, and Italian culture. Let us not allow ourselves to be deceived anew by nationalist suggestions which will be all the stronger after the present war if our fatherland emerges humiliated and depressed. It is more dignified for a people to face its own adversity than to gloat over the adversity of others and take pride in the harm done to other peoples under the mask of greatness.

From the day the liberation of Sicily began, gradually moving toward the north, the demand for the purification of the country from the laws, methods and the men responsible for our woes has been strong and constant even when it seemed that the Allies were hesitating and the government, improvised in July, 1943, was seeking their support. Now there has been a great airing out of our house which for twenty years was changed into a jail with shuttered windows and bolted doors and chains ready for those who sought to break loose from it not only physically but even spiritually.

The work of cleansing continues, partly under popular

pressure, partly by government or Allied initiative. Let us beware of feeding those prejudices and resentments that gave the impulse to fascism before it reached power and sustained it in its growth. I speak of always believing and making others believe that Italy was disliked and opposed by everybody; that there was or is a conspiracy of the powers against her; that while having all the potentialities for becoming a great power she never became one because either France or Great Britain, and before that Austria or Germany, was opposed to it; that today in this war Italy is suffering through the ill will of others and not through her own faults. There are not lacking those who think that, unable to obtain justice, Italy ought to break her social dikes and repay the others with new outrages against the co-operation of peoples, so as not to become the servant of the English or the French or the Americans or the Russians.

Such a departure would involve an inferiority complex that would have to be cured either by teachers of wayward children or by neurologists. Italy has no need of either. Her present lesson is hard indeed and tragic the experience. It will be her merit to emerge as a country made over morally before materially rebuilt, and which, seeking the solidarity of others, has solved its own problems with self-discipline and voluntary sacrifice, the true heritage of a civilized nation.

This will to be reborn through one's own merit is not to be supported by national pride or the glories of thirty centuries, but on sound, ethical principles of liberty and democracy, and by the universal tendency of the spirit of Italy that marks the specific mission of our people.

We do not know what will remain of our colonies, what our boundaries will be in Venezia Giulia and Venezia Tridentina, what economic resources will be left to us in the Europe and the world of the future.

The present war has altered the incidence of the old society which is dying and has opened new horizons to technical developments and to the economic and political structure of the new society. Whatever conditions may be made for Italy, one thing is certain, that the ethical patrimony of humanity is always the same and that it is our duty to excavate its treasures and to use them according to circumstances. In this field Italy will be second to no other country so long as she maintains a high educational, cultural and artistic level, a firm social organization and a conscious self-discipline.

Dismiss the idea that Italy for her well-being must be a great military power with capitalistic enterprises protected by the state to be able to compete with foreign countries, or that she needs powerful alliances to gain respect in international affairs. Today the dimensions of the great powers have so increased that France herself will be left behind and Great Britain will need new dominions or not a few satellite states to maintain her old dominant position.

But there is happiness too for small and medium states, if they only know how to keep their place, their dignity, their rights, their special characteristics and their influence in international life.

Many there are who dream of a millennium for all peoples, large and small, a material and economic millennium based on unattainable equality and on inhuman uniformity: a fallacy that the diversity of peoples, races and classes easily disproves. But there is an equality that no power can attenuate, the equality of human personality that every individual and every people has in itself, and must always defend against those who seek to violate it to their own advantage.

If heroic resistance by oppressed minorities, if century-old struggles by small nationalities, if the emergence into political life of countries believed to have disappeared forever, have a meaning for everyone, they have it most for Italy, who after centuries of oppression, of foreign domination and of political divisions was born of our glorious Risorgimento.

We believe that more heroism will be needed today than was necessary a century ago, because the struggles of the second Risorgimento will be harder and against greater odds, and also because it will be difficult to eliminate from people who today are Allies and yesterday were enemies not only re-

sentment for the past of war on the side of the Axis, but also
fear of the future which weighs heavily against Italy. We must
dissipate one and the other not by deceitful intrigue, but by
frank and honest sincerity toward all and with dignified gratitude to those who came to free us from foreign and internal
tyranny.

*   *   *

Garibaldi cursed those Italians who would fight against
England. In his elementary and sentimental concept of politics, he knew well that the ideals of liberty and the interests
of Italy were assured by friendship with England. Since 1860
this friendship had remained firm. The pride and stupidity
of Mussolini transformed it into jealousy and hatred; but the
fascist motto: "Hate the English!" never entered into the
hearts of the people.

Now, after such tragic events, it is the duty of Italy to re-
forge her friendship with England and to foster eternal gratitude to her, that must supersede all the resentments caused
by psychological incomprehension of the Italian soul and of
the political position of the country in the sad period of fascism and of its war.

The United States has always been loved by the Italians as
a country of liberty and initiative where live more than five
million citizens who through origin and affection may also be
called Italians.

France, sister of Italy by culture, art, religion, and common
interests, is also united in the tragic fate of the war and simi-
larity of her fall and her rebirth. France and Italy have a civil
and political mission in the new European and world order
that cannot be disjoined without damage.

Poland, whose death decree Mussolini hastened to sign after
the partition between Russia and Germany in 1939, has always been united in bonds of affection and culture with Italy.
The old links must be renewed in better or in sadder days.

To Greece, to Yugoslavia, to Albania, Italy will have to
unite herself, not only in the interests of good neighborliness,

but through the sentiment of brotherly friendship that may also be the mark of pardon and of peace. Czechoslovakia must find once again in Italy her brothers of the pact of Rome of 1918.

After the Italian people, Abyssinia was the first great victim of fascism. I bow to the Negus, a very noble figure, whose words at Geneva in 1935 and 1936 deserve to be recalled to the memory of Italians and of the whole world for their sense of dignity, of justice, of universality, that no one else seemed to possess in that fatal moment when the destinies of the world were being decided.*

Why were Italian soldiers sent to fight on the Russian front? In the name of a false crusade against communism? To the Russian people, who have shown the world how one defends one's own fatherland invaded by the foreigner, Italy owes a reparation of justice and a renewal of friendship.

One other people: the most tortured of all peoples, the Jews. Fascist Italy also stained itself with anti-Semitism, although with less ferocity than other countries. How can one repair so much evil done in cold blood to destroy a people who are the living witnesses of the Old Testament? The Italian people, who from the very first day showed displeasure and resentment against the anti-Semitic laws and helped in every way the families hit by the iniquitous orders, will repair as far as possible the damages inflicted upon them and will lend a hand to their Jewish fellow citizens who after the war return to the soil of their fatherland.†

Certainly sacrifices are being made by both sides that are fighting; but it is one thing to resist aggression in the name of civilization and Christian values and something quite different to seek a barbaric and tyrannical dominion over the world, and to obtain it not only wage war, but kill, destroy, massacre and tyrannize peaceful peoples.

---

* The opposition of the Negus to cobelligerency is comprehensible: it is enough to remember that the one to obtain cobelligerency was the winner of the Abyssinian war, later nominated vice-king.

† According to a *New York Times* dispatch, September 3, 1944, this reparation has already begun. It is worth reading the article by Richard Arvay "The Italian People and the Jews" in *The Commonweal* (New York), June 8, 1945.

That is why the Italy who has fought nazism and fascism, in spite of all the dangers, miseries and sadnesses, is redeeming herself from past faults and will return purified into the family of nations.

This catharsis that should have come with complete defeat on the field of battle has come by resistance to the German and fascist. The vision of liberty and independence, darkened by twenty years of dictatorship, gleams as a hope of the future, be it on the field of battle, in the clash of guerrilla warfare, in the pangs of hunger and thirst, in the anguish of mothers and wives, in the hardships of workers, deported soldiers or prisoners, in the tragic destruction of beautiful and glorious cities, of irreplaceable historical monuments and artistic treasures.

O my Italy, my beautiful Italy! You will return even more beautiful and happier than before, in friendship with all peoples that desire peace, in the spirit of civic progress, of social and economic righteousness, of Christian morality, contributing to the new order that will be established with the ability, the experience, the alacrity and intelligence, the genius of the people. And if the new order be not that which the ideal of peace inspires in the most generous hearts, the more difficult the first steps of a new life, the more necessary will be good will and faith in the future.

Appendices

I

The Atlantic Charter

(*August 14, 1941*)

The President of the United States of America and the Prime Minister, Mr. Churchill, representing His Majesty's Government in the United Kingdom, being met together, deem it right to make known certain common principles in the national policies of their respective countries on which they base their hopes for a better future for the world.

First—Their countries seek no aggrandizement, territorial or other;

Second—They desire to seek no territorial changes that do not accord with the freely expressed wishes of the peoples concerned;

Third—They respect the right of all peoples to choose the form of government under which they will live; and they wish to see sovereign rights and self-government restored to those who have been forcibly deprived of them;

Fourth—They will endeavor, with due respect for their existing obligations, to further the enjoyment by all states, great or small, victor or vanquished, of access, on equal terms, to the trade and to the raw materials of the world which are needed for their economic prosperity;

Fifth—They desire to bring about the fullest collaboration between all nations in the economic field with the object of securing, for all, improved labor standards, economic advancement and social security;

Sixth—After the final destruction of the Nazi tyranny, they hope to see established a peace which will afford to all nations the means of dwelling in safety within their own boundaries, and which will afford assurance that all the men in all the lands may live out their lives in freedom from fear and want;

Seventh—Such a peace should enable all men to traverse the high seas and oceans without hindrance.

Eighth—They believe that all of the nations of the world, for realistic as well as spiritual reasons must come to the abandonment of the use of force. Since no future peace can be maintained if land, sea or air armaments continue to be employed by nations which threaten, or may threaten, aggression outside of their frontiers, they believe, pending the establishment of a wider and permanent system of general security, that the disarmament of such nations is essential. They will likewise aid and encourage all other practicable measures which will lighten for peace-loving peoples the crushing burden of armaments.

(Signed) FRANKLIN D. ROOSEVELT
(Signed) WINSTON S. CHURCHILL

II

The League of Nations*

By Luigi Sturzo

Many feel a strong reluctance to give the name of League of Nations to the international body that will come into being after the war and Allied victory. Should it be known as a "Community of Nations" or a "Society of States" or a "World Commonwealth" or an "International Federation"? We go about in quest of names to indicate that we seek to build a League of Nations better than the old.

Let us leave aside questions of name, and stick to the substance of the matter. Meanwhile, to understand each other, and in the hope of some fine new name let us continue to call it a League of Nations, because we intend that not all the past should perish and that what was good at Geneva and The Hague should be brought back to life and made good use of. And since in this essay we shall try to sketch the characteristics of the future League of Nations, we shall proceed as in every scientific or practical experiment, taking the past as something achieved and the future as something to be created; thus we shall see what are the features of the new structure and what are the most significant changes.

Membership in the League: All states will be able to become members of the League; but in practice only those will be admitted that are willing to accept both the spirit and the letter of the new Covenant.

The mistake of the past, a mistake *de facto* more than *de jure,* was that of admitting to membership of the League, states that were morally or politically unable to assume the co-responsibilities of membership and which subsequently became enemies and even saboteurs of the League. This was the case with Japan who organized the first aggression against

* This article was published by the *Contemporary Review* of London in February, 1943, and reproduced in the *Reference Shelf,* Vol. 16, H. W. Wilson Company, New York, 1943.

Manchuria and for this aggression was not expelled from the League as she should have been. The same thing happened in the case of Germany and Italy. At Geneva future enemies lived cheek by jowl, and, stranger still, while those who were preparing the present war worked to undermine the League, no remedial measures were taken by the other states.

The new League must be formed first of all by the Allied Nations who signed the Washington Declaration—they number thirty at the present time,* including Fighting France. The Allies have pledged themselves to fight for liberty, justice, the rights of man, order and international co-operation; once victory is attained, it will be their duty to redeem their pledges.

There is doubt concerning Russia: we have expressed repeatedly our opinion in this matter: a common victory will mark a new era for Russia; also one is justified today in thinking that Russia, in her own interest, will co-operate loyally with the League and will deserve help and confidence. Taking the opposite hypothesis: that Russia will seek to disturb international order either by communist propaganda or by armaments in excess of the limit commonly agreed upon, the League itself would have to make a stand and recall Russia to the fulfillment of the pacts, just as the old League should have done in the case of Germany when she withdrew from the Disarmament Conference and abandoned Geneva.

It is well to remember that the old League was not lacking in means of enforcement. What was lacking was good will on the part now of Great Britain, now of France, and often of both at once. There was always lacking the co-operation of the United States which weakened the League from the very beginning. The most perfect Covenant may be drawn up, but if the will to fulfill its terms is lacking, it will remain a dead letter.

The states that have remained neutral during the entire war will have to be scrutinized one by one to ascertain whether they deserve trust and may therefore become members of the League. Those among them that have totalitarian

* At the Conference of San Francisco they were forty-six in the beginning, fifty at the end.

tendencies, deny freedom to their citizens or persecute religious, racial or linguistic minorities are not of the *same
spirit* as the founders of the League and should be denied
admission until their political system or their frame of mind
be changed.

With regard to the vanquished countries, it will be necessary to wait for the formation of new governments, the establishment of new constitutions, to decide whether and upon
what conditions they should be admitted. The League is not
a formal body but a living community. Just as a citizen must
be loyal to his country, so member states must be loyal to the
League. After a world crisis like the present, loyalty will be
presumed in the victors but not in the vanquished. The
former have fought for an ideal opposed to those of the Axis
and its satellites; the latter must therefore give certain proof
of having undergone a change, of having renounced their
ideas and adopted those of the new League. Only then will
they be eligible for membership.

Equalities and inequalities: In the Wilsonian League there
was an attempt to reconcile individualist and hierarchical
principles. The Council was formed of Great Powers, holding
permanent seats and other nations holding nonpermanent
seats, filled partly by election and partly by rotation. The pre-
eminence of the Great Powers was safeguarded but, in order
to respect the sovereignty of individual states, the absurd rule
was adopted that the validity of commitments by the Assembly
depended on a unanimous vote. One single vote was sufficient
to paralyze the whole mechanism of the League; the delegates
were obliged to resort to parliamentary devices of absence or
abstention or of backstage compromises.

All this derived from one fundamental mistake, then perhaps unavoidable owing to lack of experience with any kind
of league; today, after twenty years of hard trials, it would be
unforgivable. This mistake lay in conceiving the League as
an assembly of delegates; as such it had no effective powers
beyond those concerning its internal structure: power was
delegated by each single Government; hence the necessity for
unanimity as the member states had not given up a jot of their
sovereignty.

Are the United States, Great Britain, Russia and China

today willing to surrender something of their sovereignty and in international matters to bow with all due safeguards to the law of the majority, supposedly a two-thirds majority? If the answer is Yes, then all other states will say Yes, including the neutrals and the vanquished. But if the attitude of the United States, Great Britain, Russia and China is negative, the new league will have an even unhappier experience than the old, and will end in failure.

Let us assume the affirmative. The consequence will be that the three or four Great Powers will want permanent seats on the executive body, and this is right, they will also seek to ascertain in all earnestness the nature of the States sharing responsibilities with them, and this is even more right. This scrutiny was never undertaken in the past by France, or Great Britain, where nazi Germany or fascist Italy were concerned; because in substance membership in the League did not commit them in any way; Geneva served as a smokescreen. But when the League has its own powers and will be in a position to commit London, Moscow and Washington, or any other country even beyond the present will of their respective governments, then fellow members will be subjected to serious scrutiny.

What must be avoided at all cost is that one group should form a bloc and dominate the League; be it London-Washington-Moscow, London-Washington-Paris, London-Moscow-Paris, London-Washington-Berlin, or any similar combination. At the same time should be prevented any coalition of small or medium states that might paralyze the working of the League.

Powers of the League: No one doubts that the future League should have consultative and judicial powers like those of the Permanent Court of International Justice at The Hague. No one will wish to deprive The Hague of such a court; but changes will be required to widen its jurisdiction and improve its structure.

Nor will anyone minimize the services rendered by the International Labor Office, or by the special technical and economic commissions which worked so well, although too often hampered by a certain kind of bureaucracy that had ankylosed the activities of Geneva.

The question of the League's powers concerns the political field; and here three problems of decisive importance present themselves.

The first, the definition of aggression: a definition which must not be theoretical but practical and statutory. The associated states will have to consider as aggression, no matter what the juridical or political motives, any and all offensive acts carried out *manu militari* against a state, any military action on foreign territory, any military preparation beyond the normal and which presupposes a threat of aggression. It must be the right and duty of the League to order the cessation of hostilities between states; the side refusing to obey the League's order within the terms fixed will be deemed an aggressor and liable to sanctions.

The Covenant of the 1919 League foresaw four legitimate grounds for war; the new Covenant will have to exclude all wars between states; the League alone will have the right of armed intervention as a police measure, as a measure of sanction, and as a defense of rights; the League and the League alone will be entitled to call upon other states to join in military action the defense of the state subjected to aggression.

There are public men, writers and newspapermen who, since the failure of economic sanctions against Italy in the Abyssinian War, doubt the feasibility of such a system. Others are outright opposed to it. All of these have either no clear idea of the future League or are thinking again in terms of an impotent League. It would seem idle to argue with them; let us merely remind them that the failure of sanctions against Italy was not the fault of the system itself but that of London and Paris. The truth is that they never wanted to go to extremes.

Leaving aside economic sanctions the efficacy of which must be ultimate rather than immediate, only military sanctions can really nip in the bud any desire of a government to resort to war. Either a state will be strong enough to defy the League and the states it represents, and in such a case will by itself constitute a permanent danger to world peace so as to render necessary immediate curtailment of its offensive power, or else it will be wholly unable to face the power of the League and it will then be in no position to begin a war. Only a weak and divided and powerless League can be checkmated as the old League was, not only by Italy but even by the city of Danzig.

Disarmament and military powers: The view is gaining ground that the United Nations will have to assert the principle of unilateral disarmament for an unpredictable period, to enable the vanquished countries to abandon their aggressive mentality. This is not the place to discuss the duration of the period of disarmament to be imposed on the vanquished countries. What seems evident is that it cannot be prolonged beyond the time when a vanquished country is accepted as a member of the League of Nations. Within the League there must be no longer victors and vanquished, but only members co-operating to the same end. The military system to be fixed for all members of the League will be extended also to the vanquished countries once they have been adjudged worthy of admission.

But whatever the limits of a reduction of armaments to be achieved after the complete disarmament of the vanquished countries or in subsequent agreements among the United Nations, it is certain that a true League of Nations cannot possibly be formed without endowing it with its own military force and creating military bodies dependent upon it. If we want peace in the world, we must take the decisive step and create a real and living supernational body.

To the League we should attribute the supervision and policing of air and seas and responsibility for certain internationalized points. Plainly, not all the navies and air forces will be placed under central control; but there will have to be certain internationalized corps endowed with autonomy and their own sphere of action for the maintenance of security and order.

It is also possible to foresee a delegation of powers by the League to one or more individual member states for the fulfillment of special military missions, a kind of military mandate; similarly the League will be able to organize— entrusting its operation to the states most concerned—a sort of military cordon round any state which in violation of the pact is arming and preparing for aggression.

International control: All states and not only the vanquished states must accept the principle of international control. The vanquished states will have to submit to special control, imposed by the armistice until all their obligations under it have been fulfilled. When they are deemed worthy of admission to the League, they will pass under the same control as all other members.

Such control is necessary to ensure that members respect pacts, maintain loyalty to the League and to the moral and juridical principles upon which it is founded. The cardinal point of the new League should be that its members must all be of a like mind. If there is a repudiation of the League's principles on the part of a member, that member will have to be rendered harmless. If the League had intervened in time in the cases of Japan, Italy and Germany, as soon as their armaments and war preparations began to appear, or, even better, when those countries first changed their systems and manifested their totalitarian tendencies, the present war would have been averted.

There are Englishmen and Americans who are frightened by the revolutionary implications of such a League. But if this war is not a revolution, what other event could be? Moreover, every country will have the government it chooses. The concern of the League will be that the moral, legal and cultural principles for which we are fighting today and in whose name we shall be victorious tomorrow, should be the basis of these principles: political and religious freedom, independence, rights of human personality, justice, respect for the rights of racial, religious and linguistic minorities, and the ultimate attainment by colonial peoples of political and economic personality, solidarity and international security. The League will have the task of safeguarding the international order emerging from the new Covenant and must be endowed with adequate powers and rights acknowledged by all. The state that does not keep its pledged word and undermines the new order, even if only within its own territory, must be excluded from the League and subjected to its sanctions.

States outside the League: It must be anticipated that various and perhaps not a few states will remain outside the League temporarily or even indefinitely. Some will be small states of a special structure. Switzerland, for instance, may feel even tomorrow that neutrality is for her the best policy, and might choose to remain outside. It would be foolish to have recourse again to compromise: the League and neutrality are at opposite poles. Nevertheless, between Switzerland and the League there would be established those relations of friendship that the democratic spirit of the respective countries will make effective and co-operative.

If instead it is a question of Great Powers, the League will remain on its guard as against a potential enemy. Let us suppose that Japan after her defeat, even after acceptance of the armistice terms, will either refuse to correct her political system which would be left in the hands of militarists and ultranationalists, or refrain from applying for admission to the League. Then it would be clear that hopes of revenge were secretly fostered.

A country nourishing such sentiments in secret, against the orderly processes of the community of nations, would be more dangerous as a member of the League helped perhaps by the indulgence of London or Washington or Moscow than as an outsider under close control. The old slogan, "I accept freedom in order to have the freedom to deny it," cannot be accepted in the new order. The League must have the power both to refuse admission to a state which does not inspire confidence and to expel a state that fails to keep its pledged word.

It is obvious that vanquished states will be granted equal rights (also in regard to armaments in the measure agreed upon) if they become members of the League; but if they do not become members, either because they do not wish to do so or because they have not fulfilled the conditions of the armistice or because they do not comply with the League's pacts, they will not have the right to proportional or relative parity in armaments.

To build a new edifice on Christian and ethical principles, and on the principles of international law, is the aim of the war now being fought by the United Nations. The instrument will be a League of Nations, created upon these very principles and made effective by political and military powers which no future coalition can destroy.

III

"Provisional Peace" with Italy and the "Secret" Terms of the Armistice*

By Luigi Sturzo

This is how the story goes: on July 27, 1944, the *New York Times* published on page 6 an Associated Press news item which ran as follows:

Washington, July 26.—A British suggestion that the Allies write a provisional peace with Italy, which now has the combined standing of defeated enemy and cobelligerent, is before American authorities, it was learned today.

The plan awaits discussion with Russia and other countries interested in the Italian settlement. As now contemplated, the peace treaty would leave aside all territorial questions and probably other final claims such as reparations for later decision.

Primarily, it would serve to regularize Italy's relations with the United Nations and clarify the position of Italian war prisoners. Such a treaty would also solve the question of the Italian armistice and give considerable prestige to the Italian government, which has complained that its position is too weak.

The government of Premier Ivanoe Bonomi has asked that the Allies' armistice with Italy be published, presumably with the idea that the public reaction to its terms would force a revision. The Allies' military authorities have opposed publication now on the ground that it might prejudice operations.

* Published by *Il Mondo* (*The World*), New York, November, 1944.

Although at the time I saw no similar news item in any other New York paper, I referred quite clearly to the point in question on the occasion of a radio message to the people of Italy on July 29.

After continued silence on the part of the American press, I sought and obtained information from friends in Washington early in August to the effect that such a British suggestion had been made and favorably received by the Department of State, that only minor complications were delaying further steps in this direction. Later I learned that the main difficulty, a fairly reasonable one, was the French demand that before the question of the Italian government was settled the position of de Gaulle should be cleared up. Then I remembered that it had been reported from London at the end of June or the beginning of July that the British cabinet had discussed Bonomi's request for recognition of Italy as an Ally and, without coming to any decision, had postponed an answer until a more opportune moment. This moment seemed to me to have arrived after the recognition of the de Gaulle government in France. But days and weeks went by; de Gaulle overcame American or Anglo-American reluctance and still there was no further mention of a provisional peace with Italy. I carried my inquiry further by making a trip to Washington where I discussed the matter with Sir Alexander Cadogan on the British side and Assistant Secretary of State Berle on the American. From these conversations I derived the impression (which was not conveyed to me by any definite statement from either of my interlocutors) that some obstacle had arisen from outside quite independently of the intentions of the American and British governments.

Great expectations were aroused by the statement made after the Quebec Conference on September 26. Many satisfying things were set forth therein but, except for the agreement to resume diplomatic relations with Italy and the decision to *gradually* relax Allied control, there was no mention of the so-called provisional peace and of the secret armistice terms. Shortly afterward the British prime minister in an address to the House of Commons on September 28 said: "Obviously, no final settlement can be made with them [the people of Italy] until the north of Italy has been liberated and the basis on which the present government stands has been broadened and strengthened." We cannot say whether Churchill's words covered some secret reason for not carrying out the proposal of a provisional peace set forth in July or whether they simply implied a postponement of the question until the liberation of north Italy, which at this time was believed to be not far off.

In order to complete the story we must quote the statement attributed to Acting Secretary of State Edward R. Stettinius, Jr., who, according to the *New York Times* of October 28, said: "The resumption of diplomatic relations with Italy does not re-establish peace, nor does it settle the many questions that will have to be dealt with before a formal state of peace is declared. Only the Congress can pass upon that final step. The resumption of formal relations with Italy is intended however to facilitate the return to a state of peace, which is of course an objective of our Italian policy."

We must note that Churchill's "final settlement" and Stettinius's "final peace" have not the same practical and legal meaning. The first phrase refers to the "provisional peace" whose story we have just retraced while the second refers to Congress's approval of the *peace treaty* to be drawn up between the United States and Italy. (We do not know whether this will be a collective treaty among all the interested powers such as the treaty of Versailles and the other similar treaties of 1919 or a separate treaty such as was drawn up between the United States and its former enemies.) It is not entirely clear whether Stettinius for reasons of diplomacy was really looking so far ahead as a general peace conference. Italy can and must obtain a *provisional peace* with the Allies and be treated as a country not only at peace but actually associated with the war effort and the reconstruction program of the Allies, long before the formal ratification of peace treaties is made by the Congress of the United States and the Italian parliament.

The news of the British proposal for a provisional peace had wide repercussions in the Italian press and awakened hopes which turned out to be premature. The Allied press made no further reference to the proposal and Italian-language papers abroad neither referred to it nor discussed it. The United States Office of War Information, which should have used this news as propaganda, let the whole matter drop. I note these reactions not because I am trying to explain them (such an attempt is irrelevant under present circumstances), but merely in order to complete the story of the proposal of a provisional peace. I wish further to show that, as compared with other objectives sponsored by Italian-American groups such as (1) giving the status of full-fledged Ally to Italy, and (2) publication of the armistice terms, the idea of a provisional peace had no appeal, that is did not seem of immediate or pressing interest or advantage. These Italian-American groups merely continued to work for the two objectives mentioned above. Various of these groups have supported the promotion of Italy to the status of an Ally ever since the establishment of cobelligerency. In this connection they have made three main points: (1) the extension of Lend-Lease aid to Italy, (2) a cessation of Allied military control over the Italian government and (3) a settlement of the question of Italian prisoners of war. Many petitions have been sent to the president and many resolutions forwarded to government offices. The most important step was the motion based on regular parliamentary procedure made by Congressman Vito Marcantonio to the House of Representatives.

All these steps have great moral value and we as Italians are most grateful for them to our American friends. But from a practical point of view their only effect is to bring pressure to bear on the White House and the Department of State to the end that the United States persuade the other Allied powers to approve these plans. Such persuasion seems unlikely inasmuch as at the Cairo Conference Roosevelt consented to Italy's being a prevalently British sphere of influence and thus made American influence upon Italian affairs secondary and almost subordinate. But, after the British proposal of a provisional peace was advanced, it became plain that all subsequent proposals must hinge on this one which came from one of the three great powers involved and the power that has assumed the most direct responsibility for Italian affairs. Moreover the points regarding the change of Italy's status into that of an Ally, the easing of military control over the Italian government and the settlement of the question of the Italian prisoners of war would all be included in London's proposal. The matter of Lend-Lease aid, being entirely dependent on the United States, can and should be entirely separate; in fact, such aid can be extended to Italy even in its present status of cobelligerency.

As for the demand for publication of the armistice terms, we must remember that their publication was requested by the Bonomi government as soon as it had obtained the endorsement (or, as it is called by Americans, the recognition) of the Allies. In the news item of July 27 quoted above it was stated that Bonomi's intention in making this request was to force the Allies to modify the terms in view of the expected reaction to them on the part of the public opinion. This same point was made by Italian groups abroad.

It is plain that the Americans and the British must seize one of the horns of the dilemma: either to publish or to revise the terms of the armistice. The postponement of this choice from month to month and from one phase to another of the war in Italy increases rather than diminishes their responsibility and makes their relations with the Italian people progressively more difficult. Russia's recent publication of the armistices signed with Rumania, Finland and Bulgaria (and we may expect soon a Hungarian armistice) has deepened Italian resentment toward London and Washington and at the same time it has undermined the excuse of *military necessity* used by Stettinius in justification of the secrecy maintained for the last fourteen months.

If the author is correctly informed Badoglio is responsible for this secrecy; in consideration of the unusual circumstances in which he found himself it is hard to say whether he assumed this responsibility as a military leader or in his capacity as head of a nonexistent government. Together with the king he fled to Brindisi without any minister, counselor or even minor official to lend to them the semblance of a government. When he was obliged to sign the conditions attached to the armistice without being able to discuss them with his cabinet he took it upon himself to cover his individual action and the king's consent thereto with the veil of secrecy. And this secrecy was pleasing to the Allied authorities, who were having their first experience in Italy of the conquest of an enemy country with the intention of mobilizing its remaining forces against the Germans.

Later they came to realize that the armistice terms were either impossible to carry out or should be modified in order to avoid making an impression of excessive and purposeless severity. After the publication of the terms accorded to Rumania and later to Finland and Bulgaria it was inevitable that these should compare favorably with the treatment of Italy and cause the leaders of the two Anglo-Saxon democracies to appear in a very poor light in contrast to their Russian companion, the head of a totalitarian state. Responsibility for the secrecy is now incumbent upon the military, for when President Roosevelt declared that no difficulties stood in the way of revealing the armistice terms they hastened to make him say the very next day that there were *military necessities* in view of which, et cetera, et cetera. After this succession of events it seemed as if the bull would be taken by the horns when the proposal of a provisional peace was advanced, for such a peace would have canceled the armistice terms before they ever came to publication. And yet we see this dilemma still unsolved.

To ascertain whether it would be better to take up again the idea of a provisional peace on the basis of the British proposal or to make a fresh start altogether will be one of the tasks of the recently announced Italian diplomatic representatives to Washington and London, Sforza and Carandini. Meanwhile we shall continue to call public attention to this most important problem whose solution, we believe, cannot be further postponed. When the British prime minister said that a *final settlement* could not be made until the liberation of north Italy he must have thought that this phase of the war was fast approaching. Today we see that this is not so; the three or four lines of defense prepared by the Germans in this sector will delay for months any such longed-for event. General Alexander himself, alas, has advised the patriots to wait.

It seems as if Anglo-American policy toward Italy were to make concessions so precautiously as to make it appear that

London and Washington trust neither the Italian people nor their government. Indeed, the announced diminution of Allied control, intended to endow the government with powers which it does not now possess, has not yet gone into effect after an interval of two months. The appointment of Harold MacMillan, a member of the British parliament, as head of the Allied Commission in Rome does not mean that the whole machinery of military control will be changed.

If the promises made by Churchill and Roosevelt in the declaration following the Quebec Conference on September 26 are carried out, some of the secret clauses of the armistice would be automatically canceled, a great part of the cumbersome and paralyzing Allied control would vanish and some sort of Lend-Lease arrangement would be put into effect. Somehow or other such action must be taken, for it can be the advantage neither of the United States nor Britain that their leaders should fail to keep their promises.

There would then remain, without meaning and consistency, the secrecy requested by Badoglio, that has served the Americans and British as an excuse for their political inertia on grounds of military necessity. I refer to the political *inertia* shown toward an expectant and plaintive Italy, and also toward the third party to the Italian armistice, Stalin, who has shrouded this matter in complete silence. Did Stalin approve the British proposal of a provisional peace? Did he raise objections and if so what were they? Why have the communists in America and Britain—whether or not of Italian origin—given no support to the British proposal? Is it perhaps because it originated in London and not in Moscow?

Stalin has a way of giving indirect lessons to his Allies. It may be that he wished the publication of the armistices granted by Russia to Rumania, Finland and Bulgaria as well as the terms prepared for Hungary to precede the announcement of the new conditions which will at a given moment be laid down for Italy.

However this may be, it seems likely that the future procedure will be based on the following statement of October 13, 1943, accepting the cobelligerency offered by Badoglio: "The relationship of cobelligerency between the government of Italy and the United Nations governments cannot of itself affect the terms recently signed, which retain their full force and can only be adjusted by agreement between the Allied governments in the light of the assistance which the Italian government may be able to afford to the United Nations cause." *Webster's Dictionary* defines the verb to *adjust* as "to settle; to free from differences or discrepancies; to bring to a satisfactory state," et cetera. When such a "satisfactory state" is reached there will be neither political nor military reasons for keeping the armistice terms secret, for they will have been eliminated in the course of "adjustment." Whether or not the succeeding state of affairs is called a *provisional peace* it will in any case represent an adjustment made in relation to the contribution which Italy has been able to make to the war effort.

It is not my task to evaluate this contribution. The words of Churchill, Roosevelt and the military leaders of the Allied Control Commission testify to the fact that the contribution has been steady, important and rendered in good faith. Account must also be taken of the guerrilla warfare carried on by the Italian patriots, whose efficacy compares favorably with similar activities in any other country.

We insist on the necessity of restating the armistice terms under the guise of an *adjustment* or a *provisional peace,* because this is the only way to alter the absurd status of Italian prisoners of war by giving them their rightful liberty; only thus will Allied jurists cease to consider Italy as a formerly enemy country in everyday problems; only thus will the Italian government overcome the impossibility of taking part in international conferences where it has interests at stake, such as the Bretton Woods Conference concerning the international fund and bank for international settlements, the International Labor Office Conference of Philadelphia and the Aviation Conference recently held in Chicago.

But the principal argument for a change in Italy's status is that the Italian people should not be further wounded and humiliated for no reason by absurd armistice terms enveloped in a veil of purposeless secrecy, while other formerly enemy countries were informed within a few days of the fate assigned to them by the government of Russia, along with those of the United States and Britain; that is, the very three governments that signed both the Italian armistice and the declaration of cobelligerency. Is this too much to ask after more than a year of privation, misery and humiliation that the war has brought to an Italy now loyally fighting side by side with the Allies?

IV

*The Italian Colonies**

By Luigi Sturzo

The answer given by British Foreign Secretary Anthony Eden to the House of Commons concerning the fate of the Italian "empire" reveals nothing new. A year ago Churchill roughly declared that Italy had irretrievably lost its "empire."

The word "empire" as used by these members of the British cabinet has not the same meaning in terms of territory as was attributed to it by the Italian fascists, who applied it to the region of East Africa, comprising Abyssinia, Eritrea and Somaliland. The British, as well as many Americans, include in this term Cyrenaica and Tripolitania, which according to fascist usage were integral parts of Italy itself. The fact remains that, according to the British view, the old Italian colonies having no connection with the fascist "imperial" epoch are or should be considered lost to Italy.

Since it is in accordance with the general tradition of the British government never to act on a basis of revenge, but rather on a basis of cold calculation and self-interest, we must look for the motives of a policy which appears to us so questionable. Laying aside the overall accusations from both American and Italian sources against British policy in Italy, we must try to understand the plan that Churchill and his cabinet have been pursuing in Italy for almost two years, since no statement or press declaration has enlightened us on this question.

For greater clarification let us look at the period preceding fascism. For a long time England had pursued a cordial policy toward Italy, based on a traditional friendship and on the con-

* Published by *Il Mondo (The World)*, New York, October 1944 and by the *New Leader*, New York, April 21, 1945.

viction that Italy might serve to counterbalance any overin-
dependent or overenterprising action in the Mediterranean
on the part of France. Italy, because of its natural weakness,
was not considered a potential danger in this area.

In accord with this policy England was inclined to favor
Mussolini in his experiment in dictatorship, in spite of her
early resentment when, as a young adventurer, he occupied
Corfu and backed Poincaré's occupation of the Ruhr. The
tripartite accord between England, France and Italy concerning Abyssinia, proposed in 1925 by Sir Austen Chamberlain,
marked the beginning of a favorable policy toward fascist
Italy which lasted, in spite of the little break caused by the
"sanctions," until the "gentleman's agreement" in regard to
the Mediterranean signed in April, 1938, by the other Chamberlain, then Prime Minister.

The Mediterranean was always England's main preoccupation; so the fortification of Pantelleria, the airfields in Sicily
and Tripolitania and the increase of Italian naval power gave
rise to a certain amount of concern. This concern was mingled
with a feeling of superiority because it never occurred to the
British that the Italians would ever make war against them.
Even the "iron pact" with Germany signed by the fascist government in Milan in May, 1939, appeared to the British devoid of real meaning, especially as the Italian declaration of
neutrality after the outbreak of hostilities in September of the
same year raised British hopes or, more correctly, lessened
British doubts. Mussolini's declaration of war in June, 1940,
struck London like a thunderbolt, put an end to all fatuous
hopes and attempts at bargaining, and revealed that the Mediterranean itself was no longer safe, nor was the British Mediterranean fleet secure.

It was said in 1942 that the plan of the British admiralty,
accepted by Churchill himself, was never to allow any strong
power to command the African shores of the Mediterranean
in such a way as to be able to prevent the passage of British
shipping. The admiralty, of course, thinks in technical rather
than political terms, but when these terms are translated into
their political equivalents they go beyond technical matters
and embrace much larger problems and grave responsibilities.

It is plain that the admiralty, having burned its fingers in hot water, is afraid of cold water as well.

As we look back, we see that British political leaders not only favored Italy's involvement in African colonization but actively favored it. This was the case both in Assab and Eritrea. England asked for Italy's co-operation in "putting Egypt in order," but England alone brought to bear the force of arms, Italy having refused to do so. At last Italy gained Libya. It was foreseen and arranged with the consent of all the European powers—England the first—that Italy should take over Libya as its share in the legacy of the bankrupt Ottoman empire. Italy had only to proceed with its acquisition by means of the diplomatic and military methods then adopted by all civilized nations. From 1912 to 1932 (the real beginning of the Italian war with Abyssinia and the fascist policy of making the Mediterranean into *"Mare Nostrum"*) the British government had no fear of Italy as a potential enemy able to endanger its interests in the Mediterranean; it never suspected Mussolini of being so mad as to embark on an adventure involving war with England.

Today the situation is reversed. There is coming into being a democratic Italy which probably will be deprived of an army and of a navy. The country has been and still is the theater of a war of such destructiveness that it will take twenty, thirty, or perhaps even fifty years to recover. In its defeat it may well be forbidden to create military bases or coastal and island fortifications and it may even be obliged to cede (temporarily or not) naval bases to England. Can it be that this shadow of the old Italy inspires the admiralty with fear? This notion seems so unreasonable, one might even say so absurd, that I should be inclined to deny the existence of any such plan by the British admiralty were it not that I have been informed of the existence of such a plan and its approval by Churchill.

And what if this plan were the pretext for still another plan which for diplomatic reasons it is unwise to reveal or to discuss? Let us reason it out. A year ago a French-Canadian paper published an item of news from Algiers concerning the possibility of offering Cyrenaica or even Tripolitania to Turkey as an inducement to enter the war. There were rumors that propositions made by the British to this end (exactly what propositions were never specified) failed to overcome Ankara's fear of Moscow and so nothing came of them. Other rumors hinted that Tripolitania was to become an independent Jewish nucleus (in this way giving a guarantee to France for the Tunisian boundaries of the East) and that Cyrenaica was to be entrusted to the British since they might soon be obliged to leave Egypt even if they succeed in retaining the naval base at Alexandria. There has also been talk of giving sovereignty over part of Cyrenaica to the Senussi tribes under a sort of British protectorate. These are all mortgages on a hypothetical future. It is clear, however, that in British opinion all of Libya must change hands and cease to be an Italian colony or territory.

The Americans have made Eritrea into a supply base for the present war. We know that, although the United States is not fighting for territorial gains, it intends to increase the number of its naval bases in both the Atlantic and the Pacific and to acquire islands and other strategical points necessary to its future policy of security, commercial expansion and naval superiority in the world. It has not been stated whether or not Eritrea enters into this plan; this question is one of the postwar secrets. Some spokesmen for Abyssinia have mentioned claims on Eritrea as an outlet to the sea for their country. Those who seek to remake the world on maps have scanty notions of geography. As other more powerful interests are brought into play, however, Abyssinia may be satisfied with Italian Somaliland.

We see, then, that disposal of the Italian colonies is under way, shrouded in silence as if it were a matter of concern to no one and that the details of the disposal are developing according to the circumstances of the war and dependent on whatever advantages may be obtained with the least inconvenience. May we not ask whether the Atlantic Charter has no bearing on this case? As a matter of fact, it is stated in its first article that the contracting powers "do not seek territorial or other aggrandizements." Unfortunately the Atlantic Charter has undergone varying interpretations just as was the case with the British reservations to the Briand-Kellogg pact. One of the most serious, as announced by Eden to the House of Commons, is that the Charter will not apply to enemy countries. Eden's purpose at this time was to eliminate obstacles in the way of a cession of East Prussia to Poland in compensation for the loss of territory east of the Curzon Line.

No statement has been made about the applicability of the Charter to Italy since Italy is still, be it for better or for worse, at one and the same time, a former enemy (as witness the treatment of the prisoners of war held by the Allies), a co-belligerent (as witness the military aid rendered to the Allies by the Italian army, navy, air force and partisan units) and a friendly sovereign state (as witness the fact that there is already an Italian ambassador in Moscow and ambassadors will soon arrive in London and Washington). Which one of these three will be taken into account when the question of the Italian colonies arises? According to Roosevelt's opinion, as expressed by Attorney General Biddle, the Atlantic Charter should apply to Italy. I say "opinion," but Biddle used the word "determination" in his Columbus Day message. I hope that Biddle is not mistaken.

The Italian premier, Ivanoe Bonomi, upon receiving a report of Eden's words, demanded an explanation from the British ambassador, Sir Noel Charles. At the same time he gave an interview to the representative of the *New York Times* in which he expressed the Italian government's resentment at this treatment, more appropriate to a conquered country than to one which has been liberated. He added, quite rightly, that it will not do to constantly remind a nation that has for a year been fighting alongside the Allies and is in the process of restoring all the spiritual and political values of democracy that it has been conquered and must expect to be treated accordingly. Naturally Bonomi asserted Italy's right to keep its colonies and he voiced the protest of Italian public opinion against the untimely, one-sided and haughty declarations of the British foreign secretary. In spite of the sibylline reply made to Bonomi by Sir Noel Charles to the effect that Eden's words had been incorrectly interpreted by the press there is no substantial change in London's attitude. The future outlook remains dark, especially as Italy is in the position of having to defend her own natural borders at the Brenner Pass and in the region of Venezia Giulia. Amid powerful conflicting interests on all sides, Italy stands alone, struggling to keep on its feet.

In the matter of colonies one essential point must be stated: there is no place for a policy of self-sacrifice on the part of Italy; such a policy would meet with neither respect nor generosity from the Allies and the result would be that Italy would lower her own standing and at the same time provide a justification for those seeking to take unfair advantage of its present situation. Without entering into overrefined diplomatic subtleties it would seem best to leave things as they are in the hands of the Italian government and parliament (or constituent assembly) which must eventually re-examine all that has happened since the fall of Mussolini on July 25, 1943. It will be the task of this government to pass judgment on the responsibilities of those who played a part in the events of those months and also to ascertain and make known to the Allies the popular will of the whole of Italy, whether or not this popular will is agreeable to them and regardless of its power to shape the immediate future. No territorial concessions can be made by the present government until this popular will is able to express itself.

Some say that the colonies possessed by Italy before fascism were acquired under the impulse of a policy of expansion unsuited to its economic power and that they did not provide an outlet for the emigration of its surplus population. We may or may not agree with this proposition, but arguments for or against it are now merely academic. The problem today is this: Should we resist the attempt being made to deprive us of the colonies acquired by right of conquest before fascism? We answer Yes, even if these colonies are worthless, if they are a national liability, if they do not provide an outlet for future emigration, if they compel us to maintain a colonial army and navy to service it. We shall settle things for ourselves when we are in a position to do with our colonies what we will, to better conditions among colonists and natives alike, to come to a free understanding with France or Egypt, with England or the Negus of Abyssinia or whatever neighbors we may have. Today under the pretext of "unconditional surrender" imposed upon us after the Italian people had already clamored for peace, there are those who wish to take our colonies away from us as spoils of conquest after we have fought alongside them for a year and a half. We have every right to oppose any such division of booty and to refuse to accept any such humiliation. We shall discuss among ourselves as Italians (and not with the citizens of other nations who may have been born in Italy) the question of whether Eritrea, Somaliland and Libya can be made into assets rather than liabilities and furnish outlets for our emigration (which will remain a thorny problem after the war) and the question of whether they can develop progressively along the same lines as Tunisia, Algeria and Morocco until they can one day become their own masters.

Count Sforza has at various times put forward the idea of a joint international management of all African colonies under the direction of the League of Nations. In such a case Libya, Eritrea and Somaliland would have the same status as Tunisia, the Congo, Cameroons and other segments of Africa. But Count Sforza knows perfectly well that such ideas, like proposals voiced in the United States to the effect that the European nations should relinquish all their Atlantic, Pacific and Mediterranean colonies, are mere academic debates or pieces of sensational journalism. The truth is that no European nation will relinquish anything and it will be a miracle if there is any attempt to adopt the plan proposed by Herbert Morrison to the House of Commons in January, 1943, whereby native peoples should be gradually educated and given eventual participation in self-government. The realization of this elementary fact will prevent us from making one-sided concessions or hasty sacrifices of our colonies and will put us on the right track (already followed by the late Italian Colonial Minister Amendola) of giving the natives under our control a fuller share of their own administration. Of course what Italy must not and cannot do is to make its colonies into instruments of war and imperialism, raising suspicion among the powers interested in territories and sea lanes adjacent to our possessions. But how can anyone believe that Italy, ruined by this unwanted war, can have imperialistic aims of the sort fostered by Mussolini? Fifty years may well go by before Italy can be restored to the place it held before the march on Rome.

Bismarck, who knew what he was talking about, used to say that in the realm of politics it was difficult to look ahead for even ten years. If the British persist in taking away our colonies their vision will fall short even of ten years. Instead of being able to count on a friendship with Italy renewed and strengthened by the present tragedy that such a gesture of generosity might easily assure them, they will consciously or unconsciously turn Italy, which they have staked out as their own sphere of influence, into a restless and resentful counterpart of India.

V

Fascism and Economics*

By Luigi Sturzo

Not infrequently the affirmation is made that "Hitler and Mussolini are the consequences of the economic circumstances of their respective countries." This, in my opinion, is quite incorrect and misleading. Apart from the fact that historical events are so complex that it is impossible to isolate one cause from others, I can say from my personal experience that economic causes did not play a very large part in the case of fascism in Italy.

The economic situation there from November 4, 1918 (the time of the Italian Armistice) to October, 1922 (the march on Rome) was quite the same as that of France and even of England—difficulties in establishing equilibrium between the cost of living and the value of the currencies, unrest over salaries, and so on. As a matter of fact there were more strikes in that period in England than in Italy. Only one question was particularly Italian, and this had no connection with the Peace Conference and the economic provisions of the peace treaties. It was a very old question, one that we can find in the Roman ages, even before the Gracchi. It revives from time to time, under certain circumstances, I am sure it will rise again after the present war. This agrarian question became acute between 1918 and 1922, not because of the immediate needs of the population, but because of the psychological disappointment of the peasants. The liberal government during the war had promised distribution of the *latifundia* (large, ill-cultivated estates) and the revision of other agrarian laws. After the war the promise was not ful-

* Published by *America*, New York, April 10, and May 8, 1943.

filled. The bill introduced into the chamber of deputies by the popular group (Christian-democrats) was postponed until July, 1922. The favorable vote on the measure then was too late.

The unrest of the peasants and rural workers was the occasion for the spread of small fascist groups in Lombardy, Emilia and Romagna (the valley of the Po), the richest and happiest regions in Italy. Landowners were furious against the Popolari, the socialists and certain democrats of the chamber, and against the unions (which an American could understand very well); and they gave money and protection to the fascists who began to use violence against the unions, cooperatives and municipalities held by their opponents.

At that time the Italian people were disappointed over the decisions made by the Peace Conference on national territorial problems. The fascists raised a very arrogant and dangerous campaign for Fiume, Dalmatia, Albania, colonial mandates, the Mediterranean as *"Mare Nostrum,"* and so on. Thus the youth was excited by an imaginative sentimentalism; and too many army chiefs who were in opposition to the government over withdrawal from Fiume, the treaty of Rapallo with Yugoslavia and the reduction of armaments were pleased. They blamed the pacifism of the masses and the weakness of the ruling class for these agreements. And a flood of arms leaked from the military stores into the hands of the fascists.

Notwithstanding, the fascists got no seats in the chamber in the general elections of 1919 (of 508 seats, the socialists had 157 and the Popolari 99) and in the general election of 1921 while the socialists secured 121 seats and the Popolari 107, the fascists got only 35.

What is necessary to keep in mind in order to understand the fascist phenomenon is that the liberals and democrats (with the exception of a small group) were after all afraid that the Popolari and the socialists would soon come to control the chamber and the government and were quite in favor of the fascist purpose of checking these mass movements. Though they could not avoid the participation of the Popolari in their cabinets, they worked to reduce the growth of that new Christian-democratic party, giving help to the fascist party.

From this analysis it is clear that fascism was the consequence of a threefold reaction: the conservative economics of the landowners, the militarism of the army, and the politics of the liberal parties. As a result Mussolini was able to overcome his reactionary helpers, to get power from the king and begin the fascist revolution. In four years of struggle (1922–26) he got control of the economic life of Italy through the pseudo-corporation and the *real* authoritative system; of the army through his black militia, and of all political parties through the one-party system. The revolution was then complete and the totalitarian state began.

Americans can imagine what would happen in this country if the Ku Klux Klan with the help of some capitalist and political groups marched on Washington, occupying the White House by force and terrorizing all the people. There would be no difficulty in finding some social scientists to claim that the economic circumstances of the time (like the economic crisis of 1929, the following New Deals and so on) were the causes of the K.K.K. dictatorship and totalitarianism.

We are so accustomed to the idea that economic factors are a determining force (even those of us opposed to the Marxist theory of "historic materialism") that we forget too easily that psychological factors are more important and decisive. This is true regarding Italian fascism as well as German nazism. Above all we must consider human personality since man, with his mind and free will, is the cause of historic events. The rest is nothing but social and physical conditioning, which may be useful for good or for evil.

Understood in that sense both the following propositions are true: "Hitler and Mussolini are the consequences of the economic (and other) circumstances of their respective countries," and "Vincent de Paul was the consequence of the economic (and other) circumstances of France in the seventeenth century."

VI

The San Francisco Conference

A few days before the end of the San Francisco Conference, Marshal Jan Smuts made an important speech and substantially modified his position as stated in that other speech of his, analyzed in Chapter 9. He said that his former statement of December 1943 "was an extemporaneous speech and had been misinterpreted." At San Francisco, he abandoned his scheme of a "western European bloc" centering around Great Britain, and upheld the idea—always supported by the author—that Europe be formed into a regional unit together with Great Britain and Russia.* Smuts did not say what should be done with Germany, nor how his views could be reconciled with the system of spheres of influence, nor on what basis social and political life would be restored to Europe. Unable, at San Francisco, to deal with the more difficult problems of a world order in the making, he added a few touches to the darker side of the picture: the moral and physical destruction of Europe, the breakdown of old institutions, the prospect of poverty, hunger and revolt—a kind of race to self-destruction. What could the San Francisco Conference do for Europe? Its scope was confined to the approval of a Charter, to setting the world machine into motion. Such a gathering was never intended to settle the fate of Europe. Europe itself as such could almost be considered as absent or voiceless at San Francisco. It is all the more to the credit of such a man as Marshal Smuts that he spoke of Europe as an entity of the future to be rebuilt from the wreckage of the present.

"A Supreme European Reconstruction Council" was also proposed by Mr. Bernard M. Baruch in the eleventh of his fourteen recommendations to Congress, published on June

* See pages 217 *et seq.*

22, 1945. But, having suggested that the reorganization of Germany be used as a basis for closer understanding with Russia, he completely forgot his idea of European unity, and reverted in various ways to a scheme of spheres of influence.

The author has always maintained, here as elsewhere, that France must take the leadership in Europe, and propose a plan for unification and rehabilitation. France, however, has taken to a blatant nationalism, guided by the haughty spirit of General Charles de Gaulle. Each in turn, Roosevelt, Churchill and Stalin, have dealt with her in an ambiguous manner. France is one of the five powers upon whom rests the responsibility of preserving the peace, and yet, she is absent from the big three meetings at which the future is being molded. Meanwhile France is losing sight of her real duty to Europe and to the world.

Bearing in mind the psychology of a postwar period such as this, it is perhaps too early to speak of Europe as united, even before the ex-enemy countries have resumed their places within the international community. France thought she was protecting herself against any future danger from Germany, by having a clause inserted in the San Francisco Charter, which provides for immediate action, under the Franco-Russian pact, without waiting for a decision of the Security Committee, in case of any threat—from Berlin! The recurrences of history are indeed curious. After the last war also, France, doubting the readiness and will of the League of Nations to act, had recourse to separate alliances with Poland, the Petite Entente, and later with Russia. Unfortunately, against a growing Germany, she was unable to maintain either the Geneva system (completed at Locarno) or her eastern alliances. Let us not place all the blame upon Germany. When Hitler, in 1936, occupied the demilitarized zone of the Rhine, in violation of the Locarno agreement, France failed to set her armies in motion. When Mussolini proposed the four-power pact in 1934, France encouraged him, thereby offending Poland and Czechoslovakia. When the problem of the Sudetenland came up in 1938, France abandoned Czechoslovakia to her fate. We recall all this to emphasize the fact that ninety per cent of France's future depends more upon her policy than upon preventive pacts calling for automatic action, which at any given moment can be reduced to shreds of paper, as were the Franco-Russian and the Franco-Czecho-slovakian pacts at Munich in 1938.

France is suffering from the past of dishonor, which brought her to the Compiègne armistice and the Vichy government. Yet up to now she has done nothing to inspire the confidence and maintain the hopes of Europe or of extra-European powers, who look to France as the leading country of our civilization and culture. France is not yet a factor in practical world politics, which are still a monopoly of the big three; although she has become a party to the new worldwide dictatorship which established itself at San Francisco through the veto-right.

The regional unity of Europe, foreseen by Smuts (instead of by Bidault, as it should have been, had he not been muzzled by "the General") is not even in sight and will not be until it is possible to give European countries the place which today cannot be theirs in the International Organization.*

The effects of the occupation of Germany and Austria—divided into four distinct zones—of the spheres of influence or "security belts" of Russia and England, of the exclusion of a great part of Europe from the World Organization, added to the effects of malnutrition, disease and mortality, will within a few years produce a Europe more ruined than anything we can imagine today.

* * *

After the signature of the International Charter at the San Francisco Conference some of the criticisms made in Chapter 11 remain valid, others not. Indeed, many improvements of a technical, legal and even moral character have been made, and for these credit goes chiefly to the representatives of small or medium-sized nations, which still retain a certain freedom of initiative, and, above all, to the Australian Foreign

* Neutrals: Portugal, Spain, Sweden, Switzerland. Ex-enemies: Austria, Finland, Germany, Italy, Rumania, Hungary. Satellites: Bulgaria, Portugal, Sweden and Switzerland may request admission if they want to. Spain is barred from membership, as long as Franco is head of the state and of the government. The other countries cannot appeal to the Assembly for membership but are subject to a decision of the Security Council, which can refuse to invite them to membership in the United Nations.

Minister, Dr. Herbert Vere Evatt. However, the substance of the San Francisco policy is as originally conceived by the three heads of the Allied war effort who are responsible for future peace. This policy is based on the permanent agreement of the three, now enlarged to five, in the making of the international organization. The two new members, France and China, will, however, only carry political weight when they succeed in gaining economic and military power, which they do not today possess. Moreover, they cannot have real political influence until they can back their veto with force and resist the presence of the others.

The unanimity of the three or of the five (whichever the case) imposes upon the great powers a mutual policy of give and take, and forces them into a sort of potential hierarchy. The strongest power, or the most daring (and today everyone thinks of Russia) becomes the object of a policy of fear and appeasement.

In his writings Sir Norman Angell has many times pointed out that both World Wars occurred because the Western powers, unwilling to tolerate the expansion of Germany, did nothing to stop it but used the so-called policy of appeasement. When they faced the danger, it was too late to prevent the war. Today he thinks that "the democratic state will not acquiesce in the indefinite expansion of Russian power with its consequent totalitarian system over the whole continent of Europe, China and Asia."

It is strange that this unanimity of the three or of the five should seem to Churchill and Roosevelt (and now to Truman) a suitable means for the maintenance of good will and the promotion of universal welfare, when in fact it ties them to a policy of continual compromise that can only divide the world into zones of influence and create a state of affairs leading to a future war.

Indeed, as a result of the present political situation, the states of the pentarchy are trying to secure strategic bases, to have zones of protection, to form power-blocs, to build up fleets and armies, to introduce conscription where it does not yet exist, and to develop new inventions for an unknown future. Nobody remains armed if he is sure of not being attacked. Yet after San Francisco, and apart from the present war against Japan, the great powers are giving up disarmament, and proposing an increase of armaments. At San Francisco nobody mentioned the tenuous words of the Atlantic Charter, which promised to "aid and encourage all other practicable measures which will lighten for peace-loving peoples the crushing burden of armaments." And so it is quite evident that the new order is being conditioned by two factors, the dictatorship of the three (with their two partners) and a common fear that at any moment the equilibrium may be disturbed.

* * *

When speaking today of war as possible, one does not mean that it is probable, or at all close. One is simply speaking in terms of security. This is how one should interpret the statements of American military leaders, such as Eisenhower's demand for conscription and a permanent army, or Patton's plea that the United States guard against surprise by a well-prepared enemy. It is easy to exaggerate the danger of war in a far distant future prepared by Germany or Japan—when they will again be strong and aggressive. Today this is used as a scarecrow so that the complete annihilation of two countries may be carried out, and they can never again become enemies in the future. We do not know how history will avenge herself of all the Vansittarts and Morgenthaus of England and America. Even for the strong man and the strong country, the heel of Achilles will still be vulnerable. Nobody in 1919 thought that within twenty years Germany would be able to wage war for six years against the whole world. We cannot imagine what new inventions will be used twenty years hence, just as twenty years ago no one ever dreamed of the 1944 rockets and robots.

Should, as appears likely, Germany and Japan be out of the reckoning as first-rate military powers or political units, no one can deny that in the event of a conflict between other powers either of them, or both, might be a contributing factor, with their technicians, their troops, even improvised, (the American Army of 1942 was more or less improvised), and their economic forces. If Germany or Japan want to emerge from the position of inferiority into which they are being forced, they will certainly be delighted to take advantage of any eventual conflict between the two countries foremost today: Russia and the United States.

Neither wants war. It is stupid to imagine that Russia wants war, or is planning it for tomorrow. Marshal Stalin may reason in the same way as General Patton: let us not be taken by surprise. As a matter of fact, Marshal Gregory Zhukoff, on June 22, 1945, at the Moscow celebration of victory over Germany, stated the "necessity" for larger armies. However, today Russia has no navy to compare with that of the United States and Great Britain, nor can her aviation or industries compete with those of the other two. So she must try to form an equilibrium of potentialities to counterbalance the other great powers. That is why Stalin has annexed half of Poland, the Baltic states and Bessarabia. He is forming a "security belt" that stretches from Koenigsberg to Trieste. He occupies more than half of Germany, he wants to have his say in the administration of Suez, Tangier, the mandated or protected colonies, he wants a right of way through the Dardanelles, he is leaning toward the Persian Gulf and he will of course ask for his share of Manchuria and Korea.

This is not all. Further indirect gains will come to Russia through the communist network of the working masses of the western European democracies and the countries of the American continent. This "peaceful" expansion of Russia will certainly have its effect upon China and India. The question is whether Stalin and his advisers will be skillful enough to proceed gradually, so as to avoid any sharp conflict with the Anglo-American and Latin countries. If Stalin loses his self-control, he may become for the world what Napoleon Bonaparte, Bismarck, William the Second and Hitler were during the past century and a half. Of the four, Bismarck alone knew how to cash in on partial victories, and space them so as to reach his goal: a unified Germany in a powerful empire. Within a few years, we shall see whether Stalin has the calmness and ability to want time and opportunity for his future achievements, as Bismarck did.

Against this eventuality two different factors will operate: the unrest of the working masses of Europe and the fears of the capitalists on one hand, and international insecurity on the other.

We cannot tell up to what point the big three will be able to master this uncertain and troubled situation. We must, however, give due recognition to the good will of the present heads, Churchill, Stalin and Truman, and to their earnest desire to understand each other and get along together. There is, however, no common plan of action, nor do they have the courage to look for one, fearing that a disagreement on principles and methods might entail serious consequences. How can common effort and mutual consideration between nations rest on anything but equality of rights, respect for the personality of each state, and the freely guaranteed political liberty of the new international organization? In England, in the United States, and in the other countries of western culture, the communist parties are tolerated, but they are looked upon with suspicion, for fear that they might abuse their political freedom to seize power, and then, as in Russia, reject that freedom for their totalitarian system. In Russia, and in Russian-controlled countries, not only is there no real political freedom, but despite their so-called democracy, under the pretext of the security of the state, the rights of human individuals are violated so as to eliminate, at times with the well-known "purges," all actual and potential enemies.

The San Francisco Charter, while sanctioning the monopoly of the big three, based on the armed force of the five and other various countries in their respective spheres of influence, does not guarantee the individual freedom of the citizens of any one nation, or the individual freedom of any one nation within the regional or international framework, because no practical measures are provided for the preservation of liberty, and because there is no single and universally accepted definition of this equality of rights based on respect of law. To the San Francisco Charter principles have been added which all nations can and must subscribe to, and which correspond to the general feeling of civilized and Christian humanity. The crucial point, however, has been avoided, that of freedom; how to be affirmed, guaranteed and defended. Without freedom, it is impossible that the world become one, that peace be assured, and that the personal rights of individuals and nations be respected.

*　　　*　　　*

Italy did not have a seat at San Francisco, and her protest was rejected at a session of the Committee, which the press described as "hasty and without preparation." At the same session, it was decided that ex-enemy nations should not have the right to ask admission to the United Nations, and that the Security Council should have the power to call them in, when the time comes. In the case of Spain, a special provision was made to bar her acceptance, as long as General Franco remains in power.

The Italy of today cannot be treated on a par with Germany and Japan. Everyone is in agreement on this point. But she cannot, however, be given the same treatment as Hungary, Rumania, Bulgaria and Finland. These countries signed armistices with Russia, also promising to fight against Germany. But the contribution of these countries to the war effort can in no way be compared to that of Italy, partly because of the time and manner in which they were engaged in, partly because Germany abandoned their respective territories, or left behind only some beaten divisions. The Italian fleet, army, aviation, and patriots have contributed the equivalent of twenty months of uninterrupted warfare, and the people and government have helped the Allies with all their ability and strength. These facts have been duly recognized by the Allied heads. These facts are a title of honor for Italy which redeems the fascist past. These facts must hasten the day when Italy shall obtain a just and honorable peace, and again become a member of the family of nations.[*]

[*] Less than a month after San Francisco a new conference of the Big Three was held at Potsdam (Germany), till July 25 it was Mr. Churchill who represented the United Kingdom; after it was Mr. Attlee, following the electoral victory of the Labor Party, the new prime minister who signed the text of the Potsdam Declaration. This document does not change the points of view supported by the author in this book. Referring to Italy, the Big Three, recognizing her special position, stated:

1. "For their part the three governments have included the preparation of a peace treaty for Italy as the first among the immediate important tasks to be undertaken by the new Council of Foreign Ministers. Italy was the first of the Axis powers to break with Germany, to whose defeat she has made a material contribution, and has now joined with the Allies in the struggle against Japan. Italy has freed herself from the Fascist regime and is making good progress toward the re-establishment of a democratic government and institutions. The conclusion of such a peace treaty with a recognized and democratic Italian government will make it possible for the three governments to fulfill their desire to support an application from Italy for membership of the United Nations."

2. After an exchange of views on this question it was decided that the disposition of any former Italian territories was one to be decided in connection with the preparation of a peace treaty for Italy and that the question of Italian territory would be considered by the September council of ministers of foreign affairs."

DATE DUE

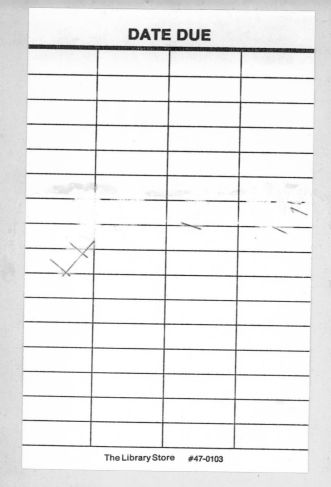